Net
Worth

Net
Worth

Shaping Markets
When Customers
Make the Rules

John Hagel III
Marc Singer

HARVARD BUSINESS SCHOOL PRESS
BOSTON, MASSACHUSETTS

Library of Congress Cataloging-in-Publication Data

Hagel, John.
    Net Worth : shaping markets when customers make the rules / John
Hagel III and Marc Singer.
        p.   cm.
    Includes bibliographical references and index.
    ISBN 0-87584-889-3 (alk. paper)
    1. Infomediaries.   2. Consumers—Information services.
3. Privacy, Right of.   4. Online information services.   I. Singer,
Marc.   II. Title.
HF5415.124.H33   1999   98-43263
658.8'00285'4678—dc21   CIP

*The paper used in this publication meets the requirements of
the American National Standard for Permanence of Paper for Printed
Library Materials Z39.49-1984.*

We dedicate this book, with love, to our families,
who give us much more than we could ever provide in return.

—Jane, Rebecca, and Rachel
—Rowena

CHAPTER

contents

Preface   ix

PART I
THE NEW INFOMEDIARIES
1   Seller Beware   *3*
2   An Agent for the Rest of Us   *21*
3   Promising Markets   *49*
4   Who Can Play?   *77*

PART II
ENTRY STRATEGIES
5   Stage One: Building the Profile   *109*
6   Stage Two: Spinning a Web   *133*
7   Stage Three: Playing the Spider's Role   *157*
8   The Economics of Infomediation   *187*

PART III
THE INFOMEDIATION OF MARKETS
9   The Unraveling of the Firm   *205*
10   Reverse Markets   *229*
11   Consumer Unbound   *247*

Appendix: The Technology Tool Kit   *261*
Further Reading   *285*
Index   *293*
About the Authors   *313*

preface

THIS BOOK BUILDS ON A NUMBER OF THE THEMES
originally developed in *Net Gain: Expanding Markets
through Virtual Communities*. Both books focus on the
potential to build new business models by using the
Internet, rather than simply by doing the same things
faster and cheaper.

Net Gain met with market success because it systematically analyzed the economic drivers for value
creation that exist on networks. It used one particular
business model—the virtual community—to illustrate the unique capabilities of digital networks and
how these might be harnessed to create a substantial
business with very attractive economics.

Our work with clients convinces us that digital
networks can make many new business models possi-

ble. These business models are co-evolving in complex patterns that define a distinctive business ecology, one that is rapidly changing as entrepreneurs search for the right combination of value drivers to build sustainable businesses.

In working with these business models, we soon realized that they all depend on the business's ability to capture information about customers and to use this information for commercial purposes. Take away this key assumption and the economics of the various business models rapidly deteriorate, and the businesses soon become very uninteresting from a value creation perspective. We decided to invest in understanding information capture in greater detail. What information about customers is most valuable? Who is in the best position to capture this information? What are the implications for other businesses that would like to use this information? How can the growing capability for ever more detailed information capture be reconciled with growing concerns about privacy?

From this work, we came up with a key insight. Digital networks such as the Internet might for the first time provide the tools necessary for customers to capture information about themselves and to deny vendors access to this information. Such an approach seemed a promising way to resolve the growing tension between the commercial value of capturing more detailed information and the privacy concerns expressed by an increasing number of individuals, advocacy groups, and politicians. It became clear that there would be an opportunity for a new kind of business—we called it an "information intermediary," or "infomediary"—to help customers capture, manage, and maximize the value of this information. We suggested in *Net Gain* that virtual communities might evolve into this kind of business, given the trust-based relationships they would develop with their members.

At about this time, we discussed the early concept with Professor Jeffrey Rayport at Harvard Business School. He immediately became intrigued by the parallels with his own work, and we decided to collaborate on an effort to flesh out this business concept. The result was an article, "The Coming Battle for Customer Information," originally published in *Harvard Business Review,* followed by a sequel article, "The New Infomediaries," published in *The McKinsey Quarterly.*

Our colleagues at McKinsey became convinced of the importance of this topic and provided the support necessary to undertake this book on information capture and the infomediary concept. As with *Net Gain,* we consider our primary audience to be senior management of large companies around the world. Secondarily, we wish to address entrepreneurs who are focused on the Internet as a promising platform for building substantial businesses. More broadly, we also want to reach the general public, especially those who seek to understand the new opportunities created by digital networks such as the Internet, as well as the challenges created by the potential for abuse of this new platform in areas such as privacy.

Our primary objective in writing this book is not to persuade people to go out and build an infomediary. As the reader will discover, we believe that infomediaries have the potential to become quite large and attractive but that few companies will in the end be able to build such businesses. Instead, our primary goal is to use the infomediary business concept to engage the reader with a broader set of themes that will be critically important to creating value on digital networks.

In general, we want to challenge a number of common views about the Internet. First, as already suggested, we urge senior managers not to view the Internet simply as a way to do the same things cheaper and faster. Although using the Internet to reduce cost and increase speed is certainly important, the most important value creation opportunities on the Internet are likely to require a fundamental rethinking of basic business assumptions and the creative use of the unique capabilities of the Internet to deliver more value to customers.

Second, we reject the notion that the Internet is uniformly

leading to disintermediation, creating opportunities for vendors to connect directly with customers while relentlessly eliminating all intermediaries that previously came in the way. Certainly opportunities for disintermediation will exist. But the Internet will spawn entirely new classes of intermediaries. In fact, the most significant opportunities for value creation on the Internet will consist of building new kinds of intermediaries that help shift value from vendors to customers.

Third, we question whether the real value of the Internet is in information access. The Internet instead is a powerful platform for connecting people or businesses with each other, enriched and enhanced by relevant information. Intermediaries play a significant role in helping connect people and in conveniently providing the information that helps enrich these relationships. Ultimately, information about people may be the most important information collected on the Internet—precisely because it helps connect people in a relevant and timely fashion.

Fourth, we are suspicious of claims that the Internet will systematically lower barriers to entry and lead to fragmentation of businesses. This may be true for certain kinds of businesses—for instance, the product innovation and commercialization businesses discussed in this book. But, in general, the Internet will lead to substantial concentration of business activity over time. Two factors will produce this result. Dynamics of increasing returns drive many of the customer relationship businesses emerging on the Internet—for example, virtual communities and infomediaries. Increasing returns tend to produce highly concentrated businesses. Another category of business—the infrastructure management businesses represented by companies that provide billing services, transaction-processing services, and advertising services, for example—is driven by economies of scale and learning. In both cases, the barriers to entry, which are relatively low today, will become more significant as the underlying economics play out.

preface

We are using the infomediary business concept as a way to develop these broader themes. Our goal is to deepen management understanding of the underlying economic and competitive dynamics that will shape the new businesses and electronic commerce emerging on the Internet. In particular, by focusing on the infomediary business opportunity, we want to direct management attention to the economic and strategic importance of customer information capture in on-line environments. Too many businesses, including many of the leading-edge entrepreneurial companies emerging on the Internet, haven't focused enough on the value of customer profiles. In many respects, we are moving from an era of competition on the Internet, which represented the battle for traffic, into a new era in which the defining battle is that for customer profiles. The winners and losers in this new era will be determined by who has rights to on-line customer profiles. Clearly, we do not want to be descriptive; our intent is to anticipate and shape companies' actions to maximize the potential for value creation on this unfamiliar terrain.

Naturally, risks and limitations are associated with such an enterprise. In some respects, we are venturing onto even more speculative ground than we did in *Net Gain*. At least with virtual communities, some businesses were already established that provided fragmentary evidence of the power of the virtual community business model. In the case of infomediaries, we are hard pressed to point to any examples of companies today that can provide anything more than distant analogies to the role we envision the infomediary playing. Nevertheless, we believe that the underlying business dynamics support and in fact demand the emergence of this kind of business.

We also have made choices to simplify the presentation of this business concept and the discussion of underlying business and competitive dynamics. For this reason, we decided to develop this business concept in a business-to-consumer context, even though we believe that this new business model will emerge in the business-to-business marketplace as well. We also have developed this business concept in a North American context, even though the services provided by an infomediary certainly have a broader, global appeal. Although we discuss the notion of an infomediary web and a host of specialized businesses that are likely to play a key role within this kind of web, our work focuses on the economics and business model of the infomediary itself. We have also briefly referred to the likely extension of the infomediary business into traditional physical markets, but we have not developed in detail the specific issues involved in moving from digital markets to physical markets. As mathematicians are fond of saying, we leave the application of this concept to other domains in the capable hands of the reader.

By focusing on the infomediary business concept, we run the risk that some readers might think we believe that this is the only viable, or at least the most attractive, business concept on the Internet. This is certainly not the case. We are using this particular business model because we believe it is particularly helpful in highlighting and developing important broader themes for business managers venturing onto the Internet. As the reader will discover, we certainly believe that infomediaries will become large economic entities with significant implications for other businesses operating in both digital and physical markets. Nonetheless, we believe that a broad range of other business models will also provide significant value creation opportunities. One of the challenges for business managers will be to determine which business model is appropriate for their particular company, given their unique resources and aspirations.

Finally, by writing a book on infomediaries, we do not in any way suggest that virtual communities, the focus of *Net Gain*, have lost their power and appeal. On the contrary, the virtual community business model continues to show great promise.

As *Net Gain* emphasized, virtual communities are not easy to develop, but their economic rewards are significant. Many companies focused on the latter message and rushed to add a bulletin board or chat area to their Web site, proudly announcing the formation of a new virtual community. These companies have been disappointed when few came and even fewer stayed in their "community." They failed to hear the message that virtual communities are a complex mixture of social and economic interactions which must be aggressively cultivated and managed. Those who did hear this message have generated rapidly growing traffic, expanding usage rates, reduced churn rates, and high member response rates to targeted (and appropriate) marketing messages.

We suggested in *Net Gain* that virtual communities might evolve over time into infomediaries, and we continue to believe they are attractive candidates to play this role. *Net Worth* simply tries to develop in more detail what we mean by infomediaries, the appeal that infomediaries will have, the dynamics of that particular business model, and the implications for a broad range of businesses.

This book is organized in three broad sections. Part I, "The New Infomediaries," provides a broad overview of the infomediary business opportunity. It describes the unmet customer needs that will give rise to infomediaries and the range of services that infomediaries might offer to address these needs. This section also discusses the specific market arenas that might first spawn infomediary businesses and the existing businesses that might take advantage of this opportunity.

Part II, "Entry Strategies," goes into considerable detail regarding the three stages of evolution of an infomediary business. The final chapter in this section analyzes the economic performance and economic drivers shaping value creation in an infomediary business. This section will be of greatest interest to those who actually want to build an infomediary business. For other readers, it will help give a more tangible understanding of how infomediaries might actually emerge and what drives their economics.

Part III, "The Infomediation of Markets," steps back and explores the broader business implications of infomediaries. It also raises public policy issues that will both shape and be shaped by infomediaries. This section will have perhaps the broadest appeal in clarifying the way infomediaries will reshape the economic, social, and even political landscape.

Acknowledgments

As with *Net Gain,* this book has been substantially influenced by our continuing interactions with a diverse set of clients around the world. There is no greater discipline than having to go before the senior management of a leading company and explain how and why certain business issues will affect them. Even more helpful is the need to provide actionable recommendations that can generate substantial, lasting, and positive impact on the business. The demands of client service relentlessly focus our work, providing the setting to be creative, yet constantly grounded in the need to return to the "So what?" question. No matter how creative and exciting the opportunity, it matters little unless that opportunity can be translated into specific actions the client can take to improve performance.

In keeping with our policies of client confidentiality, we cannot acknowledge the help and encouragement we have received from individual clients and client executives. Nevertheless, we certainly wish to express our gratitude for the opportunity to test and refine our perspectives in so many different environments, both in the United States and around the world.

Within McKinsey & Company, many colleagues and partners have collaborated to shape and refine the perspectives presented in this book. The leadership of the Electronic Commerce Practice—in particular, Yuji Akaba, Jonathan Auerbach,

Ennius Bergsma, Sanjeev Dheer, Wilfred Griekspoor, Eric Labaye, Gottfried Liebbrandt, Tomoko Namba, Takashi Nawa, Mike Nevens, Nagi Rao, Greg Reed, George Riedel, Paul Roche, Anders Thulin, Magnus Tyreman, and Holger Wohlenberg—has contributed to the thinking presented in this book. We would particularly like to thank Jeff Brown and Mike Nevens, who carefully read an initial draft of this manuscript and provided counsel and suggestions to tighten the perspective and make it even more compelling.

We involved a number of other colleagues at McKinsey to build knowledge and provide perspective for this book. From beginning to end, Joyce Dickerson proved herself a valued thought partner by bringing us uniquely valuable insights into the capabilities of established companies, the fast-changing landscape of new players, and the evolving technologies that will enable infomediation. Dennis Layton-Rodin helped us develop the economics of infomediation and contributed other important perspectives. A broader team, made up of Lorraine Harrington, Wendy Harrington, Steven Hoffman, Abhi Ingle, Linda Kraemer, Ryan McDonough, John Real, and Wiebke Sinz, committed extra hours to developing valuable material and providing intriguing suggestions for this book.

The origins of the perspective developed in this book can be traced back to a team assembled almost four years ago to begin to understand the dynamics of information capture in on-line environments. Key members of that team included Justin Colledge, Michael Faralla, Ian McKerlich, Nina Pustilnik, and Toni Sacconaghi. It was Justin Colledge, the most junior member on the team, who first came up with the notion of an infomediary to help customers capture information about themselves. Other people who contributed valuable perspectives to this first team included Andrew Abela, Michael Sherman, and Michael Zeisser.

Members of other teams in the electronic commerce arena who have contributed ideas, comments, and suggestions in the course of our writing this book include Jed Dempsey, Guido Frisiani, Kristina Klausen, Daan Knottenbelt, George Kurian, John Ouren, Vincent Rerolle, Jeffrey Russakow, and Tom Stephenson.

We have also benefited substantially from the long-standing commitment of McKinsey's Marketing Practice to Continuous Relationship Marketing. The list of leaders and practitioners in this area who have influenced our thinking by anchoring it in the reality of contemporary information-based marketing is too long to include here. But a few have done so over the longer-term—David Court, Margo Georgiadis, Joshua Goff, Tim Gokey, and Mike Sherman—and have otherwise created a fertile environment for a next generation of ideas and strategies to take root.

In this book, we have relied heavily on the work done by a team assembled within McKinsey to better understand the global forces shaping business environments. This team focused on the importance of interaction costs, the role of technology in systematically reducing these costs, and the implications for industry structure. Members of this team included Byron Auguste, Pat Butler, Ted Hall, James Manyika, and Lenny Mendonca.

We also have drawn on the work of another McKinsey team that has helped explore the power and potential of web-based strategies as an alternative, or supplement, to traditional joint ventures or alliances. The Electronic Commerce Practice and the Strategy Theory Initiative within the Strategy Practice jointly sponsor this team. Members of this team have included Eric Beinhocker, Ken Davis, Tetsuya Mori, Somu Subramaniam, and Lo-Ping Yeh. Todd Hewlin, Todd Hutchings, and Mary Kate-Scott have provided significant insight into the potential application of web-based strategies in the financial services arena. The Strategy Theory Initiative in general has given us a powerful framework and tool kit for understanding how business strategy must change in highly uncertain market environments.

As always, many people within McKinsey have contributed to our thinking without formally being part of any team. Although we will inevitably leave many of these colleagues out, we wish to give special acknowledgment to Kevin Coyne, Detlev Hoch, Conor Kehoe, Rod Laird, Will Lansing, Nick Lovegrove, Bill Pade, John Rose, Jonathan Shapiro, Jack Stephenson, and Dennis Sweeney. Some of these people have now left the firm and are putting their ideas into practice.

Lang Davison, of McKinsey's Communications Group, went well beyond editorial support to engage in the substance of the book in a way that made it a far better product. He worked with us from concept to final manuscript delivery and, as he did with *Net Gain,* went above and beyond the call of duty to ensure that we stayed on course and sharpened our perspective to make it more relevant and accessible. Bill Matassoni and the entire Communications Group have been unstinting supporters of our efforts from the outset, providing us with ready access to the *McKinsey Quarterly* to develop many of the original concepts that made their way into this book. Gene Zelazny worked his usual magic on many of the charts that help to illustrate and support the text, and Clementine Griffin effectively translated these ideas into book-ready graphics under very tight deadlines. Our exceptional assistants, Carrie Howell and Jeanne Porter, continued to exceed expectations by taking on many of the support tasks required to develop and deliver this manuscript in a timely fashion.

Outside McKinsey, we have already indicated that Professor Jeffrey Rayport at Harvard Business School played a central role in refining and enhancing the infomediary business concept. His collaboration on the two articles that developed this concept was essential to sharpening the definition of the opportunity and the requirements for addressing the opportunity. We are deeply indebted to his insights; they provided a strong foundation to build on.

We owe a special debt to Corey Peck, who worked closely with us in building the economic model that proved invaluable in understanding the economic potential and the underlying dynamics that drive value creation in the infomediary business model. We also have been heavily influenced by a continuing relationship with the Santa Fe Institute—in particular, by discussions with Brian Arthur and Stuart Kauffman. Our work with the institute has given us a deep appreciation of the need for new mental models and tools to manage businesses in complex, highly uncertain market environments.

This book would not have been written without the support and encouragement of Kirsten Sandberg. She saw the potential of the ideas when they were still in very preliminary form and patiently but persistently encouraged us to take on the challenge of developing them into a book. She provided enormous help in sharpening both the ideas and the language so that they would make for a more compelling read. Her enthusiasm and insight not only made this book possible, but also made it a far better book. Her colleagues at Harvard Business School Press helped to accelerate the editing and production process so that we are able to deliver this book to the market on an accelerated schedule—although still not quite on Internet time. We also remain grateful to Tom Kiely, our former editor at the *Harvard Business Review*. He, too, saw the potential of the ideas presented here and provided us with our first forum outside McKinsey for presenting the infomediary concept in a focused way.

Despite all the help we have received along the way, we must in the end take full responsibility for the views expressed in this book. We have ventured well beyond the horizons traveled by most of our colleagues. The view is refreshing, and we welcome others to join us. Until then, we hold ourselves solely accountable for the reports we send back to the mainland.

THE NEW
INFOMEDIARIES

seller beware

THE RIGHT TO BE LEFT ALONE.
Film actress Greta Garbo craved it. Justice Louis
Brandeis defended it. And the Fourth and Fifth
Amendments to the U.S. Constitution uphold it.

In the landmark case *Olmstead* v. *United States* in
1928, Brandeis wrote: "The right to be left alone is
the most comprehensive of rights, and the right most
valued by a free people."

But protecting that right is becoming more difficult. Each day, marketers expose Americans to some
12 billion display ads, 3 million radio ads, and more
than 300,000 television commercials. The unsolicited
electronic junk mail known as "spam" now constitutes
some 10 percent of all worldwide e-mail. The average
U.S. consumer receives roughly 1 million marketing

messages a year across all media, or about 3,000 messages per day. Worse yet, companies are using private information ferreted out of daily commercial transactions, financial arrangements, and survey responses to inundate consumers with still more commercial messages (and sometimes to deny them credit or insurance).

The very words marketers use to describe their methods of finding and connecting with customers—military metaphors such as *target, campaign, deploy, blitz,* and *capture*—betray an increasingly "us versus them" mentality about how companies treat consumers. Telemarketers call consumers at home at all hours of the day and evening. Direct marketers stuff their mailboxes with unsolicited catalogs and junk mail. Relationship marketers demand more and more of their personal information. Who can blame consumers for feeling besieged?

The rise of the Internet, with its ability to help companies more easily obtain information about customers, brings privacy issues center stage. Consumers and the groups that protect them, such as the Electronic Frontier Foundation, worry about privacy. They worry that businesses will use the Internet to capture customer information (without consumers' knowing it) when consumers visit corporate Web sites and, by merging this information with a wide range of other publicly available data (such as credit histories, phone bills, and medical records), will be in a better position to leverage vast databases of customer information.

Who can blame consumers for feeling besieged?

Lawmakers and advocacy groups in many different countries are marshaling their forces against the perceived threat. In the United States, for example, legislators have sponsored a comprehensive consumer health care bill of rights at both national and state levels. Consumers are acting on their own behalf as well. Some have requested that marketers remove their names from telemarketing and direct mail lists. Others take part in "Buy Nothing Day"—a 24-hour moratorium on consumer spending sponsored during the Christmas shopping season by Adbusters, a group that vows to hold the marketing strategies of consumer products companies "up to public scrutiny and to set new agendas in their industries." Others provide false information in on-line registrations, surveys, and forms. Still others participate in "TV Turnoff Week." And some go so far as to respond to ads calling for focus group participants in the classified section of local newspapers and then deliberately give false information to questioners.

These actions may well represent a broader consumer backlash.

- A 1996 DIRECT survey found that 83 percent of those surveyed said there should be a law requiring an opt-in procedure for names to be included on direct mail lists.

- A 1998 survey of more than 10,000 World Wide Web users by Graphic, Visualization & Usability (GVU) found that 72 percent of Internet users believed there should be new laws to protect privacy on the Internet and that 82 percent of users objected to the sale of personal information.

- A 1998 *Business Week* poll found that 53 percent of respondents said government should pass laws now for how personal information can be captured and used on-line, a figure three times higher than the number of consumers who support the idea that the government should let trade groups develop voluntary privacy standards.

These survey findings are borne out by recent warnings from trade groups and organizations that oversee corporations. In 1997 the U.S. Federal Trade Commission warned businesses to adopt strong privacy guidelines to avoid government legislation. In 1998 the U.S. comptroller of the currency (who oversees nationally chartered banks) cautioned banks to take steps to protect consumers' privacy or risk new government regulations. That same year, the National Retail Federation suggested voluntary guidelines for U.S. retailers that would let customers know beforehand what types of personal information were being collected at the cash register—and how retailers planned to use that information.

Few marketers seem to have recognized the importance of the issue to consumers.

- In late 1998, Geocities, a popular Internet site that allows consumers to put up free Web sites, agreed to settle FTC charges that it had misled its 2 million members by secretly selling their personal information to marketers. The charges resulted in a 15 percent drop in Geocities' stock on the Nasdaq.

- Pacific Bell requested in 1998 that regulators allow it to call unlisted numbers with unsolicited sales pitches. Regulators turned the company down after consumer groups and California legislators blasted the proposal.

- America Online decided to sell its members' phone numbers to a telemarketing company in 1997, reversing itself later after members protested.

- American Express announced plans in 1998 to sell extensive information on its cardholders to merchants, despite considerable criticism from privacy groups.

- Blizzard Entertainment (maker of the popular Starcraft on-line game) admitted in 1998 that it copied personal information without consent from consumers' computers via the Internet.

- Giant Foods and CVS (a supermarket and a drugstore chain, respectively) decided in 1998 to stop sharing medical information with a marketer paid to send customers prescription reminders and promotional literature for new drugs—but only after critics called the practice unethical and a violation of privacy.

- In 1998 GTE Corporation inadvertently published the unlisted phone numbers and addresses of up to 50,000 California customers, some of whom, such as police officers and crime victims, could have had their personal safety compromised. The blunder led to 25,000 calls to the company, 400 e-mails, and 1,500 requests for new phone numbers.

Beneath the current antagonism, marketers and consumers share a set of very real common needs—consumers need the goods and services vendors sell, and vendors need consumers to

Marketers are wearing out their welcome

buy these goods and services. But the fact that it is economical for companies to send out junk mail and catalogs with the expectation of a 2 percent response rate means that 98 percent of what consumers receive is irrelevant to their needs and interests. Inundated with so many irrelevant messages, consumers feel beseiged by marketers. Marketers are beginning to wear out their welcome with the people they need the most.

The high cost of shopping

Ironically enough, consumers have never been more alone—despite the 3,000 marketing messages they receive each day. With ever more products launched, and the complexity of many products on the rise, the time and money that consumers spend searching out the best possible product at the best possible price may be higher than at any time in the past, particularly for those high-ticket, complex items they purchase infrequently.

More troubling still, consumers continue to be vulnerable to the risks of moral hazard and asymmetric information—the perennial standbys of consumer rip-off.

Complex products

Consider the home computer. Computers are impressively complicated machines to purchase, install, and operate. Anyone who has tried to buy one (and some 60 million American households have at least one) knows the frustration of talking to salesclerks who don't have a clue about which features are really important. Worse yet are salesclerks who overwhelm the customer with technobabble in a sincere effort to be helpful. Do you want your computer with a 1GB Jaz drive with 12ms access time and 5.5Mbps data transfer? How about an STB nVidia 4 MB 3D AGP video card? or a 1000LS monitor?

And the fun doesn't stop when you've made the purchase. Most consumers find setting up their new computer a challenge, to say the least. The *New York Times* reports that home computer vendors receive some 28 million technical support calls every year. Microsoft alone receives approximately 15,000 cries for help a day. After setup comes learning how to get on the Internet—another formidable task.

Consumers may expect such challenges when it comes to buying computers. But what about cars, televisions, washing machines, even the lowly coffeemaker? For many of the products consumers buy, particularly those they don't buy very often, the time and money they spend searching out the best product at the best possible price are going up.

Some readers may question this assertion. After all, the telephone (and the yellow pages) let your fingers do the walking, and the advent of the Internet has made searching out products even easier. Research shows that, for some products, the telephone and the Internet have greatly reduced the search time needed to find them.[1]

But consumers experience this ease of search primarily for products they purchase relatively frequently and for which they don't have to conduct much research. It's a snap to dial up Amazon.com and order a best-seller, or to go to Travelocity and find the best airfare between Dallas and Rome. But what about more complex purchases, like an air conditioner or a health club membership?

If you want to do it right, buying an air conditioner for a particular room requires a complex calculation. The variables include

- The length of the walls in the room you want to cool and whether they're facing north or are shaded.

- The materials the walls are made of (masonry up to 8 inches thick? uninsulated?).

- The ceiling area of the room, in square feet, and the insulation above the ceiling.

- The floor space.

- The number of doors and arches.

- The type and orientation of the windows (and whether or not they have shades).

- The number of people who normally use the room (more body heat means you need more air-conditioning power).

- The total wattage of appliances being used, and how many hours you'd typically use the air conditioner in the given area.

Rather than figure all this out, of course, most consumers simply head for the appliance store and throw themselves on the mercy of the salesclerk.

Or consider a health club. As *Consumer Reports* points out, "Joining a health club can be as tricky as buying a used car. You have to find a club that matches your needs, navigate the nuances of a contract that may lock you in for a year or more, pay a substantial fee—for a fancy club, perhaps $500 for initiation and $75 a month—then exercise enough will power to exercise your body more than once in a blue moon."

The problem with either of these purchases is the risk involved. Will the salesclerk really know which air conditioner will best match the customer's needs, or is he more likely to steer they buyer toward the product at hand or the highest-margin item? Will the salesperson at the health club fill customers in about their cancellation rights? Will the club really buy the new equipment and install the whirlpool next month as it claims? The Federal Trade Commission frequently pursues rogue health clubs for high-pressure sales tactics, bait and switch, and unfair billing.

These kinds of risks to consumers arise from what economists call "asymmetric information," which occurs when the seller knows more about the quality of a product than the buyer does. The textbook case is the used car. The used-car dealer may know that the sedan he's selling is a lemon with a bad clutch and worn brakes, but the buyer, kicking the tires and looking at the new paint job, won't know about these defects. Even if the buyer hires a mechanic to look at the car, chances are the seller is still going to know more about it. The buyer therefore runs the risk of paying more than the car is worth.

The problem of asymmetric information has increased dramatically with the number of new on-line vendors. Not only are consumers unable to physically inspect a product in cyberspace, but they often don't know whether the company selling it is big or small, new or established, legitimate or illegitimate.

Consumers can fall victim to "moral hazard" as well. The classic case of moral hazard comes from the pre–managed care era of health care, when a consumer could purchase complete medical insurance coverage and then proceed to visit the doctor more often than he or she would have with limited coverage. With the advent of managed care, the shoe is on the other foot—the consumer, not the insurer, is at risk. Now that physicians are under pressure from the cost-conscious HMOs that employ them to reduce treatment costs, consumers no longer blindly trust their doctors to put their interests ahead of the HMO's, their employer's. Physicians may give their primary loyalty to the HMO rather than to the patient. (Of course, vendors can also fall prey to moral hazard, as when consumers falsify information on surveys.)

Needle in a haystack

Product proliferation also plays a part in raising the interaction cost of purchasing products and services: there are simply more products out there than in the past. Companies used to introduce their products once every five years or so. Intensified competition and improved innovation now mean that companies modify or replace products on six-month cycles. Technological innovations have reduced minimum scale and made it easier for smaller companies to enter and compete successfully in many markets—bringing with them still more products. Information technology, meanwhile, helps companies expand their reach from local markets to global markets, increasing the choices available to the customer in any local market. Widespread deregulation (in the form of trade liberalization and the removal of restrictions on entry into specific industries) also encourages entry by new vendors.

An explosion of choices for consumers

The advent of the Internet has released an explosion of choices for the consumer by removing the constraint that used to hold back the proliferation of products—limited retail shelf space. With the Internet, shelf space constraints disappear. By logging on to the Internet, consumers can access all products offered for sale within a particular category.

As the range of potential choices expands, the time and effort required to sort through them also expands. Because different vendors offer these different products, difficulty comparing and evaluating products increases. Vendors, in an understandable effort to differentiate their offerings, seek to design and represent their products in a slightly different way, making straightforward comparisons virtually impossible. In the case of consumer electronics, for example, vendors will often take the same model of VCR or "boom box" and change the model number, color, and perhaps a marginal feature or two to allow major retailers to differentiate their offerings from those of other retailers.

These problems are difficult enough when the customer is actively searching for a product to meet a specific need. The problem becomes even more severe when customers are *browsing* for products—in other words, when they don't know in advance what product they want. The may not even be planning a purchase. As product offerings proliferate, the effort required to browse through thousands, if not millions, of product variants within specific categories becomes like searching for the proverbial needle in a haystack.

A widening gulf

Behind the continuing invasion of consumer privacy and the constant expansion of product choices lurks an unrecognized truth about consumers and marketers: their wants and needs are misaligned. Marketers gather customer information and create loyalty programs to build deeper and more lasting "relationships" with customers, but the customer's demand for selection and comparison is sharply at odds with a deep or exclusive relationship with any one vendor. Marketers want all the information they can possibly get hold of about customers, but customers demand that their privacy be respected and protected.

The apparent conflict has its roots in the marketing approaches that have come into fashion over the last 10 to 20 years. Approaches like database marketing, relationship marketing, permission marketing, and loyalty programs aim largely to help marketers overcome a fundamental lack of information about the customers they *don't* know by giving them more information about the customers they *do* know.

The limitations of relationship . . .

"Relationship marketing"—also known as "one-to-one marketing"—first came into fashion in part because companies were (and still are) limited in the type of information they can obtain about people who aren't already their customers. United Airlines, for example, identifies business travelers who fly extensively on United and often upgrades service to those travelers to increase loyalty to United. But it has much less ability to identify an American Airlines frequent flyer who happened to book a flight on United. From United's perspective, this passenger is a relatively uninteresting one because she doesn't appear to travel much; therefore she doesn't receive special attention or service. If United had access to integrated travel profiles of *all* its passengers (even people who have never flown United before), it could be much more effective in targeting and serving highly profitable business travelers.

Because companies aren't as well positioned to learn about people who are not yet their customers, relationship marketing focuses companies largely on collecting additional information about the customers they do have. The idea is to set in motion a virtuous cycle in which companies deliver additional value to customers. Customers are in turn motivated to provide additional information to companies, which those companies can then use to deliver yet more value.

This is why relationship marketers put so much emphasis on

"share of wallet" within a product or service category as a key measure of success. To capture as much information as possible about the customer, the product vendor must capture the full range of the customer's business within a particular category. For one-to-one marketing to work to its full potential, there isn't room for more than one vendor. Any notion of customers' spreading their business among multiple vendors undermines the ability to build rich profiles of customers—and to capture a high share of their transactions.

Companies using relationship marketing are thereby at odds with the customer's need for selection and comparison. Moreover, the relationship marketer's need to capture as much information as possible often leads it to intrude on customers' lives to an increasingly intolerable extent.

. . . and permission marketing

Another approach to marketing is known as "permission marketing."[2] Permission marketing explicitly acknowledges the importance of obtaining permission from customers before blitzing them with advertising messages and criticizes the "interruption" marketing programs in which advertisements are inserted in media or delivered in unsolicited ways, such as a phone call at dinner. Advocates of permission marketing instead propose contests and sweepstakes in which customers will participate in exchange for agreeing to receive certain marketing messages.

Permission marketing begins to address the challenge of finding and reaching customers in a less intrusive way than traditional marketing approaches. It introduces the notion that vendors should be prepared to pay customers either in kind or in cash in exchange for their attention. But permission marketing fails to address the challenges marketers face in accessing information about customers who purchase from competing vendors. Even in the case of customers who do business with a particular vendor, that vendor never really knows whether its customers are giving it 10 percent of their business or 100 percent. Unable to get information about customers whom the company doesn't already have, the company must revert back to its old techniques of interruption marketing to get more business from existing customers.

An economic force works against permission marketing per se as follows. The high value of an acquired customer enables marketers to profit from making so many calls and sending so many pieces of direct mail—even when consumers reply only 2 percent of the time. Moreover, marketers don't bear the cost of the interruption—the consumer, who pays for it with his or her time, bears it instead.

Thus we have a widening gulf between marketers and consumers. Not long ago, consumers regularly responded to marketing surveys. Today most will complete surveys only if they receive rewards in cash or in kind. Customers once provided companies with referrals for new business; today they rarely give out such information for free. Ten years ago, many consumers responded politely to telemarketers who called them at home during the dinner hour to conduct surveys. Today people resent the imposition on their time. Soon consumers will demand that telemarketers compensate them, just as people now routinely receive compensation for participating in focus groups.

The Internet only makes the dilemma more acute. As the Internet lowers barriers to market entry and the number of product vendors expands, marketers will confront growing competition for customers' attention. Most will increase their use of advertising, direct mail, telemarketing, and spam. Numbed consumers will pay less and less attention, prompting all the more advertising in response. These same dynamics will play themselves out as companies use the Internet to capture ever more detailed customer information, and consumers will respond with demands for stricter government controls on information capture and use.

Power shifts to the consumer

The current conflict between marketers and consumers also results from the economics of information capture. Consumers have become all too aware that companies' ability to collect information far outstrips their ability—or inclination—to deliver meaningful value in return. As we've seen, the primary use of customer information by companies today instead seems to be to generate growing volumes of junk mail and unsolicited telemarketing calls. It seems that one of the easiest ways for companies to generate value from the customer information they've captured is to sell it to third-party list companies. The list companies in turn resell the information to a variety of companies that use it to target their direct mail and telemarketing offers. Consumers increasingly recognize that they are selling their "privacy" cheaply to companies that are using it to forward their own interests.

Are consumers selling their "privacy" cheap?

Seen in this light, the privacy backlash for many consumers may have less to do with the desire to keep information about themselves confidential and more to do with the pragmatic assessment that the returns for the information they divulge are, simply put, unsatisfactory. Consumers are rational beings, after all. Most have shown that they are willing to release personal information if they can profit by doing so. In a doctor's office, consumers share intimate details about their health in exchange for appropriate medical care. They share intimate details about their finances with financial advisers because the quality of advice they receive depends on a detailed understanding of this information. They insist that the airline record their frequent-flier numbers so that they may receive miles good for upgrades, free flights, and a growing array of other products and services. In all of these exchanges, the key is for consumers to receive sufficient value in exchange for divulging their information.

Several new technologies will soon enable consumers to challenge marketers for control of their information. (These, and the other technologies discussed in this chapter, are more fully defined in the Appendix, "The Technology Tool Kit.") In the on-line world, these technologies include

- Anonymization software, which allows on-line users to shield their identity as they surf the Web.
- Cookie suppressors, which defeat a Web site's ability to plant information in an on-line user's computer that can be used to identify the user and track his or her behavior.
- E-mail filters, which allow on-line users to screen out unwanted spam.
- Anonymous payment mechanisms, which allow on-line users to buy something without revealing who they are.
- Reverse cookies, which will allow consumers to keep track of and store a record of their own on-line behavior.

In the physical world, these technologies include

- Smart cards, which act like credit or ATM cards but which "remember" their transactions.
- Digital cash, which is like physical-world cash, except that it's used on-line.
- Set-top boxes for televisions, which will allow the consumer to record his or her television-viewing behavior.

These technologies, alone or in combination, will for the first time enable consumers to seize control of information about themselves and choose whether to keep it private or share it with product and service vendors or a third party.

Taken together, or in combination, these technologies allow consumers to obtain much more comprehensive and accurate profiles of their own commercial activities than any individual company—or plausible combination of companies—could hope to collect. Through these technologies, users will be able to choose whether to release or withhold information about themselves. Their decisions will hinge, in large part, on what companies offer them in return for their data.

As these technologies simplify information capture for consumers, they complicate it for companies. Anonymizer sites can cloak the identity of consumers as they surf the Web, shielding the information from vendors. Consumers can use smart cards and reverse cookies to capture and store the names of vendors and transaction amounts (although the ability to obtain details about the specific items a consumer buys will require a common set of standards and protocols).

Consumers will challenge marketers for control of their information

set of standards and protocols). The smart card or reverse cookie user can then routinely download this information into a PC to produce an integrated profile of his or her purchases. More ambitious consumers could merge this information with data collected on viewing meters attached to their television sets to obtain a profile that combines viewing habits with purchasing patterns. Marketers would be willing to pay handsomely for such information.

Thus, in one elegant stroke, these technologies will offer a solution for people worried about privacy. If they don't wish to reveal information, the technology makes denial possible. But if they choose to make information available in return for something of tangible value—as the evidence suggests most consumers will—they will have that opportunity. And so should the seller beware—and be ready with an offer to the consumer.

The rise of the infomediary

Consumers won't have the time, the patience, or the ability to work out the best deals with information buyers on their own (nor will vendors have time to haggle, customer by customer). In order for consumers to strike the best bargain with vendors, they'll need a trusted third party—a kind of personal agent, information intermediary, or *infomediary*—to aggregate their information with that of other consumers and to use the combined market power to negotiate with vendors on their behalf.

In this book, we argue that companies playing the infomediary role will become the custodians, agents, and brokers of customer information, marketing it to businesses (and providing them with access to it) on consumers' behalf, while at the same time protecting their privacy. These new entities will emerge from combinations of companies that provide unique brand franchises, strong relationships with their customers, and radically new strategies. They will become the catalyst for people to begin demanding value in exchange for data about themselves. By offering a variety of agent and targeted marketing services, they will help consumers reduce the "interaction" cost of searching for goods at favorable prices in an environment of proliferating, increasingly complex products.

Because their value to the consumer will come, in part, through lowering the interaction costs consumers face, infomediaries will emerge first in markets where product lines are rapidly changing and complex, and where pricing is opaque or complicated in ways consumers have a hard time understanding. Products in these markets often require substantial research to evaluate and have prices that are hard to compare. Because customers will interact with an infomediary primarily over the Internet, and because the infomediary's services will be essentially information based, infomediaries will also find fertile ground in markets where products and services have high information content and can be delivered in digital form.

The infomediary's role will, in fact, be a very traditional one. As consumers take ownership of their own behavioral and transactional data, they'll create a new form of information supply. By connecting information supply with information demand, and by helping both parties determine the value of that information, infomediaries will build a new kind of information supply chain. Thus will they bridge the widening chasm that separates marketers and consumers.

This book explains how the senior managers of today's biggest corporations—as well as farsighted entrepreneurs—can benefit by taking the customer's side in matters of privacy and information capture. Those who recognize the opportunity to truly champion the customer (rather than simply paying lip service to the idea) will be able to build infomediaries that generate considerable revenues and market value. Companies that choose not to form infomediaries must pay close attention as infomediation invades the markets where they compete. Infomediaries will be the catalyst for sweeping forces that the Internet (and information technology in general) has already set in motion. Companies will ignore these forces only at their own risk.

Notes

1. "A Revolution in Interaction," *McKinsey Quarterly* 1 (1997): 4–23.

2. Seth Godin, president of Yoyodyne Entertainment and author of *eMarketing* (New York: Berkeley Publishing Group, 1995).

2

an agent for
the rest of us

CAPTURING INFORMATION ABOUT CUSTOMERS
and using it for commercial purposes is hardly a
new idea. Entire industries—the direct-marketing
business and the credit information business, for
example—have been built on this activity. But the
infomediary should not be confused with other businesses that trade in customer information.

Traditional direct-marketing "list" or database
companies typically own the marketing data in their
databases and build their business on buying and selling this information to third parties. The potential
for abuse of the information, either in the benign
form of junk mail or in more harmful forms, is high.
The entire focus of these companies is to help vendors find and sell more products or services to cus-

tomers. Credit bureaus operate in much the same way. They focus on helping vendors and lenders reduce credit risk, rather than helping customers get better deals on products or loans.

In contrast, infomediaries do not "sell" or even own the customer profiles they manage; they act as custodians or agents on behalf of their clients. In this role, infomediaries must act aggressively to represent the interests of their clients and help them optimize the value they receive from vendors.

Traditional direct-marketing companies, such as mail-order companies, either develop and market their own products or at least take inventory in the products of others. This gives them a considerable vested interest in selling more of their own products or services. In contrast, infomediaries seek to mobilize as many suppliers of products and services relevant to their clients as possible. In fact, the infomediary has few, if any, products of its own to sell and does not take inventory in the products of others. Instead, it helps deliver appropriate marketing messages and facilitate transactions, and in return it receives a commission for helping to connect buyers and sellers.

The few analogues to infomediary businesses tend to be traditional (often noncommercial) associations or precursors to infomediaries on the Internet. Many associations have emerged to help customers. The American Association of Retired Persons (AARP), which emerged as an association to help senior citizens protect and extend government benefits, now provides a broad range of services designed to help senior citizens get discounts on products such as health insurance and automobile insurance. The American Automobile Association (AAA), which started by helping stranded motorists, now helps motorists get low-cost auto insurance and other services. Even earlier, churches and labor unions provided their members assistance in getting more value from vendors in their communities.

These analogues are quite limited relative to the potential of the infomediary as outlined here. In most cases, these associations and institutions provide help by aggregating buying power across large memberships. Because these analogues focus on buying power, they rarely capture detailed profiles of individual members in any systematic form, and they resist pressures to tailor offerings to individual members. The focus on buying power also tends to limit the range of products and services that can be offered to members. These analogues concentrate on products or services that are broadly needed by their membership. To strengthen buying power, they offer only a limited number of options within any product or service category. Furthermore, because most of these associations are not profit driven, they have a difficult time expanding the range of members served or the range of product categories represented.

More recently, we've seen a complex ecology of business enterprises emerge on electronic networks. Transaction aggregators like E*Trade and General Electric's TPN Register are creating electronic marketplaces that facilitate transactions between buyers and sellers. Virtual communities like Motley Fool and Mediconsult explicitly seek to help their members extract more value from vendors, by creating environments that integrate information and communication capability so that customers can compare notes and then bargain with interesting vendors. Portals like America Online and Yahoo! are trying to position themselves as a "first stop" for anyone seeking access to the Internet, a place where people can quickly and conveniently find the resources that are most useful to them. In various ways, these enterprises are new kinds of *inter*mediaries, focusing on the opportunity to capture information about their customers and, using this information, to help customers connect with vendors.

What if every consumer had an agent?

But most are still missing some key ingredients of the *info*mediary business model. For example, information capture for these businesses is still largely a by-product of other business activities on the network. Few, if any, of these businesses are explicitly negotiating with their customers to capture information about a broader range of their activities on the network. Few of these businesses have developed the necessary skills to use the information they are already capturing to maximize the value delivered back to the customer. Chapter 4 explores in more detail the requirements for these kinds of network-based businesses to evolve into infomediaries.

Consumer advocates

To get a better idea of how infomediaries differ from other businesses, we need to look more closely at the role infomediaries will play for consumers. In this role, the infomediary will become the consumer's advocate, or agent.

Film, stage, and television actors know they've reached a certain level of accomplishment in their career when they attract the services of an agent. Good agents know nearly everything about their actors—whether they can mimic a Russian accent, work out of the country for extended periods of time, or get along with a particular director or producer. With this knowledge and the best interests of their clients' career in mind, agents search out appropriate employment opportunities for actors and receive a percentage of the actors' earnings in return.

Writers' agents play a similar role. They get to know their authors' work and become familiar with the preferences of publishing houses and editors, the better to find the right fit between book and publisher. Once a manuscript is ready for sale, the agent uses his or her contacts within the industry to hold an auction in which publishers bid for the rights to the manuscript. (Similar auctions generate bids from Hollywood.) The agent then receives a percentage of the writer's advance in return for his or her services.

What if consumers had an agent—not for the books they

might write or the acting they might do, but for their role as consumers? A "consumer agent" could get to know clients' wants, needs, and preferences—as well as their disposable income and demographic profile—and could use this knowledge (as well as knowledge of vendors) to create a kind of "reverse market" each time a client wants to buy something. (In contrast to conventional markets, in which vendors seek out and often have the upper hand over customers, customers seeking out and extracting value from vendors characterize reverse markets.) If clients wanted to buy an automobile, for example, an agent could help them sort through the various cars in their price range and then solicit (and help evaluate) bids from interested car dealers. Consumer agents could play this role for purchases ranging from refrigerators to air conditioners to espresso makers to family vacations in Bali—all for a percentage of the price of the product or service being purchased.

In fact, consumer agents already exist—at least for wealthy consumers. Private bankers help affluent investors buy the financial products that best suit their investment portfolios. Personal shoppers help well-heeled clients buy fashionable clothing at retail. Agents also exist for consumers who don't have a lot of money to spend on apparel or financial products; these "agents" go by the name of "shopping clubs" or "warehouse clubs." Shopping and warehouse clubs perform a limited agent function for their members by purchasing products in volume and passing along the savings to their members.

Travel agents also play a limited agent function by helping their clients select travel destinations and navigate complex reservations systems in return for a commission. To earn these commissions, however, travel agents frequently place their own interests ahead of their clients' by directing clients to travel providers, such as tour groups, that offer the highest (or volume-driven) commissions.

But travel agents and shopping or warehouse clubs can't get

to know each client well enough to help him or her sort through the enormous volume of product information available via the World Wide Web and more traditional channels. It would be too expensive for them to do so. Holding reverse auctions for consumers and helping them select the best offer would be even less economically feasible. That's precisely why there aren't true agents for ordinary (that is, nonwealthy) consumers—it simply costs too much to provide them with effective agent service.

The consumer quandary

But let's imagine for a moment that consumer agents were economically feasible. To effectively meet the consumer needs we described in Chapter 1, they would have to play four roles:

1. Lowering the cost of searching out the product or service that best suits the consumer's needs.

2. Determining the best possible price for that product or service.

3. Shielding the consumer from unwanted intrusions by marketers, at the same time alerting them to new products that truly meet their needs and preferences.

4. Protecting the consumer's personal information and, if the consumer so desires, marketing that information to vendors.

In the early 1990s, the emergence of software agents gave consumers hope that technology might play at least the first two of these four roles. Software agents—a.k.a. "information agents," "knowbots," "infobots," or "netbots"—would go out and search electronic networks and databases for specific product and price information and then comparison shop on the consumer's behalf. The idea was for the software agent to handle the electronic data intelligently so that consumers didn't have to.

But software agents proved a disappointment. For one thing, the lack of standards and protocols between Web sites meant that agents were unable to compare any product features other than price. This left them unable to suggest which product offered the best value—only which one was the cheapest. For their part, vendors soon rebelled against an agent that could read only price; some found a way to block software agents from their Web sites.

New technology has since allowed software agents to handle this search function more effectively. One technology, developed by a company called Junglee, allows software agents to put data from different vendors' Web sites in comparable format— a process called "wrapping the data." And so-called configuration tools now walk consumers through a set of questions about how they intend to use a particular product or service and then focus the agent's search accordingly.

But software agents are still only as good as the information they're given. The more "intelligent" a software agent is about the consumer, the more independently it will act, and the better its results will be. "Intelligence" in this case means being extremely sophisticated about what consumers want, like, need, and value—their hobbies, income, profession, what movies and books they like, whether they have children, what kind of cars they own. Many consumers are hesitant to divulge such intimate details about their lives to anybody, let alone to an electronic entity that might expose their information inappropriately as it crawls across the Web. They

> **Infomediaries will provide the best of both worlds: lower interaction costs and increased privacy**

fear that information given to software agents will lead to an on-slaught of predatory advertising or even more insidious abuses.

Consumers consequently find themselves in a catch-22: if they give an electronic agent personal information, they run the risk of having their privacy compromised. If they withhold their personal information, there's little chance that a software agent will be of much benefit to them. Thus the ability of software agents to lower search costs and find the best value for consumers collides head on with consumers' need to have their privacy and information protected.

The infomediary solution

Infomediaries will give consumers a way out of this quandary. By explicitly pledging to help consumers get as much value as possible for their information—while also vowing to protect that information against abuse—infomediaries will provide consumers with the best of both worlds: lower interaction costs and increased privacy.

Their ability to do so stems from their ability to build an extraordinarily deep and broad informational profile of each consumer. This profile will give the infomediary the unique ability to shield consumers from unwanted intrusions. It will enable the infomediary to lower consumers' high interaction costs. And it will help the infomediary protect consumers from the perils of asymmetric information and moral hazard. Last but not least, the customer information profile, as we'll see, will also prove irresistible to vendors.

Seizing the opportunity to simultaneously protect and enrich consumers will require the infomediary to play three broad roles for clients in which they provide the following:

1. A set of privacy tools that will help them prevent vendors from obtaining information about them during their commercial interactions.

2. A set of profiling tools that will help them capture detailed information about themselves.

3. A range of services that will maximize the value of these profiles to the infomediary's client.

The privacy tool kit

Given consumer anxiety about their personal information, the infomediary's first priority will be to prevent vendors from capturing data about its clients. In on-line markets, vendors can capture a significant amount of information about customers who do nothing more than simply visit their Web site. The vendor can record which site consumers have come from, which pages they viewed while on the vendor's Web site, how long customers spend on each Web page, which product listings they examine, and which Web site they go to next when they leave the vendor's Web site. If the customer registers with the vendor or makes a purchase with a credit card, the vendor can then connect this profile with name, mailing address, e-mail address, credit card number, and whatever other information customers volunteer in the process of registering or purchasing.

To prevent vendors from obtaining data in these ways, infomediaries will furnish each client with a privacy tool kit consisting of software installed on the client's computer as well as an infomediary-issued payment mechanism (initially a credit card, but likely to become a smart card as this technology evolves). The software will give clients an anonymous e-mail address equipped with a filtering technology that will block unwanted spam. The infomediary will also connect clients with a home page on the Web that will allow them to visit other Web sites without revealing anything about their location or identity, and provide them with an easy-to-use "cookie cutter" to prevent vendors from capturing profiles of customers' visits to a Web site and storing this information in a cookie file stored in the customers' own browsers. (These tools are discussed in more detail in the Appendix.) The credit (and, later, smart) card will give them anonymity in their physical-world transactions as well.

The privacy tool kit accomplishes two objectives. First, it denies access to the consumer's name and address (e-mail and snail mail), thereby protecting him or her from unwanted marketing messages. Second, it creates a bargaining opportunity for clients: vendors that want access to information about clients will have to offer something of value in return.

A simple example will help illustrate how the privacy tool kit will work. Customers who buy a lot of books may not want a profile of their book interests or purchases floating around the Internet. What if the customers were looking for or buying books on alcoholism, shyness, interviewing for a new job, or finding a lawyer? In the wrong hands, this information might be damaging to them. Even innocuous book purchases like travel books or books on music might lead to a barrage of commercial messages from vendors trying to determine potential product interests. Remember, on the Internet, customers don't even have to buy the books—the mere fact that they looked for information about such books can be recorded and marketed to others. The privacy tool kit would cloak customers in anonymity, allowing them to browse and purchase without giving away information about themselves.

The profiling tool kit

Once privacy is assured, infomediaries will begin to assemble an informational portrait of their clients. Largely by observing what clients do during their on-line sessions—which Web sites they visit, how much time they spend at each Web site, what kind of content they access, and what purchases they make—infomediaries will gather the information they need to

act effectively as the client's agent in future searches and transactions. (We'll be examining, in later chapters, the kinds
of descriptive and behavioral information such a profile will
contain.)

Profiling software, installed on the client's computer, will
allow the infomediary to observe the client's on-line behavior.
Lest the idea of the infomediary watching its clients' on-line
behavior seems frightening, infomediaries will give their clients
the option of switching off this software at any time and browsing on their own. (Similarly, clients will continue to have the
option of using noninfomediary-issued credit cards at any
time.) The infomediary will be able to take the information
captured by the profiling software and download it to centralized servers maintained by the infomediary, in either real-time
or batch form, at periodic intervals. The infomediary will then
combine the record of on-line activities with transaction
records from the credit card (or smart card) to create a complete
profile of both on-line and traditional retail activity.

By installing profiling software directly on clients' computers—and by giving clients a credit card with which to concentrate their off-line purchases—infomediaries minimize the
need for clients to provide information through surveys or
questionnaires. This both reduces inconvenience for the client
and increases the accuracy of the profile, because people will
often intentionally or unintentionally misrepresent their purchase intentions or true needs and preferences if asked through
a survey or questionnaire.

The value of this kind of customer profile should not be
underestimated. Unlike profiles of customers captured by vendors, customer profiles captured by an infomediary will provide
a much more complete and integrated view of customer transaction activity, needs, and preferences. (This will become clear
in Part II of this book, as we look closely at the differences
between today's profiles and those that will be assembled by

infomediaries.) They will also provide a unique platform for infomediaries to deliver a broad range of valuable services.

The profiling capability highlights the importance of trust. Given the value of this information and its sensitivity to clients, consumers must be able to trust completely that the infomediary will prevent unauthorized access to this information and guard against its potential abuse. In this the infomediary will have to inspire the same level of trust that lawyers command through the client-attorney relationship and that doctors maintain with their patients. The unprecedented profiling capability offered by the infomediary requires complete confidence that the infomediary acts only in the interests of its clients. Any indication of divided loyalties or uncertainty about the priorities of the infomediary will have a chilling effect on clients concerned about their privacy. For this reason, "vendor-facing" infomediaries—those that seek to capture information about customers on behalf of vendors—will likely not succeed. Only "customer-facing" infomediaries are likely to succeed in persuading customers to cooperate in capturing detailed and integrated profiles of their activities.

To return to our example of on-line book buying, the profiling tool kit will provide a detailed profile, not just of all book purchases, but also of all books customers "looked at" on-line. This profile will cover all booksellers the customer visited. It would even extend to related content sites—

The infomediary plays matchmaker between customers and vendors

for example, which book reviews did the customer read in particular Web sites? All of this information would be collected simply by tracking customers as they visit various sites on the Internet—there would be no need to fill out time-consuming questionnaires or purchase logs. Not only will booksellers find enormous value in this profile, but vendors of many different kinds of products or services might also learn about purchase intentions by using book purchases as a "leading indicator" (for example, purchase of travel guides often suggests an impending trip or vacation). The challenge for the infomediary will be to assure customers that these profiles will be protected and used only to advance the interests of the customers, subject to explicit directives from customers regarding privacy.

Services to maximize the value of client profiles

The privacy and profiling tool kits provide a powerful platform for delivering a broad range of services to clients. These tool kits create a unique asset—detailed and integrated client profiles—which will be available only to clients and the infomediary. The value proposition of the infomediary will be to maximize the value of this asset for its clients, consistent with their privacy preferences, through a range of profile-based services. Clients will measure the performance of infomediaries accordingly.

The infomediary's service line to consumers will include filtering services, agent services, targeted marketing services, purchaser identification services, and various data management and analytic services. Each is discussed below.

Filtering services. Filtering services, as the name implies, filter out unwanted marketing messages to consumers. The infomediary will construct a filter to review incoming commercial e-mail and automatically weed out unsolicited messages that do not match the needs or preferences of its clients. Clients can specify in advance any categories of vendors or products they want to include in, or exclude from, this filter service.

Book-buying clients, for example, might indicate that they have no interest in unsolicited commercial messages from booksellers. In this case, the filtering service would lead to a total block on all commercial messages from booksellers. On the other hand, clients might want to receive selected messages about new books that are truly relevant to them. In this case, the infomediary could use the profiles captured through the profiling tool kit to determine which kinds of books are likely to be of greatest interest to their clients and to weed out unsolicited messages about books their clients wouldn't be interested in.

Customers will still receive unsolicited messages via the postal system, of course, but even these should decline over time. As consumers make more and more of their off- and online purchases through the infomediary, vendors will simply become less and less aware of their customers' identity. It will soon become uneconomical for vendors even to send out solicitations randomly. As for unwanted spam (if that's not redundant), the infomediary will filter it out before the consumer gets it.

Agent services. If filtering services go to the heart of consumer anxiety about privacy, agent services address the growing difficulty consumers face dealing with proliferating, and increasingly complex, products. As we demonstrated in the previous chapter, consumers face increasingly high interaction costs when they seek out the right product at the right price—particularly for the high-ticket items that they purchase infrequently. The infomediary's agent services will help lower these interaction costs by helping consumers who are searching out products to find the right one. Then, if customers so desire, the infomediary will solicit bids from relevant vendors. An infomediary might be able to contact relevant car dealers, for example, and solicit bids on the specific model of car the client wishes to buy. Vendors may be reluctant to participate in these auctions, but the infomediary's ability to deliver not just one but large numbers of qualified customers over time will help to overcome this reluctance.

The infomediary will be able to play this matchmaking role thanks to the sophisticated understanding of the consumer's needs and preferences that it has gained from its customer information profile. This matchmaking ability will only expand over time as subsequent transactions and interactions make the infomediary smarter about its clients. As familiarity increases, the amount of time and effort clients must invest in searching out the products that meet their unique needs will decrease.

For example, the infomediary's agent services can help clients find books that are difficult or impossible to find. That obscure book of poetry, history, or cooking—even if it's out of print—becomes more accessible through an agent service. Of course, many Web sites today offer this capability. Customers choosing to use these Web sites, however, risk compromising their privacy through the information they must provide about themselves to initiate the search. In contrast, the infomediary can search anonymously and even make the purchase anonymously on behalf of the customer. Along the way, the infomediary begins to learn preferences, so that customers don't have to "teach" the agent each time they initiate a search. The infomediary agent learns, for example, that a particular customer prefers only hardcover first editions in fine condition when searching for out-of-print novels.

Targeted marketing services. The infomediary will also sell its clients' willingness to receive advertisements and other marketing messages from vendors. Let's say a client is in the market for a new television. The client would notify the infomediary, which would then line up all the vendors interested in sending a marketing message to this "qualified lead." Or suppose a client is searching for the right airline to book a flight for a vacation to Bali. The infomediary would pass through to the client messages from resorts that meet the client's preference profile (for example, upscale resorts catering to couples without children and offering scuba diving and tennis facilities).

For reasons we explain later in this chapter, the opportunity to address consumers as they're considering a purchase is a privilege for which vendors will likely be willing to pay handsomely. They'll also be well disposed to pay to get their messages to clients who are not actively in the market for their particular product at that particular time. After all, the vast majority of consumer advertising works on this basis today.

Each time the client agrees to receive a message from a vendor, the client will be compensated by the vendor through the infomediary. To protect the privacy of its clients, the infomediary will never sell its clients' names or profiles to vendors. It will simply provide vendors with a way to reach clients with their message. The marketing messages will be delivered via e-mail through the infomediary to protect the client's privacy. Upon receipt, clients can choose whether or not to read or respond to them.

Clients might also consent for the infomediary to send them marketing messages relating to a particular product or service every time they search for that product or service on-line. These messages would be prescreened to make sure they meet the client's needs and preferences profile. For example, clients who are audiophiles might indicate to the infomediary that they are willing to receive messages about the latest audio components coming to market.

It's important to note that clients must first request targeted marketing services—they'll never be subjected to unwanted messages or inundated with spam. They can also specify in advance how many of these messages they wish to receive and the specific categories of vendors or products they want included in the service. The only clients who will receive these targeted marketing messages are those who have requested them.

The targeted marketing service will also provide a way for the infomediary to get smarter about its clients as it observes their response to messages. Did they read the message? Did they request more information from the vendor? Did they actually purchase the product? Each delivery of a targeted marketing message adds new insight for the infomediary about the clients' needs and preferences. This new information will help the infomediary to be even more selective and helpful to clients with the next wave of targeted marketing messages. In this way, the infomediary will shield its clients from unwanted intrusions, while allowing messages to pass through that are relevant to their current needs. Infomediaries will thereby lower interaction costs for their clients, while increasing their privacy.

When it comes to book buying, for example, the targeted marketing services of the infomediary might provide a valuable form of "browsing" to complement what the infomediary's agent services can do. Agent-based searches, after all, are of little help when the client isn't even aware of the existence of a book in the first place. Book buyers usually depend on their friends to suggest books they might like, based on an understanding of their preferences. Or they might depend on a book reviewer whose tastes and opinions they trust. Or they might visit their local bookseller. But such approaches can mean that customers miss out on books that might truly interest them.

The infomediary, through its targeted marketing services, will take a much more systematic approach. By watching its clients' purchases and on-line browsing activity, the infomediary will begin to approach selected book vendors and solicit messages from them on books that are relevant to their clients. As a result, each time they open their e-mail, clients will find a carefully selected set of marketing messages matching their preferences.

Purchaser identification services. Thanks to the privacy tool kit that the infomediary will install for them, infomediary clients will have the option of remaining forever anonymous as they browse the Web and make purchases on-line. Those who are willing to reveal their identity, however, will stand to profit from doing so: they'll be paid a small fee by vendors every time they divulge who they are or what their e-mail (or snail-mail) address is. This fee may take the form of a monetary payment, or a discount in the price of the product sold, or the tailoring or customization of the product to better serve the client's needs.

The infomediary will facilitate the transaction by setting up a payment process for vendors to pay clients, by providing a mechanism for the release of the customer's information upon payment, and by negotiating the terms of information disclosure. For example, the vendor will need to contractually commit not to sell to third parties any information it receives through the infomediary.

Of course, by revealing their e-mail address, consumers run the risk that the vendor will send them advertisements or unsolicited messages in the future. Any such messages will then be filtered by the infomediary. But infomediaries won't be able to filter messages arriving by mail or telephone, so consumers who choose to give out their snail-mail address or phone number will do so at their own risk.

Our book-buying client, for example, might be willing to reveal his or her identity because he or she values the services or recommendations of the bookseller.

Customers can choose to remain forever anonymous Through the infomediary's purchaser identification services, the identity of the purchaser might be selectively offered in return for a frequent-purchaser discount or for a tailored service such as a notification service for books written by a certain author the client enjoys. The infomediary would of course impose restrictions on the use of this information by the vendor—for example, the information might be restricted to discount offers only and could not be used to send unsolicited messages. The transfer of this information to third parties would also be prohibited. Vendors that failed to uphold these restrictions would be deprived of purchaser information in the future.

Data management and analytic services. The final service that infomediaries will perform for their clients is to format and deliver a variety of regular reports summarizing transactions and other activities on the network (and in the physical world as well, once smart cards are up and running). Infomediary-supplied analyses will help clients improve their efficiency and effectiveness in such areas as financial budgeting, time management, and expense account management.

In addition to capturing information about clients, the infomediary will also be able to capture detailed information profiles about vendors as a by-product of transaction activity conducted through infomediary services. For example, if a client is interested in purchasing a computer, the infomediary will be able to generate a report summarizing the number of computers sold by major vendors to clients of the infomediary; the number of complaints received, by vendor and computer model; and the number of computers returned to vendors. In this way, the infomediary will provide clients with a kind of mini-*Consumer Reports*.

Individuals don't have an easy time collecting this kind of information themselves—at least not if they want to do it routinely. The infomediary can automate much of this process, provide value-added analytic services, and even benchmark clients against each other in specific categories.

Of course, infomediaries won't be able to provide all these data management and analytic services right from the start. Assembling in-depth vendor profiles, for instance, will first require winning the participation of a large number of vendors. We address this challenge in subsequent chapters.

Book-buying clients, for example, might discover from regular summaries of their purchase activities that they purchase a substantial number of their books in the course of a year from particular publishers and could then use this information to request targeted marketing messages from these publishers.

The economic value of the infomediary
to the client

What will all these services be worth to consumers who sign up with an infomediary? In addition to the value generated by having their privacy interests protected, clients will realize a small portion of the economic value of the infomediary's services in the form of cash payments sent to them regularly by the infomediary. A much larger portion of the economic value will be realized in the form of broader selection and better prices as a result of systematic reductions in interaction costs.

The basic membership in an infomediary service—including the necessary privacy and profiling tool kits—will be free. Filtering, targeted marketing, and purchaser identification services will also be free. Clients will pay the infomediary only when they wish to use agent services. Even in this case, clients will pay only when they actually purchase products generated through an agent search. At that point, clients would pay the infomediary an agency fee of $2\frac{1}{2}$ percent of the purchase price of products purchased through the agency service.

The cost to clients of participating in an infomediary service is therefore negligible. They pay nothing unless they use the agent search service. Even then, the $2\frac{1}{2}$ percent fee is likely to be relatively modest compared to the savings clients experience from the greater selection and price transparency made possible by an agent service. Assuming clients save on average 15 percent of the purchase price of products sourced through an agent service, the savings will far outweigh the fee paid for use of the service.

In dollar terms, assuming 15 percent savings on the purchases that are likely to be addressable with agent services, infomediaries will generate roughly $1,340 in annual savings for the average client household. (This estimate assumes that the average infomediary household spends roughly $8,900 per year on goods and services that can be sourced through an agent service.) Deducting the 2½ percent fee charged by the infomediary yields net annual savings of $1,110 for the average client household. These savings do not take into account the time clients save by not searching for products themselves, nor do they attempt to quantify the value to clients from discovering more appropriate products as a result of lower interaction costs.

Clients will also receive cash payments in return for providing selected vendors with access to their information profiles, either through the purchaser identification service or the targeted marketing service. (This part of the infomediary's service will take time to unfold, as infomediaries build enough vendors to generate the payments.) The amount of the cash payment will, of course, depend on the privacy preferences of individual clients. Clients who choose to remain totally anonymous and not receive any marketing messages from vendors will forgo cash payments in return for the assurance of their privacy. Clients who are comfortable with the controls imposed by the infomediary on access to their information profiles, and who see the value of selective disclosure to vendors, could generate cash payments for themselves. The average infomediary client could receive as much as $260 in cash payments per year from the purchaser identification service and the targeted marketing service.

Clients will receive cash for giving access to their profiles

Considering the net savings to the client from using the infomediary's agent services and the revenue generated for the client from purchaser identification and targeted marketing services, each infomediary household would generate an average total quantifiable value of roughly $1,400 annually. This represents almost 9 percent of the total household spending activity likely to be handled by the infomediary. Roughly 20 percent of this benefit will be in the form of cash generated from the client profiles, and the remaining 80 percent will be in the form of net savings on products purchased.

Why vendors will benefit

It's easy to see why consumers might want to participate in a service that promises to both protect their privacy and provide them roughly $1,400 worth of value every year. But why would vendors decide to participate in a service that will make them pay for their access to consumers and for the information they previously got for free?

Despite the higher up-front costs, most vendors will soon realize that infomediaries can give them unprecedented access to customers. And not just to any customers, but to desirable ones who are looking to buy something they need. As mentioned in the previous chapter, vendors today struggle to obtain information about people who are not yet their customers. As low response rates to direct mailings prove, marketers can only guess whether they can convert noncustomers to customers. Marketers may now be able to afford mailing and calling even when 98 percent of customers ignore their entreaties. But the unaccounted-for intrusion cost to consumers has created a backlash that makes infomediation—or government regulation—inevitable.

Infomediaries will build more detailed and comprehensive information profiles about customers than vendors could ever have hoped to create on their own. Properly constructed information profiles will allow marketers to more reliably reach and convert prospects into customers. Vendors will see their cost of customer acquisition—for many companies their highest marketing cost—significantly decline. They will also reduce churn and increase cross-selling, while gaining more cost-effective insight into opportunities for product enhancements and customization.

By protecting the interests of its clients, and by building an integrated profile of their descriptive and behavioral information, the infomediary will create a new and differentiated supply of customer information that will be extremely valuable to vendors.

Portal to the consumer

Infomediaries will supply their service line to vendors through a "portal" service that will connect vendors with the customers they want to reach. This will include three broad service offerings: customer acquisition services, targeted marketing services, and market research services.

Customer acquisition services. The infomediary's first service to vendors will be to deliver them a steady flow of potential customers. This service will be provided free of charge to vendors and will be an outgrowth of the agent services described above. As the infomediary's search agent software finds the best fit between a particular product or service and its client's exact needs and preferences, the infomediary will facilitate, or "introduce," the vendor and customer. Leads generated in this fashion will have high conversion rates for vendors and will be especially valuable for marketers in categories with infrequent purchases and high costs of finding customers (examples include automobile sales, many categories of financial services, and computer equipment, to name just a few).

These services will prove far more effective than conventional mass-marketing advertising in traditional media. Even if infomediary clients were to respond to targeted messages only 10 percent of the time—and one could imagine much higher rates of response given the ability to query the database in fine detail—vendors would experience a five- to tenfold improvement over the average response rate of direct marketing programs today.

Vendors will get unprecedented access to customers

This low-cost avenue for customer acquisition will also have other benefits for both vendor and infomediary because it will likely make vendors more willing to accept open standards for how they represent data about their products on their Web sites.

The customer acquisition services of the infomediary will deliver to booksellers, for example, a steady stream of customers searching for specific books. Many will search for these books based on price, but other factors will also drive searches, including the availability of the book, shipping options, and, in the case of out-of-print books, the condition of the book.

Targeted marketing services. Working with an infomediary will not only give vendors a stream of qualified leads but also enable them to conduct more targeted searches against specific criteria in order to identify appropriate customers for their marketing messages. Let's say, for example, that a computer manufacturer seeks women who work at home, have school-age children, have purchased graphics-intensive computers and peripherals in the past, but haven't purchased a computer in the past two years. The infomediary's targeted marketing service could search its database, identify the number of matches, and negotiate with the vendor to deliver targeted marketing messages to clients who have indicated a willingness to receive such messages.

Vendors could also specify to the infomediary that they are

interested in sending an advertisement or marketing offer to any infomediary client who happens to be searching or browsing a particular subject area or product category. (Recall that clients would first have had to declare themselves willing to receive messages under such circumstances, and at no time would the infomediary provide the vendor with a list of clients, identify those clients by name, or communicate individual profile information.) This differs from the "selling-search words" provided by portals like Yahoo! because the messages can be more specific to the individual, instead of to a category. For example, if a client is searching for vacation information, and the infomediary knows the client has small children and enjoys the outdoors, the infomediary could deliver a message about vacation opportunities in mountain cabins, rather than the generic vacation information a typical portal would deliver. The infomediary will also be able to monitor the client's behavior across Web sites. Portals can observe behavior only at their own site. This will give the infomediary (as we will see later in this book) a much richer client profile than the portal would be able to assemble.

This service will enable vendors to target their marketing efforts very precisely. They'll be able to combine delivery of the message with the option of immediately buying the product or service. And they'll be able to measure the performance of the message based on purchase response rates, not just on requests for more information.

To go back to our book-buying example, targeted marketing services will allow booksellers and publishers to reach those readers who are most likely to be interested in specific book titles, authors, or genres. Subject to the privacy constraints imposed by the infomediary's clients, booksellers will be able to present new books directly to the most attractive readers and offer them the opportunity to purchase these books as soon as they receive the marketing message.

Market research services. Besides enabling vendors to more precisely target their marketing messages, infomediaries will help them improve their market research. Infomediaries will be in a strong position to provide market research services for vendors by "looking across" broad aggregations of client profiles. The value to the vendor would be in identifying patterns to help in either targeting marketing messages more effectively or increasing customer retention and repurchase.

For example, the infomediary might work with a vendor to identify characteristics of segments of customers who are buying competitors' products. It might turn out that competitors are much more effective in selling to senior citizens, either because their messages are tailored to that demographic or because some feature of their products is more appealing. This insight might emerge first from studying purchase patterns across infomediary clients and then from following up with targeted focus groups recruited from purchasers of the competing products. Such market research can be done today, but in most markets the costs of identifying purchasers of competitive products, assembling enough purchase data to be meaningful, and then comparing this data with detailed personal profiles of the purchasers is time consuming and expensive.

Once again, we can get an idea of the value of this service by looking at it in a specific industry context. Today, the only timely information available to book publishers about book purchases comes from limited store samples; publishers can only infer sell-through information based on unsold book inventory returns, a lagging (and expensive) indicator. This lack of information creates substantial advantage for large national retail book chains, because they are the only ones with large enough data samples to understand demand patterns. But even these retailers have limited ability (except through frequent-buyer clubs) to track book purchases down to the individual consumer. The infomediary could provide considerable value to both publishers and retailers by aggregating meaningful demand pattern data and by providing insight on the ability of specific authors or genres to appeal to certain demographic segments.

A virtuous circle between customers and vendors

Working with an infomediary will create advantages for both vendors and consumers. Vendors will be forced to make a number of changes in the way they think about and use customer information. They will be forced to reassess and overhaul forecasting and inventory management processes—leading to substantial operating savings and asset leverage—in order to reflect the value of much more detailed information regarding customer demand patterns. They will also be forced to reengineer their research and development processes to take full advantage of information about customer needs and preferences.

Customers, meanwhile, will become more open about what they share with vendors as their privacy becomes better protected and their personal information generates value. Customers will find that, by providing information about themselves to the infomediary, they can substantially reduce search costs and increase the likelihood of purchasing the best possible product at the lowest price. They will also discover that the infomediary, by comparing their profiles with the profiles of other clients, can help connect them with helpful and valuable products and services of which they were not aware. Relying on the infomediary, clients will find that they can extract value from vendors in return for more information about themselves, whether that value is in the form of cash payments or tailored products and services.

Thus infomediaries set in motion a powerful virtuous cycle: the more value vendors learn to deliver to customers in return for access to customer information, the more willing infomediaries' clients will be to let them have that access. And the more access vendors have, the more value they will be able to deliver, and so on.

The infomediary addresses real unmet needs of customers while at the same time delivering value to vendors. Certain markets are much more likely to provide fertile ground for infomediaries in the near term than other markets are. Our next chapter describes which markets infomediaries are likely to find the most promising.

3

promising
markets

TECHNOLOGY SEERS HAVE FOR YEARS FORECAST
the arrival of a frictionless economy. "Frictionless," in
this case, means an economy free of interaction costs,
or what economists call "transaction costs." As we
explained in Chapter 1, these are the costs of searching, coordinating, and monitoring that consumers
(and companies) incur when they exchange goods,
services, and ideas. McKinsey research shows that
interaction costs at the economywide level represent
more than a third of the U.S. GDP. In less-developed
economies, interaction costs are even higher.[1]

Thanks to information technology and other factors, interaction costs are indeed falling rapidly. Consumers, however, have not fully benefited. In some
markets, consumers have profited from lower prices
as margin gets pulled out of the distribution channel

by new intermediaries and redistributed, in part, to them. But few, if any, of these intermediaries have focused on the interaction costs consumers incur as they search for and buy products and services. Fewer still have identified privacy as an important consumer issue.

In the first two chapters of this book, we asserted that infomediaries will emerge to target this opportunity. In so doing, they will extend the benefits of the frictionless economy to the average consumer household, particularly in those product and service areas in which consumers continue to experience high interaction costs. This chapter explores a few of the markets—such as personal financial services and health care—that we believe are ripe for infomediation and describes how infomediaries will emerge there.

Friction-filled markets

First, let's define those characteristics that make markets favorable for infomediaries. In general, the most promising markets for infomediation are those in which, due to market inefficiencies, both consumers and vendors incur more costs than necessary. For the consumer, these inefficiencies create high costs to find products and services, and can cause them to buy a suboptimal product, pay too much, or not buy at all. Market inefficiencies can also result in pricing that doesn't match the product's value, in customers' paying more than they should have, and in vendors selling less than they could have. On balance, both consumers and vendors are worse off as a result of these inefficiencies, although vendors sometimes benefit through higher prices.

Infomediaries will deliver value to their clients by focusing,

"Frictionless" markets rarely benefit consumers.

especially in the early stages of their development, on markets in which consumers and vendors experience substantial inefficiencies in locating each other, and in which pricing is opaque or complicated in a way that consumers have a hard time understanding. These products are often ones that require substantial research to understand and evaluate, where prices are hard to compare.

High search and distribution costs

When asked, most consumers will say that they shop around for the best price for products and services, but McKinsey (and other) research shows that these efforts are in fact quite limited. For many consumers, the time and cost of finding vendors and comparing prices limit their appetite for searching and shopping, even for major items like automobiles, mortgages, and insurance. Instead, customers commit to these major purchases after only one or two phone calls, or one or two visits to vendors.

Although there are many important determinants of individual shopping behavior, the time and cost associated with the process of getting information are critical. The difficulty for consumers is getting enough knowledge or experience to see beyond the company-provided literature or advertising to assess and differentiate attributes of a product or service. In the absence of such information, many consumers default to associating higher prices with better product attributes and vice versa—which isn't always, of course, an effective means of differentiation.

Markets with high search costs for consumers also tend to be characterized by high distribution costs for vendors. The cost of finding customers, as well as the cost of delivering information about product features and benefits, is the primary driver of these distribution costs.

In markets with high search and distribution costs, infomediaries can leverage profiles of their clients to identify relevant information and well-matched products and services for their clients. Infomediaries can also use their customer acquisition and targeted marketing services to lower customer acquisition costs for vendors.

Pricing distortions

Infomediaries will also take root in markets where customers have difficulty finding the market price for a specific product or service due to poor or costly information. These difficulties are in part due to the fact that many vendors price discriminate, charging one customer one price for a product and other customers another, according to what the market will bear. In general, pricing gets distorted when products and services are bundled or priced in indirect ways, as they are, for instance, with checking accounts, where consumers pay some combination of explicit fees and in some cases forgo interest revenue. Consumers are thus unable to meaningfully compare providers based on explicit charges. Infomediaries will be able to get good traction in product markets with these types of distortions. Again, they represent a chance for consumers to find the best provider for their needs through both agent and filter services.

Other important economic features of attractive markets

Other markets ripe for infomediation include those in which

- The profitability to vendors of individual customers varies widely.
- Products and services have high information content.

- Customers can easily purchase and use products and services "remotely," away from the presence of a retailer or a manufacturer.

Widely varying customer profitability

In industries where customer profitability varies widely, some customers inevitably subsidize others, meaning that they pay more so that others can pay less. Subsidies happen for a number of reasons, including different levels of product or service usage by the customer, different levels of customer loyalty, different costs to serve different customers, and the pricing-related reasons described above. Where profitability varies for any of these reasons other than cost, an infomediary, through its agent and filter services, can help individual consumers recapture the part of their profitability that subsidizes other customers. The infomediary can also help vendors to properly price, or avoid, customers who need to be subsidized. Infomediaries will do so by delivering good prospects to vendors and by efficiently matching offers to consumers.

Some customers inevitably subsidize others

High information content

Because customers will interact with an infomediary primarily over the Internet (and because the infomediary's agent and filter services are essentially information based), products and services with high information content will offer more opportunities for infomediation than those that are less easily digitized. (Products with high information content include, for example, computer goods, mortgages, and local and long-distance phone service.) The advantage of information-intensive products and services is the consumer's (and the consumer agent's) ability to evaluate them through specifications rather than through physical characteristics. These products will lend themselves well to the infomediary's search and filter functions.

Digitization and remote purchase

Goods and services that can be purchased and delivered digitally (such as airline tickets, hotel reservations, stocks, news, and software) also present good opportunities for infomediation. Digitized and remote-purchase products and services (such as information, education, entertainment, and financial services) won't require the more complicated handoff and multiple-step search and selling efforts that physical-world products often do.

This tendency to gravitate toward digitized and remote-purchase products—as well as the fact that most interactions with the infomediary will take place on-line—also explains why infomediaries will likely get their start with consumers who have computers and who can and will search out products and make purchases on-line.

The best markets for consumer infomediation

Which markets exhibit these characteristics? To approach this question systematically, we took each of the above market characteristics and applied them to the product and service categories on which Americans spend the most. As shown in Table 3-1, we ranked each spending category on a scale of 1 to 5, with a maximum score of 5 for each attribute; the highest any spending category could achieve was 35. This ranking yielded 15 categories in which infomediaries have strong opportunity to benefit consumers, as shown in Table 3-2.

TABLE 3-1 Household Spending

	Average annual spending per household ($)	ECONOMIC FACTOR					OTHER		
		High search costs	Pricing distortions	Varying customer profitability	High information content	Absolute size	Remote feasibility	Privacy benefits	Total score
Food	4,505								
• Food at home	2,803	1	1	2	1	4	1	1	11
• Food away from home	1,702	1	1	3	1	3	1	1	11
Housing	10,465								
• Owned dwellings*	3,754	3	3	5	3	5	3	2	24
• Rented dwellings	1,786	3	2	3	2	3	3	2	18
• Miscellaneous	899	1	1	3	2	2	2	1	12
Utilities, fuels, and public services	2,193								
• Electricity	870	2	2	2	1	2	3	1	13
• Telephone	708	2	2	3	2	2	4	1	16
• Miscellaneous	107	1	2	2	1	1	2	1	10
Household operations	508	2	2	3	2	1	1	1	12
Housekeeping supplies	430	1	1	2	1	1	3	1	10
Household furnishings and equipment	1,403	3	4	4	1	3	2	1	18

Scale = 1 to 5, with 5 indicating highest correlation.
*Excludes payments made on mortgage principal.

TABLE 3-1 Household Spending (*continued*)

	Average annual spending per household ($)	ECONOMIC FACTOR					OTHER		
		High search costs	Pricing distortions	Varying customer profitability	High information content	Absolute size	Remote feasibility	Privacy benefits	Total score
Apparel	1,704	2	2	4	1	3	1	2	15
Transportation	6,016								
• Vehicle purchases	2,639	3	4	3	1	4	3	1	19
• Gas and motor oil	1,006	1	1	2	1	2	1	1	9
• Maintenance and repairs	653	2	3	3	1	2	1	1	13
• Vehicle insurance	713	3	3	3	2	2	4	2	19
• Public transportation	355	1	1	2	1	1	1	1	8
• Miscellaneous	650	2	1	1	1	2	1	1	9
Health care	1,732								
• Health insurance	860	2	2	3	4	2	3	2	18
• Medical services	511	2	3	3	4	2	1	5	20
• Miscellaneous	361	1	2	3	3	1	2	4	16
Entertainment	1,612								
• Fees and admissions	433	2	1	2	2	1	2	2	13
• Television, radios, sound equipment	542	3	2	3	2	1	2	1	14
• Miscellaneous	637	1	2	2	3	2	3	2	15

	Average annual spending per household ($)	ECONOMIC FACTOR					OTHER		
		High search costs	Pricing distortions	Varying customer profitability	High information content	Absolute size	Remote feasibility	Privacy benefits	Total score
Reading and education	634	2	2	3	3	2	2	2	16
Personal-care products and services	403	2	2	3	3	2	1	3	16
Alcoholic beverages	277	1	1	3	2	1	1	3	12
Tobacco products and smoking	269	1	2	4	1	1	3	4	16
Personal insurance and pensions	2,967								
• Life and other personal insurance	374	4	3	3	3	1	3	2	19
• Pensions and social security	2,593	3	3	3	3	2	2	2	18
Cash contributions	925	2	1	2	2	2	2	2	13
Miscellaneous services†	766	3	3	3	3	2	3	2	18
Total	**32,275**								

Scale = 1 to 5, with 5 indicating highest correlation.
†Legal and accounting fees, funeral expenses, finance charges excluding home or vehicle.

We further classified these spending categories into two spending groups—essentials, and consumption and lifestyle—each of which is more or less initially accessible to different infomediaries depending on their capabilities, brand, customer base, and alliance and "web" partners. Because essentials tend to score higher against the market characteristics that are favorable to infomediation, infomediaries are likely to build from an initial position in these product areas. (These classifications are applicable mostly to consumers; the last section in this chapter addresses infomediaries' opportunity to provide services to small businesses.)

Essentials

The two biggest purchases the average consumer makes are a house (or apartment) and a car, either of which can also be leased. Given the complexity of these purchases and the number of product and vendor choices involved (not to mention the

---

TABLE 3-2
Categories of Opportunity

Owned dwellings	24
Medical services	20
Vehicle purchases	19
Vehicle insurance	19
Life and other personal insurance	19
Rented dwellings	18
Health insurance	18
Household furnishings and equipment	18
Pensions and social security	18
Miscellaneous services	18
Telephone	16
Personal-care products and services	16
Reading and education	16
Miscellaneous health care	16
Tobacco products and smoking	16

myriad other purchases, such as insurance, that go with them), housing and transportation are two of the most promising markets for infomediaries to take hold.

As a whole, the group of essential purchases listed in Table 3-3 represents almost 50 percent of household expenditures and includes a large portion of big-ticket, periodic purchases, as well as services purchased on a recurring basis, such as telephone expenditures, which the consumer needs to search for. In addition, many of these products and services include an important financing or financial services component.

Infomediaries will identify customers interested in purchasing the more costly of these products and services, such as dwellings and vehicles, by tracking their browsing and search behavior on-line.

Housing. Housing represents the largest single expenditure for most consumers, not just for the house or apartment itself, but for all the purchases and new vendor relationships that go with

---

TABLE 3-3
Essential Household Purchases

Housing
• Owned dwellings	24
• Rented dwellings	18
• Telephone	16
• Electricity	13

Transportation
• Vehicle purchases	19
• Vehicle insurance	19

Health care
• Medical services	20
• Health insurance	18
• Miscellaneous	16

Financial services
• Pensions and social security	18
• Miscellaneous services	18

it. Three types of entities are targeting the "home purchase and ownership" opportunity: real estate brokers, mortgage companies, and Internet portals.

Most notable among the mortgage brokers is E-Loan (www.eloan.com). Initially an on-line mortgage service, E-Loan has expanded to include thorough information on mortgages and tools to demystify and simplify the mortgage decision-making process. E-Loan offers extensive rate comparisons and product variety. Two E-Loan services that fit well with the infomediary model are its "monitor a loan" and "rate watch" services. "Monitor a loan" allows a client to enter his or her existing mortgage data and receive e-mail notification from E-Loan when mortgage rates drop enough to justify a refinance. "Rate watch" allows the client to preset loan rates and terms they're looking for (for example, 10-year fixed, 7 percent, < 1 point), and E-loan sends notification when loan rates drop to that level.

Infomediaries will track consumer behavior on-line

Realtor.net, the official site of the National Association of Realtors, stands out in this market from the real estate perspective. Realtor.net offers searchable listings of over 1 million homes, as well as information on neighborhoods and neighborhood services. Interested clients are provided with name and contact information for the broker handling the property, thereby continuing to support the local realtor market. Although Realtor.net offers links to neighborhood and relocation services, such as child care, change-of-address services, and moving companies, as well as mortgage information (through a partnership with Rate.net), Realtor.net doesn't offer any personalized services or notification services. Another real estate site, Coldwell Banker (www.coldwellbanker.com), allows users to input desired house specifications (location, number of bedrooms, and so on) and receive an e-mail from Coldwell Banker when a house matching their specifications comes to market.

Finally, the portals have captured the best of both worlds by partnering with real estate and lending groups to create full-service sites. For example, Yahoo! offers a wealth of information and resources on home buying, real estate listings, mortgage financings, and so on, at realestate.yahoo.com. It has done so by partnering with E-Loan, CyberHomes, InsWeb, The School Reports, and Virtual Relocation.com, among others. Yahoo! Real Estate offers perhaps the most complete set of services, with services interacting as a collection of independent services offered by individual companies.

Although each of these types of businesses contains elements of what an infomediary would offer in the home purchase and ownership market, infomediaries will have the opportunity to take control of this market by providing an integrated, single-source, highly personalized experience. The infomediary could offer resources for buying a home, such as buying tips, mortgage loans, personal financial management, and neighborhood information.

The infomediary could also act as the intelligent search agent for the best home ownership resources, such as homeowner's insurance, second mortgages, refinancing recommendations, home redesign services, neighborhood news and information, community chat services, contractor recommendations, and so on. And it could provide a conduit for extremely well timed, targeted messages that would be initiated by clients' searches for these home ownership services.

The infomediary would start by making a few simple inferences. Customers who look at on-line real estate or rental listings in a particular city, for instance, might be considered reasonable prospects for moving to that city. Add a couple of trips to the city and some searching for information from moving companies or about the weather, and the infomediary could make pretty strong inferences that would allow it to deliver targeted messages from real estate brokers, mortgage companies, homeowners' insurance providers, and furniture and appliance manufacturers. Subsequent to the purchase, a large number of service providers and local vendors would be interested in getting access to this new customer: utilities, grocers, dry cleaners, and pharmacists, to name just a few.

These types of opportunities aren't available just for home purchasers. Renters changing homes also undertake significant levels of spending and establish a whole new set of relationships. As consumers search on-line rental listings and engage in other behavior indicative of a move, an infomediary would be positioned to play many of the value-added roles described for new home buyers.

The key for the infomediary will be to get better and better at making inferences about the meaning of behavior, particularly for critical major events such as moving.

Transportation. Few markets attract more controversy over pricing than the car market. Saturn's promise of a no-haggle car-buying experience gained national publicity and praise, for example. And in a recent survey, used-car dealers retained their ranking as the least-trusted profession (pharmacists were most trusted, followed closely by the clergy). Allegations of hidden charges, overpriced extras, and high-pressure tactics—most of which are the result of a high degree of information asymmetry—make the experience less than enjoyable for many. More and more consumers are doing their homework in hopes of being able to negotiate the best deal. Increasingly, new car buyers are using the Internet to look up car specifications, reviews, and pricing before making a purchase.

These behavioral changes make sense given the value consumers place on their automobiles. For starters, cars are typically the second most valuable asset most people own, outranked only by their home. On average, consumers spend almost $6,000 annually on transportation, including vehicle purchase, fuel, insurance, repairs, fees, and financing. A car is also a visible and personal belonging that, to some, carries certain attributes that become affiliated with its owner.

These characteristics combine to make the automotive market an attractive one for infomediation. Indeed, an active online market for automobiles already exists. Car-buying services like Auto-by-Tel and Autoweb.com accept orders from buyers on the Internet and forward them to dealers who have agreed to sell at preestablished discounted prices. Roughly one in five auto purchases is made by a buyer who has consulted the Internet or a traditional car-buying service first, so it's not surprising that a recent survey by J. D. Power & Associates found that only 10 percent of dealers viewed the Internet as a help, whereas 48 percent saw it as a threat. Auto-by-Tel has secured a network of 2,700 dealers around the country and stopped allowing new dealers to join the network.

In addition, interaction costs are particularly high, as reflected by the typically large price differentials to consumers across different dealers. Traditionally, the time and cost of traveling to different dealerships and playing the elaborate negotiation game has discouraged consumers from really shopping around for the best price. Five, ten, even twenty percent purchase price differences were not uncommon. The Internet erases traditional geographic boundaries, allowing low-cost dealers to market their wares to anyone surfing the Web.

Finally, although the level of uncertainty isn't as pronounced as it is in the computer equipment market, where rapidly changing technology can make a product quickly obsolete, the automobile market continues to undergo technological change as car manufacturers roll out new models at record speeds. Moreover, customers interested in a convertible would have to visit several different dealers (say, Porsche, Mazda, Saab, and

BMW) to see the cars and get the details, which makes it nearly impossible to do a side-by-side comparison. The Internet makes all this possible . . . except, of course, for the test drive.

The infomediary will also lower the interaction costs of all the other purchases that accompany purchasing an automobile. Car buyers may need financing, for instance, and insurance. They may also want cell phones, advanced stereo systems, and GPS equipment. Profile-based targeting and agent services could help vendors find the most desirable customers (for instance, insurance companies will be interested in those with the best driving records) and help customers find the best values.

Health care. The health care market is particularly well suited to infomediation. The topic has mass appeal, as indicated by the proliferation of Web sites and the fact that over 50 percent of Internet users express an interest in content related to health care. Technological and therapeutic advances, an increasingly active and aware consumer, and the rising cost of health care have unleashed a host of changes in the industry that make it an attractive, albeit challenging, market for infomediation.

Consumers and employers alike are proactively seeking information to help them evaluate the full range of health care options. Those looking to choose a health plan (HMO, PPO, fee-for-service) often visit Mediconsult (www.mediconsult. com). Those looking for medical information often browse at Healthfinder (www.healthfinder.gov/). And a popular site for those trying to evaluate the cost and quality of health care services is the Medical Cost and Quality Assistance home page (www.mecqa.com/).

Of the more than 6,500 health care–related Web sites identified by Yahoo!'s search engine, the vast majority are information-based, as opposed to product-based, sites. The sites provide access to drug databases, disease-specific community groups, profile-based news updates, referral networks, age/gender/race-related health concerns, and so on. Sites range from being broad and untargeted (PharmInfoNet.com, run by VirSci Corp., a software provider to the pharmaceutical industry) to those focused on demographic segments (AARP) or targeted to a specific life stage (babycenter.com, run by a privately held new media company called BabyCenter, Inc.).

Infomediaries will be able to succeed in the health care market because interaction costs are significant, the product has high information content, the need for privacy is high, and it takes a lot of time and effort to search out the most effective treatment and the best treatment provider. And, as we mentioned in Chapter 1, health care is an industry where consumers, because of their loss of faith in traditional providers, are subject to the risks of moral hazard. As the battle for cost reduction continues, consumers no longer blindly trust that their physician will always look out for their best interests. For example, many question whether their relatively short hospital stay was based on their own best interests or those of the hospital or health plan.

Consumers demand to keep medical information private

Another important factor is that health care is a sector where both consumers and providers face significant technological, and to a lesser degree regulatory, uncertainty. The rapid introduction of new products from pharmaceutical companies, medical device manufacturers, and biotech companies is exceeded only by the impressive pace of research discoveries and the promise of even more effective treatments in the not-too-distant future. Infomediaries can help customers get the information they need most, when they need it.

Finally, health care is a market in which customers demand privacy. One's health condition is personal, and consumers don't want their neighbors, friends, or employers to know that they're inquiring about treatments for AIDS or sexually transmitted diseases, mental health problems, addictions, alternative medicines, and a range of other health concerns. The ability to cloak oneself in anonymity is of utmost importance here.

Privacy concerns around health care may cut two ways for an aspiring infomediary. On the one hand, privacy is at the core of the infomediary value proposition. On the other, consumers may be less likely to explicitly or implicitly reveal private details about their health conditions than, say, about their housing or automotive needs. This likelihood means that infomediaries will need to think about the sequencing of arenas in which they operate and the extensibility of their domain expertise and brand as they extend infomediary services across product and service categories. Clearly, a customer relationship company like a health care provider would be more credible, earlier, than would a bank for this important essentials category. We'll discuss these sequencing issues in Part II of this book.

Financial services. Financial services are ubiquitous today. They are part of the financing and insuring of homes, the leasing of rental property, and even health care. As a result, an infomediary that understands emerging needs in these areas, based in particular on search behavior or agent services, can identify and help consumers meet these directly related financial service needs.

The category we refer to as "Financial services" in Table 3-3 includes a variety of products and services that consumers use to meet their payments, financing, savings, and protection needs. These products are ideal for delivery over networks, as they are nonphysical goods that do not require costly land-based delivery services.

Purchasing financial services isn't easy for consumers. Most consumers seek tailored information to help them improve their decision making. For any given product, constantly moving pieces (rates, terms, points, fees, and so on) frequently perplex the unsophisticated or out-of-date buyer. But financial services demand an increasingly high level of personal involvement, given how they affect an individual's quality of life, as well as the quality of life of his or her heirs.

Pricing also varies widely in this market. Consumers with identical needs for credit, checking, and insurance products typically pay a range of amounts for the same products. In addition, from a vendor's perspective, customer profitability varies widely in this arena. Both revenues and costs differ from customer to customer. In particular, personal servicing and bad debt costs can vary by orders of magnitude, yet these differences are predictable based on a customer's particular profile.

The high value that consumers place on privacy also makes financial services an attractive market for infomediation. A number of studies have indicated that one reason people don't consolidate their financial affairs with fewer providers is concern over privacy. But more complete profiles would enable many financial service providers to make better offers to their customers. Today customers are constrained by their unwillingness or lack of time to provide multiple prospective vendors with detailed personal information. An infomediary can clearly help resolve these trade-offs.

On-line players like HomeShark and NextCard focus on the search costs and pricing questions. By completing a profile, customers can quickly find the best pricing for two of the most important credit products that they can use. Today the privacy policies of these players limit the infomediary role that they could play, but they indicate the unmet need for lower-cost, higher-efficiency solutions in this market.

Another early mover in the financial services market is Intuit. The Quicken customers organized around Quicken.com amount to a self-selected vertical market with surprisingly similar demographics and profile characteristics. The site offers an array of products of interest to this group, including insurance, investments, and mortgages, as well as advice on taxes, retirement planning, borrowing, saving, and investing. Once at the site, customers encounter recommendations for books that can be purchased through Amazon.com, read the latest business and money-related news, or chat with fellow users and featured experts. Customers can use the Quicken.com site to search for the best rates on certificates of deposit, car loans, personal loans, checking accounts, and money market accounts. Quicken.com also provides links to thousands of financial services providers—banks, credit card companies, savings and loans, and tax preparation firms. Of course, customers can also purchase any of the Quicken family of products at the site.

Quicken.com has aggressively built out many of the features an infomediary might offer—in particular, analytic tools and search capabilities that help customers find the best financial products or services. What they've yet to do is to offer customers privacy and profiling tools on-line or enable customers to maintain their anonymity and capture their own profile information while they visit other Web sites. As a result, if customers leave the Quicken.com Web site, Intuit loses the ability to track and offer them broader agent, targeted marketing, purchaser identification, and analytic services based on the customer's profile. Intuit can only offer on-line services to customers if they come to the Quicken.com Web site, stay at that site, and deal only with vendors who agreed to be represented on that Web site. Quicken.com is still, in the end, a much more closed system than the infomediary's will be in this product category.

Consumption and lifestyle

Infomediaries will also have many opportunities in product and service markets that are less essential in nature. Consumption and lifestyle spending categories represent 30 percent of household expenditures and include mainly replenishment goods, shopping items, small point-of-purchase spending, and bigger-ticket discretionary spending, such as furniture and entertainment (Table 3-4).

These products and services are often branded and purchased without any search being undertaken (with the partial exceptions of household furnishings, travel, fees and admissions, and education). For this reason, and because of their point-of-purchase intensity, infomediaries will find good opportunity in these categories to offer targeted messaging, filtering, and purchaser ID services.

Household furnishings and equipment. This category might not be an obvious one until you realize that it includes consumer electronics and, most particularly, personal computers, software, and peripherals. Computer equipment and software are tailor-made for infomediation—and are currently, in fact, the biggest on-line retail category (although travel is closing in fast). First, consumers must navigate their way through an excess of product offerings. Most consumers need help just understanding features, let alone price. They're justifiably concerned that their purchase will quickly become obsolete, or that they'll overpay for the product or get shortchanged on performance and service. For all these reasons, the computer

---

TABLE 3-4
Consumption and Lifestyle Household Purchases

Household furnishings and equipment	18
Personal care products and services	16
Reading and education	16
Tobacco products and smoking	16
Apparel	15
Fees and admissions	13
Alcoholic beverages	12
Food at home	11
Food away from home	11

equipment and software market is ripe for infomediaries to help consumers select and purchase the product that best suits their needs, wants, and price range.

Second, computers and software lend themselves nicely to on-line evaluation, and consumers have already established their willingness to purchase PCs through remote channels, thanks to direct PC retailers like Gateway and Dell.

Interaction costs are high in this market, as indicated by the wide range of prices for essentially equivalent products. Personal computer prices run the gamut from $500 to $10,000. Third, as noted above, uncertainty abounds due to rapid technology change.

On-line players such as Gateway, CompUSA, and Dell currently let consumers pick the type of computers they want, but often there is no help available when they get to the difficult configuration stage.

An infomediary that noted a customer browsing for computers could begin by offering advice, recommendations, and product specials on multiple brands of notebook computers, as well as on long-life batteries, international connectors, carrying cases, software, personal information managers, and so on.

Entertainment and travel. Infomediaries have a good chance to get going in entertainment and leisure-time activities as well. On-line discount travel services and airline Web sites already allow consumers to find the best prices and to mostly serve themselves. At these sites, consumers become self-service reservation agents, inputting desired travel dates and times, class of service, and departure and arrival cities. They're rewarded with a list of available flights and their relevant details (ticket price, airline, flight times, in-flight services).

> **The infomediary can look "across" spending categories**

The on-line market for travel is growing rapidly. A recent search on Yahoo! for travel-related sites yielded 13,051 matches. However, the big three consumer travel sites—Expedia (www.expedia.com), PreviewTravel (www.previewtravel.com), and Travelocity (www.travelocity.com)—have yet to take full advantage of the opportunity to capture and hold customers. Each offers basic services for searching for travel needs (flights, cars, hotels, packages) and taking payments, and they go so far as to send e-mail to members when fares on specific routes drop to a preset amount. In each case, the customer must enter desired information rather than having a model where the Web site gains knowledge and insight by tracking the customer's behavior.

One site, called BizTravel.com (www.biztravel.com), appears to be the furthest along in enabling a suite of services that an infomediary would offer. Targeted at the business traveler, BizTravel.com offers the typical range of searches for travel, cars, and hotels. Not only does BizTravel.com track the client's reservation, it also offers the following services:

- Sends a pager alert to both the traveler and whomever else needs to know (such as an assistant, car driver, significant other) if a flight is delayed or canceled.

- Sends a nonurgent alert with additional information (for instance, seat upgrades) via pager, fax, or e-mail.

- Sends travel plan notifications to designated recipients (assistants, significant others).

- Offers real-time flight tracking.

- Keeps track of all frequent-flyer and frequent-stayer programs, making balances available.

Although targeted at a smaller audience (business travelers), BizTravel.com's intention is to drive higher loyalty and usage by offering customized services to customers who travel frequently and appreciate the benefits of having an integrated travel service.

Infomediaries will be able to go even further by evaluating fares and other elements of a specific itinerary or by monitoring fares and costs for discretionary trips. An infomediary could, for example, let its clients know when fares to the cities where their relatives live dip below a certain level. Obviously, some of these agent services are available from other providers of on-line travel and information services, but the infomediary's full profile of client preferences, as well as its ability to execute transactions, should give it the advantage.

But an infomediary could deliver much more to clients than simply turning them into their own reservation agents and acting as agent for them in "reverse markets." The infomediary can also use its understanding of its clients' prior travel, interests, and financial situation to suggest new places to travel, related goods and services, and the best ways to save money while traveling.

Imagine an infomediary client who visits California's Napa Valley periodically and has visited the south of France once or twice, and who is a regular buyer of wines and high-end olive oils from these regions. The infomediary might reasonably infer that this client would have a strong interest in seeing targeted messages about a number of products and services: bed-and-breakfast vacations in Tuscany; mail-order purchases of domestic and imported wines; perhaps even an e-mail from a small olive oil manufacturer in Tuscany that sells direct to customers around the world. Based on the client's response to these messages, the infomediary would get smarter about the client as time went by. Perhaps this client also makes regular purchases from bicycle stores. Wouldn't Backroads Bicycle Touring or Butterfield & Robinson have just the right bicycle tour through wine country?

Its ability to look "across" interest and spending categories this way—and to help customers identify previously undiscovered opportunities that will meet their interests—gives the infomediary a clear advantage over other providers of travel information.

Other consumption and lifestyle goods. Infomediaries will also be interested in other products and services in the consumption and lifestyle category. These will present a different set of challenges, depending on whether they are "shopping" or "replenishment" goods or services.

Shopping goods are products that have no identifiable search behavior associated with them. Examples include apparel, reading materials, food consumed outside the home, and some houshold furnishings. Indeed, some of these are impulse purchases, meaning that customers are both in the market for these things and not in the market at the same time, depending on whether something sparks their impulse. Targeted offerings best address shopping goods and, to a lesser extent, services, once customer profiles are established through other sources—for example, a mortgage application and the accumulations of on-line search behavior. An infomediary that has an accurate profile of a customer's demographics, income, mortgage payment, automobile, vacation travel, and on-line search behavior would be better able to target the on-line equivalent of individual pages from a variety of mail-order magazines, obviating the need for (or trouble of) a mailbox full of catalogs.

Other products in this category frequently require shopping as well, but are also replenished frequently—for instance, personal-care products and tobacco products. For these types of products, an infomediary could well act as an agent, representing large numbers of customers and negotiating volume-based purchases and, conceivably, new low-cost distribution methods that would benefit both its customers and vendors.

The small business opportunity

Infomediaries will also make inroads into the fast-growing small business market. Privacy issues may not be quite as important to businesses as they are to consumers, but search costs are equally high.

As Table 3-5 shows, the small business arena offers many analogous opportunities for infomediaries when we compare it with the consumer arena. The opportunities will become the province of a focused small business infomediary—one that brings customers and a relevant brand to bear. Some significant part of the small business opportunity will be available to infomediaries that secure the individual business owner as a customer and then provide agent services in categories with relatively high correspondence between consumer and small business needs. These categories include automotive and

TABLE 3-5
Consumer versus Small Business Spending Categories

Consumer spending category	Small business analogue	Relevance of consumer infomediary service to small business
Housing	Office/commercial space	Low
Transportation	Transportation	High
Health care	Group health care	Medium
Financial services	Financial services	Medium
Household furnishings and equipment	Office furnishings and business equipment	Medium
Travel and entertainment	Travel and entertainment	High
Other consumption and lifestyle goods	—	None
—	Raw materials	None

travel and entertainment, where the services offered by a consumer infomediary are highly relevant for a small business infomediary.

Categories with medium correspondence will include financial services, health care, and furnishings and business equipment. In these business categories, there is some vendor and product overlap, but significant distinctiveness to business vendor and product usage would limit a consumer infomediary's relevance for all but the smallest businesses.

In the category of low correspondence we place office and commercial space, where the nature of the need is similar to that for consumer housing, but where the vendor and product net are unique. Finally, there are some categories where businesses have either unique or no analogous needs—specifically, raw materials inventories and the lack of a real analogue for consumer consumption and lifestyle goals.

As this chapter demonstrates, the markets in which infomediaries will get their start represent a fairly broad cross-section of consumer spending. As we'll see in the next chapter, however, few companies are well positioned to take advantage of this opportunity.

Note

1. "A Revolution in Interaction," *McKinsey Quarterly* 1 (1997): 4–23.

4

---

who can play?

AS FOND OF CONSUMERS AS THEY MIGHT BE, the senior managers of today's biggest corporations can't be expected to form infomediaries out of the goodness of their hearts. Fortunately for consumers, infomediaries promise to be a very profitable venture for the companies that organize them.

Chapter 8 of this book goes into considerable detail about the sources of an infomediary's revenues, profits, and market value. At this point, suffice it to say that successful infomediaries could generate more than $4 billion in revenues by their tenth year of existence and more than $20 billion in market value. Skeptics (or converts) might wish to skip directly to Chapter 8 in order to verify this for themselves. They'll need to come back to this chapter, however, to evaluate their own chances of forming a successful infomediary.

The truth is that few of today's companies have what it takes to become an infomediary. Most lack either the customer relationships that will be necessary to get started or the risk-taking culture that will be necessary to succeed. Not that infomediaries will start from scratch—the considerable investment needed and the advantage of starting off with customers already in place will militate against the possibility that a start-up will capture this opportunity. Instead, the likely scenario is that infomediaries will emerge from a strategic combination of businesses that already exist.

Few companies have what it takes to become an infomediary

One possibility is an alliance between an Internet-based and a more traditional business (recent pairings along these lines include NBC and CNET Snap!, and Disney and Infoseek). The Internet-based business would bring the ability to move quickly, along with essential organizational attributes such as risk taking, a speed-driven culture, strong leadership, institutional "paranoia," and innovation. The more traditional business would bring deep pockets and, more importantly, customer relationships and extensive customer profiles.

This chapter reviews candidates for the infomediary role and evaluates their strengths and weaknesses.

Key attributes

Aspiring infomediaries will encounter two primary challenges as they set about building an infomediary business. The first is the ability (and the credibility) needed to build trust with customers. Trust is the infomediary's lifeblood. How else will it persuade its clients to divulge their most sensitive information?

The second challenge is to gain access to an existing set of customer relationships and customer profiles. Infomediaries will need an *existing* set of relationships and profiles because it will be too costly and time consuming to build one from the ground up.

Without existing customer relationships and profiles, aspiring infomediaries will have to invest more to acquire clients and vendors and will generate correspondingly less revenue in the early stages of development because, in the absence of profiles, they offer less value to both clients and vendors. Chapter 8 suggests that, even with existing customer relationships and profiles, aspiring infomediaries will need to invest over $200 million. For infomediaries starting without these assets, the required investment will more than double. More importantly, aspiring infomediaries without existing relationships and profiles will need longer to build the critical mass of client and vendor relationships necessary to deliver value. These aspiring infomediaries will be significantly disadvantaged relative to competitors that can deliver value more quickly through existing customer relationships and profiles. Competitors that can accelerate entry and build position more quickly will crowd out disadvantaged entrants even if those entrants can afford the additional investment required.

Building trust

When it comes to meeting the first challenge, companies today may have further to go than they think. Most companies would assert that their customers trust them, just as most politicians would assert that voters trust them. Many customers do trust companies to deliver safe products and services. The essence of a brand, after all, is the trust consumers have that the products or services of a specific company have certain attributes on which consumers can depend. Consumers may perceive a particular brand as reliable, for example, or as a good value, or as being consistent with a certain lifestyle.

But trust in specific products or services is very different from trust in companies to handle sensitive personal information responsibly. It's one thing to trust a Toyota to run for hundreds of thousands of miles, or to rely on the local telephone company to provide a reliable dial tone to the home. A different (and higher) level of trust is required for parachutes, for example, or for toddlers' toys, food, or pharmaceuticals. When it comes to sharing sensitive information, companies will have to leap an even higher hurdle. Will the makers of the well-known brand be willing to protect (or even capable of protecting) that information from abuse? Trusting a company to provide the best soft drink, computer, or retail experience is very different from trusting it with information about how much money one makes or whether one is seeing a psychotherapist.

Even when such trust *does* exist, it may be too narrow in scope to support a broad-based infomediary business. For example, to obtain a mortgage, customers may be willing to provide a mortgage company with sensitive financial information, but not a more detailed statement of their financial transactions. A health care company may build sufficient trust with its customers for them to provide sensitive information regarding their health; but would they so easily fork over sensitive financial information?

Consumers will also demand security from the companies that handle their personal information. (Banks may be advantaged in this regard because of their long experience preventing, detecting, and responding to fraud.) What if the *National Enquirer* hires professional hackers to become the digital world's answer to paparazzi? Infomediaries will have to convince potential clients that it can provide the security that clients will need in order to hand over their information.

Access to information

A second challenge that aspiring infomediaries will face is access to an existing information profile of prospective customers—preferably one well populated with valuable behavioral data that the infomediary can search, from which it can infer possible offers. As we've explained in previous chapters, an infomediary's services to both clients and vendors depend on the existence of just such a profile.

Infomediaries starting without an existing database of client profiles must purchase profile information from third parties, ask new clients to fill out time-consuming forms, or limit services until they accumulate an appropriate profile as the client uses privacy and profiling tools. None of these options is attractive.

Any combination of companies trying to launch an infomediary would therefore be smart to start out with at least one player that has relationships already developed with a broad range of customers and profiles of these customers accumulated in specific transaction categories. It's too time consuming and expensive to build customer relationships from scratch, let alone to create a database of customer profiles.

Even those fortunate enough to have an existing database of profiles will have difficulty broadening such a database beyond the narrow slice of customer purchasing behavior that they see in their own transaction categories. In most cases, the profile will be very narrow in scope, even if there is a lengthy relationship with the customers profiled.

Consider the example of an airline that has accumulated a database of detailed profiles of its frequent flyers' flight preferences and patterns. The first limitation of this database will be that the profiles cover only the airline's own frequent flyers— the airline has very limited information about the frequent flyers of other airlines. The second (and broader) limitation of the database will be that its profile will provide information only on where and when passengers have flown. It will have very little to say about passengers' broader travel preferences or activities, much less their other preferences or purchase activities. What

Infomediaries will emerge from alliances between traditional and internet companies

kinds of hotels does the traveler tend to stay at? Where does the traveler like to eat? What kinds of suitcases does the traveler buy? Is the traveler interested in art museums or nightclubs? Airlines capture precious little of this information in the customer profiles they assemble. Travel agents, of course, are in a better position to capture a broader travel profile of each client, although they might be hard pressed to offer insight about the restaurant, nightclub, or luggage preferences of their clients. Relative to airlines, travel agents would know more about fewer travelers, given the fragmentation of the travel agency business.

Difficulty broadening databases means that even those companies with an existing database of customer profiles will be challenged to build their base of customers—and therefore their access to information about customers—beyond the transaction categories with which they've started. This will in turn require consummate marketing and relationship management skills in order to quickly expand the scope of clients and vendors served. Finding clients and vendors, and then building relationships with them, will be urgent priorities.

Other attributes

Marketing skills will be essential on many levels. Segmenting the marketplace to identify the most receptive clients and vendors, developing highly leveraged marketing programs to reach these clients and vendors as cost-effectively as possible, capturing and packaging information so that it will have the greatest value to clients and vendors—all these will demand sophisticated marketing skills that extend beyond individual product categories.

As we'll see in Part II of this book, infomediaries will need a specific sequence of actions to build and preserve trust-based relationships with clients. One action is building a "web" of customers and companies that infomediaries can leverage to make their entry strategies a reality. Chapter 6 will detail these web-based strategies, in which combinations of companies aspiring to build infomediaries will create and manage looser relationships, with a broader range of companies, than most are used to today. To do so, companies will develop relationship skills that extend well beyond conventional skills at negotiating and managing alliances and joint ventures. These skills demand a deep understanding of the economics of various potential web participants and the kinds of economic incentives that will compel each participant. Successful players will understand that the most enduring form of influence is not in the "control" embedded in detailed legal contracts, but in the ability to address the deepest economic needs of other businesses.

The right culture and mind-set will be essential. Infomediaries will need strong leaders, a risk-taking attitude, sustained paranoia, the ability to move quickly, and a capacity for rapid innovation. These "softer" cultural attributes will persuade other businesses to join the "webs" organized by infomediaries, as will the ability to influence the perception of risk by other participants. Bold, fast-moving, and innovative infomediaries will reduce perceived risk and thus magnify the impact of the economic incentives the infomediary creates. In the absence of these attributes, participants will perceive more risk, diluting the impact of economic incentives and seriously hampering the competitive position of the infomediary.

The contenders

Certainly no one company possesses the full range of these attributes. In fact, in most companies, certain attributes, when present, almost guarantee the absence of others. The small, entrepreneurial start-ups that have begun to carve out early positions on the Internet certainly excel at some of the organizational attributes necessary. But these smaller companies begin with few, if any, existing customer relationships and certainly lack extensive profiles of their customers. Trust and credibility are often at issue. Deep skills in marketing and relationship management are usually lacking. For example, most Internet-based businesses still experience very high visitor churn rates (70 to 80 percent annually isn't unusual) and, despite substantial accumulation of usage profile information, have invested little in the systems or people necessary to analyze this information and deliver value back to the customer.

Big companies are especially lacking in the "softer" attributes required for success. How many have a strong personal leader, rather than a management team, at the helm? Strong personal leaders, as exemplified by Bill Gates at Microsoft and Andy Grove at Intel, are typically more successful than management teams at building a broad web of business relationships in highly uncertain markets. They are more successful, among other reasons, because they ensure consistency and conviction in recruiting other businesses to join their "web," which helps reduce perceived risk.

Big companies lack risk-taking cultures

How many have created or maintained cultures where risk taking not only is rewarded, but also is a requirement for success, and where the driving question is not How good is the analysis? but What actions have you taken to preempt others? Building an infomediary will require managers to take many risks, including innovating with new products and services, scaling operations very quickly, defining standards for data presentation and capture, and defining architectures for privacy and profiling tool kits. How many are really prepared to bet the company in order to build credibility among other potential web participants? As Chapter 6 describes, infomediaries must commit to specific data standards and technology architectures that represent true "bet the company" propositions. If these standards and architectures are not widely adopted by other businesses, the infomediary will have a difficult time recovering. How many have combined the paranoia and innovation necessary to create the relentless drive to stay one step ahead of everyone else?

Given the realities of traditional markets, companies possessing deep, trust-based relationships with a large installed base of customers tend to be tightly integrated and cautious organizations with a strong cultural bias against either boldness or dependence on other companies for key elements of customer value. After all, they've built trust with their customers by tightly controlling all elements of the offer and by refusing to bring anything to market that isn't extensively tested and guaranteed to work.

We can get a better feel for their strengths and limitations by looking at each of these contenders in more detail. These candidates fall into two broad categories: entrepreneurial, Internet-based companies; and larger, more-established companies operating in traditional markets.

Internet-based candidates

The rise of the Internet has spawned a rich ecology of new businesses that have the potential to evolve into infomediaries over time. The more promising among these businesses include

- Portals
- Virtual communities
- Transaction aggregators
- Specialized advertising network businesses

Portals. Portal businesses are essentially traffic aggregators. These businesses seek to become the first stop for network users as they venture onto the Internet. They offer to help connect users with the network resources that are most relevant and useful to them. Examples of these kinds of businesses include America Online, Yahoo!, Excite, Microsoft's Start, and CNET's Snap!

These businesses typically leverage either an access or a search asset in order to attract on-line traffic. In the case of America Online (AOL), the company provides physical network access as part of its service. While it tries to maximize the time that subscribers spend in its own proprietary content areas, AOL also provides an entry point to the Internet and helps guide its subscribers to broader Internet resources that might be useful to them. Yahoo! and Excite, on the other hand, leverage search engines to help users locate resources on the Internet, while Microsoft's Start leverages its parent company's leadership in desktop operating systems and browser products to establish another entry point for Internet users. CNET has taken still another route by combining strong marketing and traffic aggregation skills with partnerships with companies having strong access positions—either Internet service providers like GTE or computer manufacturers like Compaq.

All of these companies have demonstrated strong marketing skills in their competition with a broad range of other Internet businesses to generate traffic. Each is clearly among the top 20 Internet businesses in terms of traffic generation. The traffic they generate broadly represents network users, not one specific segment of the network population. They have built successful businesses driven by a clear understanding of leverage. Rather than trying to provide all the content resources themselves, they have relied primarily on providing a connection service, helping their users to connect with the resources of other companies.

Generating traffic doesn't mean building trust

This allows them to "piggyback" on the investments others have made in content. And they are all led by strong founders who understand the need for urgency and who are prepared to take considerable risks to build pre-emptive positions on the Internet.

Although all of these characteristics strongly position portal businesses to play the infomediary role, there are some missing elements. Generating traffic and building deep, trust-based relationships with Internet users are two very different tasks. Portals excel at the former but wrestle with the latter. Churn rates are high, and many Internet users use more than one gateway. The questions earlier posed about trust need to be applied here. Users may trust a gateway to have a reliable search engine or directory, but does this necessarily mean that they would trust a gateway to collect and manage the most sensitive information about themselves? This kind of trusting relationship will likely continue to elude most portals until they consciously begin to ally themselves with customers instead of taking the traditional vendor-focused view of customers as assets to be exploited for revenue.

Even if portals do succeed at establishing trust, most will still lack the ability to capture or effectively manage detailed profiles of Internet usage, much less the ability to turn this information into tailored offerings for the customer. Portals are moving quickly to build such capability (either through acquisitions or through internal skill building), but they are still far behind traditional database marketers in this regard. Investments by major media companies in portals (for example, Disney's investment in Infoseek and NBC's investment in CNET's Snap!) appear designed to help accelerate traffic generation but offer little in terms of profiling capability or targeted marketing skills. Portals will need different kinds of partners to supply these capabilities if they want to build infomediary businesses.

Virtual communities. Virtual communities build on network users' widespread desire to connect with each other around common areas of interest. Virtual communities create environments to facilitate and enrich such connections by integrating published content, communication resources (bulletin boards, chat rooms, and e-mail), and commerce capabilities relevant to these areas of interest. Rather than focusing on bilateral communication (between the organizer and each member, or between specific vendors and each potential customer), virtual communities generate a rich web of personal relationships among the members themselves. ParentSoup, Third Age, Motley Fool, Mediconsult, and @griculture Online represent early examples of virtual communities emerging on the network.

Virtual communities have some key assets that would be valuable to an infomediary business. They typically start with a very strong customer, rather than vendor, focus. Their role is to help customers get the best possible value from the vendors they deal with, an orientation critical for an infomediary. As a result of this orientation, virtual communities have been able to build strong, trust-based relationships with their members. Churn rates go down substantially, and usage rates increase as members develop loyalty to and identification with their virtual community. Virtual communities ask for and receive very sensitive personal information from their members because of this trust. The leading virtual communities are also aggressively building preemptive positions on the Internet and have demonstrated a high capacity for innovation as well as risk taking.

But virtual communities also lack some key attributes required for success as an infomediary. Given a narrower focus than gateway businesses—as well as the inherent lead times required to build trust-based relationships with members—virtual communities tend to have substantially smaller traffic flows than the major gateway businesses. Furthermore, some virtual communities define their focus much too narrowly to provide attractive platforms for an infomediary business. A virtual community targeting Barbie doll collectors may be able to build a profitable niche business, but won't have sufficient reach to build a viable infomediary business. On the other hand, virtual communities targeting such areas as financial management, travel, or health care may have a more attractive platform to evolve into the infomediary role. Virtual communities are generally ahead of portals in terms of developing database-driven marketing and relationship skills, but their skills are limited compared to those of sophisticated database marketers in traditional businesses.

Transaction aggregators. Transaction aggregators are a third Internet-based business that could contend for the infomediary role. Transaction aggregators create on-line markets enabling a critical mass of vendors and customers to connect with each other and conduct transactions based on the rules and procedures defined by the transaction aggregator. Although some transaction aggregators like Amazon.com and Onsale take inventory in the products sold, an increasing number of transaction aggregators simply play a facilitating role and collect a commission on the transaction without ever taking ownership of the product. Examples of emerging transaction aggregators on the Internet include Amazon.com, Onsale, E*Trade, Auto-by-Tel, Compare.Net, General Electric's TPN Register, and Cendant's NetMarket.

Many transaction aggregators have built substantial traffic

and established relationships with a broad range of customers and relevant vendors. They understand in depth the requirements for transactions to occur and have created a range of value-added services to facilitate these transactions. In the course of facilitating these transactions, they are building detailed transaction profiles of the customers and vendors doing business in their markets. They also understand the advantages of leverage and have creatively relied on a variety of other companies to deliver key elements of the total value required by the customer. As in other Internet businesses, management teams that are bold, aggressive, and willing to take considerable risk in order to build preemptive market positions lead the leading transaction aggregators.

With some exceptions, such as General Electric's TPN Register and Cendant's NetMarket, where the companies leverage a broader market position established in more traditional markets, most transaction aggregators are focusing at least initially on narrowly defined transaction categories, such as electronic components, books, records, and stock trading, to ease the challenge of building a critical mass of buyers and sellers. Such focus makes sense given the untimely demise of early transaction aggregators like Nets Inc., which tried to go too broad too quickly. This narrow focus on specific transaction categories, however, may create too narrow a platform to support a viable infomediary business.

Transaction aggregators may struggle to translate the trust they've established as a transaction intermediary into the trust that customers will need to turn over their personal information. The fact that few transaction aggregators have shown much interest in customers beyond their role in generating commissions for the transaction aggregators' business will not be in their favor. Furthermore, transaction aggregators have built narrowly defined transaction profiles that reveal little beyond transaction histories. Transaction aggregators might infer buying preferences from this information, but unless they offer robust search capability, they won't have direct indications of buying preferences from the customers. They'll also lack the demographic and behavioral data that infomediaries will capture in the process of profiling client activity across a wide range of Internet Web sites. For example, when a customer purchases a toy, was it for her own child, or was it for the neighbor's child? Which content sites does a customer tend to visit before making a purchase? (Without this information, marketing messages cannot be targeted in a timely fashion.) Few transaction aggregators have developed the skills required to use narrow transaction profiles to drive marketing or relationship initiatives.

Specialized advertising network businesses. A fourth category of Internet business that might evolve into an infomediary is the advertising network organizer. Companies like DoubleClick and 24/7 Media sign up networks of Web sites and manage advertising campaigns across them. Others, like MatchLogic (owned by Excite, a major gateway company) and AdKnowledge, manage advertising campaigns across Web sites for vendors or advertising agencies. These companies have developed sophisticated information capture and analytic tools to help Web sites participating in their networks to describe the traffic they're generating and to target the right "eyeballs" for the right advertiser. In the process of building their networks, they've built a broad set of relationships encompassing both Web sites and advertisers.

The primary asset these companies have relative to the infomediary business is a detailed understanding of the tools and skills required to capture information about customers and to package this information for advertisers. Most importantly, they've developed the infrastructure required to aggregate information capture beyond one Web site. This allows them to develop a more integrated view of traffic on the Internet. As a result, they probably have a more detailed view of customer activities on the Internet than any other single Internet business. These businesses combine their information capture capability with the marketing and relationship management skills required to build strong networks of Web sites and advertisers. Again, like other Internet businesses, the leaders in this category demonstrate bold, innovative, and risk-taking behaviors such as "betting the company" by investing millions of dollars to build advertising networks on the Internet, at a time when most advertisers are holding back from spending in this unfamiliar medium.

These companies lack experience of direct interaction with customers, much less any reservoir of trust by customers. They represent classic vendor-focused businesses. Their entire orientation is to help vendors find and reach as many customers as possible and, in the process, help Web sites maximize the ad revenue they generate from the traffic visiting their Web site. Thus far, they have accomplished this role by remaining largely invisible to the customer—few customers know they even exist, much less what role they play. (Their lack of visibility to consumers would, by the way, make these companies interesting candidates for an "Intel-inside"–style awareness-building campaign.) Shifting focus to become custodians of information generated by the customers themselves and then helping customers to maximize the value of this information relative to the vendors would likely represent a major challenge for this kind of business. Even if they could make the required shift in mindset, convincing customers to trust them in this role would be difficult given the prior focus of their business. In addition, the profiles they are accumulating tend to focus more on usage activity (which Web sites and Web pages the user tends to frequent) than on transaction activity (which specific products or services the user tends to buy).

In summary, each of the Internet-based businesses reviewed above has relative strengths and weaknesses, summarized in Table 4-1. There is no obvious winning model as they are currently configured.

TABLE 4-1
Infomediary Potential for Internet-Based Businesses

Type	Advantages	Disadvantages
Portal	• High traffic generated by good marketing skills • Frequent visits by customers • Broad range of topics, which provides potential for broad profile • Strength in building partnerships • Innovative and risk taking	• Little experience building trust-based relationships • Lots of trial, not much loyalty • Little to no experience managing profiles • Historically vendor focused versus customer focused
Virtual community	• Customer focused rather than vendor focused • Strong trust-based relationships • Innovative and risk taking	• Small traffic flows • Depending on scope, may be too narrow to build adequate profiles • Unproven database-driven marketing and relationship-building skills
Transaction aggregator	• Profiles include transaction data • Skilled at building partnerships • Skilled at handling transactions • Innovative and risk taking	• Many are not broad enough • Although trusted to enable transactions, not necessarily a trust-based relationship • Profiles show transaction history only • Unproven database-driven marketing and relationship-building skills
Advertising network	• Understanding of tools and skills required to capture customer information • Infrastructure to capture information across Web sites • Broad perspective on consumer behavior • Experience managing networks of business relationships • Innovative and risk taking	• Profiles contain usage data only, no transaction data • Completely vendor focused rather than customer focused • Not a trust-based relationship—no brand-name recognition or awareness

More traditional candidates

What types of larger companies might be in the best position to evolve into infomediaries? Two types of companies are likely candidates. First are companies with strong relationships with a broad range of customers. Within this category are the fiduciaries (such as financial institutions and health care companies) that already deal with highly sensitive information about customers; the retailers and direct marketers that act as intermediaries between customers and vendors; and the media companies that have established strong relationships and credibility with specific audiences (such as special-interest magazines and newspapers). Some of the larger software companies such as Microsoft and Intuit might also be able to leverage a large installed base of customers to offer network-based services.

The second group of companies includes those that have developed large databases about customers, as well as the skills required to manage and extract value from these databases. These companies tend to have well-established relationships with a broad range of vendors but are relatively invisible to the customer. Within this category one finds credit profile providers and marketing data providers such as Experian and Acxiom.

Nonprofit organizations of various types represent another group of potential infomediaries. For example, many universities have strong relationships with a large number of alumni and have built extensive databases on these alumni for fundraising purposes. Organizations like the American Association of Retired People (AARP) and the American Automobile Association (AAA) have large memberships and have built a reputation for helping their members obtain good value in certain products and services. Even religious and fraternal organizations have broad, trust-based relationships with their members and might find opportunities to leverage this asset into an infomediary business. We won't discuss these in depth here because our focus is on more commercial players.

Customer relationship companies. *Fiduciaries* represent the first type of customer relationship companies that have the potential to evolve into infomediaries. These are typically businesses in the financial services or health care markets. In these markets, the ability to protect customer confidentiality and to build enough trust among customers that they feel comfortable providing confidential information about themselves is almost a prerequisite for doing business. As a result, these businesses might be viewed as natural candidates for the role of infomediary. Although fiduciary businesses certainly have advantages relative to many other kinds of product businesses, even these advantages may be limited in scope. For example, is the trust they've generated sufficiently deep and broad in scope to support an infomediary business?

Among the fiduciaries operating in financial services, the large regional and money center banks such as Wells Fargo or Citibank are probably the best positioned to evolve into the infomediary role. These banks are building the scale necessary to reach and serve a broad customer base. Unfortunately, the aggressive merger and acquisition programs they're using to build this scale run the risk of undermining the trust they've established. Will customers who trusted their local bank give the same trust to the larger, more impersonal institution that has acquired the local bank?

Another difficulty for banks is the evidence that the average bank customer is spreading his or her business across multiple financial institutions more than ever before. Is this a warning signal that, as it becomes easier to deal with multiple institutions, the average customer will adopt a much more transactional view of financial institutions and resist efforts by these institutions to establish deep relationships across a broad range of financial services?

Like financial services players, health care institutions are also going through a process of consolidation. In health care, the impact on trust is even more pronounced. As physicians and other health care providers become increasingly integrated into health maintenance organizations (HMOs)—organizations perceived to have cost reduction as one of their primary goals—many physicians are losing their position of trust with consumers. The popular image of the caring family physician is rapidly being replaced by the image of a large, impersonal institution serving the interests of insurance companies and employers at the expense of the patient's health.

Will customers trust big companies with their personal information?

HMOs like Kaiser Permanente and HealthNet are generally in a good position to gather integrated data about patient billings and treatments, not to mention data about treatment outcomes. But many HMOs are still trying to sort out their heavy investments in information technology. They're a long way from being able to effectively capture and mine data about patients—even if customers trusted them enough to safeguard that information once they'd captured it.

Financial services and health care institutions are also hampered by their legacy information systems, most of which are characterized by a product-centric view of the market. A bank can tell who has a deposit account and who has a mortgage but is often unable to say with confidence who has both. Health care institutions have similar difficulties in developing integrated profiles of their patients across multiple medical specialties and facilities. These legacy systems are now being painfully and expensively overhauled to capture integrated views of the customer, but most of these institutions are still wrestling with the inability to generate integrated views of their customers.

Perhaps the biggest liability that fiduciaries bring to the table, however, is their heritage as fiduciaries. Fiduciaries traditionally have developed cultures that avoid risk, reward caution, and suspect innovation. (Much of this culture has to do with the considerable government regulation these industries have experienced.) Such cultures have served fiduciaries well in the past, but now they find themselves struggling to develop cultures more appropriate to intensely competitive markets (and to the role of an infomediary).

Retailers and direct marketers represent a second type of customer relationship company that might evolve into an infomediary. The large-scale players among retailers and direct marketers generally have a broader reach than fiduciaries in terms of the range of products or services sold. Retailers like Wal-Mart, Home Depot, and Nordstrom tend to be skilled at establishing relationships with a broad range of vendors and aggregating customers relevant to these vendors.

Direct marketers like Fingerhut, L.L. Bean, and J. Peterman have highly developed targeted marketing and vendor relationship management skills. Some of these catalog businesses will naturally pursue the infomediary opportunity as they move on-line.

Although these companies offer breadth of business relationships, their relationships with customers tend to be much more transactional in nature than those enjoyed by fiduciaries. With some notable exceptions, the depth and scope of trust is likely to be limited to narrowly defined product attributes such as availability, quality, or price. Most retailers' and direct marketers' interests are more aligned with vendors than with customers, which limits trust. Once a retailer or direct marketer takes ownership of a vendor's product, the inventory risk provides strong motivation to sell the product at the best possible price to as many customers as possible. Few retailers or direct marketers take the customer's perspective and view their mission as extracting as much value as possible from vendors on behalf of customers. Wal-Mart represents an important exception to this general pattern, although even at Wal-Mart substantial investment in bricks-and-mortar retail outlets and product inventory inevitably limits customer focus.

Direct-marketing and retailing companies capture substantial information about transactions, but they do so as a by-product of making the sale, not because customers have offered information on their own. As with fiduciaries, the information systems of retailers in particular are still highly product-centric, able to track in detail the movements of a particular stock-keeping unit, but relatively silent about whether a certain customer tends to buy one brand over another. Direct marketers have the advantage of tracking individual customers more readily than most retailers, but even in this case the information is transaction-specific. Most direct marketers have very limited insight, except as might be extracted from the transaction information itself, about a customer's broader needs or preferences. Some retailers and direct marketers are implementing loyalty programs of various types to capture even more information, but the results of these programs have been uneven at best.

Given their strong audience relationships—and relationships with advertisers—*media companies* are a third type of customer relationship company with the potential to evolve into the infomediary role. These are special-interest magazines (such as *Travel & Leisure, Prevention,* and *Field & Stream*), some focused cable channels (such as MTV, ESPN, and Discovery Channel), and major newspapers. But not all media companies would seem to have sustainable relationships with specific audiences. The one exception, of course, is Disney. Disney's focus on a particular audience segment—parents with small children—has enabled it to build relationships with a broad range of advertisers seeking to reach that audience segment. Virtually all the other major media conglomerates—companies like News Corp., Time Warner, Universal, and Bertelsmann—lack either a consistent audience focus, information capture across their multiple media properties, or a brand name that influences purchase decisions.

Even the media businesses that have a specific audience focus and well-established advertiser relationships will confront some significant challenges in building an infomediary business. Once again, there is a question of what kind of trust these media businesses have built with their audiences. Certainly the audiences trust the magazine or newspaper to deliver uesful information or entertainment, but would they trust the business enough to turn over detailed information about themselves? Few of these media businesses have any profile of the individual members of their audience beyond their names and addresses. Some, like cable channels or print media purchased at newsstands, don't even have that. Notable exceptions include *Reader's Digest* and *Prevention,* which have built active direct-marketing businesses around their flagship magazine property.

Certain *software businesses* represent a fourth type of customer relationship company that could evolve into an infomediary. The leading candidates are Intuit and Microsoft, which have established relationships with a large number of customers and are regarded as leaders in the computer industry. Because the privacy and profiling tools required for the infomediary business are likely to involve software residing on the desktop computer, these companies would be viewed as natural candidates to offer these tools. Both Intuit and Microsoft are aggressively building out service businesses on the Internet to complement their shrink-wrap software application businesses; this could provide a convenient platform for expanding into infomediary services on the Internet.

But the scope and depth of the relationships and trust built by these software businesses are open to question. Customers may be very loyal to Intuit for helping them to organize their personal finances, but they do this largely from their desktop without turning over to Intuit any sensitive personal information. Similarly, customers may trust Microsoft to deliver high-quality application software and can rest assured that they're unlikely to be stranded with an obsolete application if they buy from Microsoft. But are they likely to trust Microsoft enough to turn over sensitive personal information? Also, because many software purchasers buy their products in retail stores or through other forms of intermediaries, companies like Intuit and Microsoft depend on customers to submit registration forms, just to identify their names and addresses. Beyond this basic information, software companies today generally have limited profiles of their customers.

Other customer relationship candidates include *telephone companies* and *electric utilities*. These companies have direct-billing relationships with many customers and collect some information from them in the course of providing their core services. They have strong brand names in their service areas, although, with some exceptions, they don't have strongly developed marketing capabilities. Because of regulation, however, these companies generally don't operate in highly competitive markets, and, as a result, they must transform their corporate cultures to succeed in an intensely competitive Internet environment. Although many countries are deregulating aspects of these industries, companies operating in these industries still must contend with cumbersome regulatory regimes. For example, U.S. regulators still restrict telephone companies from using customer information acquired in their core telephone business for other commercial purposes.

Companies that rate products and vendors are another category of business that might become contenders for the infomediary role. J. D. Power has built an extraordinary reputation among many consumers for its rating service on automobiles. It has more recently extended this service into other well-known consumer services like airline travel. Morningstar provides trusted ratings on mutual fund performance. *Consumer Reports* and *Good Housekeeping* are examples of magazines that have developed well-known ratings services. Zagat's has rapidly built a reputation for reliability in restaurant ratings. These companies have strong brand names, widespread customer trust in their objectivity, and deep expertise in certain product categories. They will certainly become important resources for infomediaries to help their clients evaluate vendor offerings. In some cases they might actually develop their own infomediary services. To do this, they would need to develop direct marketing and large-scale transaction-processing skills.

Customer database companies. Virtually all of the customer relationship companies described here have built databases of their own customers. As we've attempted to make clear, however, most have only a limited view of consumers who are not their customers. Customer database companies, in contrast, specialize in aggregating across multiple vendors information about customers. They package and resell this information to vendors to help them more efficiently target customers for their products or services. In other words, these are specialized information intermediaries (collecting information about customers is their primary business), but they are vendor-centric information intermediaries. Their primary goal is to help vendors become more efficient in acquiring customers, not to help customers become more efficient in dealing with vendors. The paradox is that, although they possess some of the core skills required to be a successful infomediary, they also possess a mind-set and existing relationships that are likely to make it very difficult to exploit these skills aggressively in building an infomediary business.

Two broad types of companies compete in the customer database business and might emerge as potential candidates for the infomediary role. First are the *credit information providers* clustered around the three largest data collection companies—Experian, Equifax, and TransUnion. Second, there are the *marketing data providers,* which focus on helping vendors target customers for their products and services. These providers are dominated by companies like Acxiom, Donnelly Marketing (for consumers), and Dunn & Bradstreet (for business), which specialize in collecting data from a variety of sources to create customer profiles.

Customer database companies excel at the skills required to collect data. They know how to manage extremely large databases and package information in ways that are helpful to vendors. They augment their own skills through relationships with still more-specialized companies that possess focused data-mining and analytical/statistical skills for specific kinds of credit or marketing applications. Although relatively invisible to the consumer (except when credit applications are turned down), these companies have built strong brand names and relationships with vendors who rely on their databases to make key decisions in their businesses. Because most of these companies have been in business for a long time, they have already accumulated detailed profiles of most consumers and small businesses in the United States, including addresses, transaction histories, and a broad range of personal information, such as age, sex, number and ages of children, education, hobbies, and magazines read.

Database companies have detailed profiles— but do customers trust them?

Clearly the biggest hurdle for these businesses to surmount if they seek to become infomediaries is customer distrust. In the eyes of most customers, these companies are, at worst, responsible for credit application denials and, at best, help marketers clog mailboxes with junk mail and interrupt meals with unsolicited telemarketing calls. What would it take to persuade customers to actually hand over additional information about themselves to these companies? Even if the trust hurdle were overcome, customer database companies lack deep marketing skills of their own, particularly in the consumer market. They may understand what data would be required to help target a marketing campaign (although, even here, credit bureaus fall short), but they generally have less insight about what the marketing message should be to maximize impact.

In summary, each of the traditional companies has relative strengths and weaknesses, summarized in Table 4-2.

Who will rule?

If no one company is the natural owner of this business opportunity, who in fact will come to own the opportunity? As we suggested at the beginning of the chapter, the broad range of organizational capabilities required suggests that infomediaries will be likely to evolve not just from a single company, but from a combination of companies with complementary capabilities. The best candidates will combine the capabilities of a smaller, entrepreneurial company with the deep skills and assets of a larger, well-established company.

Such an organizational entity could emerge in several ways. First, a smaller entrepreneurial company could negotiate a privileged relationship with a larger company to gain access to the skills and assets of the larger company without giving up a significant ownership position to the larger company. More likely, however, the larger company will insist on carving out a significant ownership position in the smaller company in return for helping to build a substantial business that will ultimately develop the primary relationship with the larger company's customers. Disney did this initially with Starwave and then with Infoseek. American Airlines, through its Sabre group affiliate, has done this with Travelocity, which is a major transaction aggregator for travel services.

An outright acquisition is likely to be the wrong answer for both parties. It risks destroying the unique and essential organizational culture of the smaller company. It also removes

TABLE 4-2
Infomediary Potential for Traditional Businesses

Type	Advantages	Disadvantages
Broad base of customers		
• Fiduciaries	• Trusted relationship with customers • Rich data set on existing customers	• Trust may not apply outside particular business • Trust declining, particularly in health care • Data stored in product-centric legacy systems • Little experience with database marketing • Regulation can restrict use of data • Generally not risk taking or innovative
• Retailers and direct marketers	• Broad set of products sold, thereby creating broad profile • Skills managing relationships with vendors	• Transactional relationship with customers • Typically vendor focused rather than customer focused • Data stored in product-centric information systems • Narrow profiles
• Media	• Many have sustainable relationships with specific audiences • Potential to know customers well and to build profiles	• Not necessarily a trust-based relationship • Minimal, if any, profiles kept
• Software	• Large installed base of customers • Experience with technology • Some have trusted brand names	• Little exposure to end users themselves; difficult to get profiles • Not necessarily trusted organizations

Type	Advantages	Disadvantages
Deep database of customers		
• Database marketing and credit bureaus	• In-depth profiles of customers across vendors • Data collection and management skills • Little, if any, brand recognition among consumers	• Lack of trust among customers • Vendor-focused mind-set and relationships • Lack deep marketing skills
Nonprofit organizations		
	• Strong relationship with constituency • Deep profiles kept for fund-raising purposes • Broad, trust-based relationship	• Frequently lack a commercial focus • Likely lack resources to invest

the key metrics and incentives necessary to retain the senior management of the smaller company and preserve the commitment of the larger company's senior management. Unless the management of the smaller company participates significantly in the value creation upside of the venture, that management is likely to be recruited away by ventures that do offer this upside. On the other hand, the senior management of the larger company needs a market-based measure of the value created by this entrepreneurial venture, to ensure that the larger company doesn't focus excessively on near-term profit-and-loss performance.

The best way to provide this measure of value created is to have some portion of the equity of the venture traded on the open market. The most promising way to resolve these competing needs therefore may be a partial acquisition in which a substantial portion of the equity of the venture remains in the hands of the entrepreneurial management team, a portion of the equity is publicly traded, and a portion of the equity is held by the acquiring company to ensure that it has the necessary motivation to ensure access to its assets.

This kind of ownership structure might be built in one of two ways. It might be created through a partial spinout, in which the assets of the larger, established company are spun out into an independent entity partially owned by the parent company. This independent entity would recruit a management team consisting largely of Internet "veterans" who have demonstrated the ability to build businesses on the Internet and who could help create the appropriate organizational culture. This spinout entity would then be able to build appropriate relationships with other Internet businesses.

A slightly different approach would be a partial "spin-in," in which a larger, established company acquires a significant minority equity position in a leading Internet company. This larger company would contribute not just money, but also access to key resources like brand name or customer profiles, in return for a minority equity position.

In either case, the key objective would be to leverage the relevant assets of larger, established companies with the culture and organizational skills of the more entrepreneurial, Internet-based company. Some early examples of these kinds of relationships, although not focused on building an infomediary business, would include the relationships established between CBS and Sportsline, and Disney and Starwave.

It won't be enough to simply put two promising companies together, however. Aspiring infomediaries must launch a carefully sequenced entry strategy if they are to dominate the competition. The second part of this book examines the entry strategies the infomediary will need in order to build profiles of its customers and to leverage them with both customers and vendors.

PART

II

ENTRY
STRATEGIES

C H A P T E R

stage one: building the profile

IN THE OPENING PART OF THIS BOOK, WE asserted that infomediaries will help consumers get value in return for their information, while helping them protect that information from abuse. They'll do so, we suggested, by getting to know their clients' wants, likes, needs, and values, and by deploying software agents to lower their clients' costs of searching out the right products and services at the best possible price. The economic model discussed in Chapter 8 indicates that the average infomediary household, after two to three years of building a rich profile with the infomediary, will benefit from these services (through lower purchase prices and cash payments for their information) to the tune of about $1,400 a year.

Vendors will also benefit, as infomediaries assemble information profiles of their clients. For the first time, marketers will be able to answer some long-elusive questions about consumers in a cost-effective manner.

- **Who** are the most attractive consumers?
- **When** are these consumers in the market?
- **Where** can marketers reach these consumers?
- **What** do marketers need to offer these consumers to win their business?

With today's customer information, companies can barely answer these essential questions. With today's information, even the most skilled marketers receive at best a 5 percent response rate to their direct-mail or telemarketing efforts. (A response rate of 2 percent or lower is much nearer the norm.) As a result, marketers spend 20 or more times trying to convert prospects to customers than they would had they perfect information. Their cost to acquire customers is therefore 20 times higher than it needs to be. Perfect information may never be available, but infomediaries that are able to improve the quality and timeliness of the data in customer profiles will go a long way toward increasing the effectiveness of the needs assessment and targeting process for marketers.

Most marketers are unable to get the information they need about target customers until after they've already purchased. Worse yet, much of the customer information that marketers *do* have—even from the best sources—is riddled with inaccuracies. In the third-party databases used by many of today's best marketers, values are typically missing for at least 10 to 40 percent of the individuals for whom measures exist. Furthermore, the measures themselves are frequently estimated based on census tract or survey data, giving them a high degree of error.

Infomediaries will capture four basic types of information about their clients (Table 5-1). *Descriptive data* will provide

TABLE 5-1

Infomediary Client Information Profile Categories

Primary data category	Example data elements
Descriptive data	• Name • Address (home, work, phone, e-mail) • Date of birth • Gender • Income • Credit card debt outstanding • Mortgage debt outstanding • Total investments • Marital status • Children (number, ages, gender)
Transaction history	• Amounts spent • Vendor • Purchase category • Date • Channel (on-line)
Direct preference measures	• Purchase detail (product, vendor attributes) • Response history (to types of marketing messages and product offers) • Measure of media usage (what kinds of media, individual time spent)
Trigger events	• Indicators of life events (relocation, college graduation, birth of a child) • Measures of product information browsing or requests (starting to browse on information regarding a specific travel destination, asking a vendor for product information in response to a marketing message) • Cluster product purchase event (home purchase, moving plans drive need for furnishings, insurance, new set of local service providers) • Direct client interest (client informs infomediary of interest in purchasing new car, buying furnishings, refinancing mortgage)

"geodemographic" information, including name, address, age, and income. *Transaction history* will spell out what the consumer has purchased in the past, which is generally a useful indicator of what will be purchased in the future. *Direct preference measures* will indicate what

Marketers spend 20 times more than necessary

kinds of messages a consumer responds to, which media the consumer enjoys, and what kind of product and service features he or she prefers. And *trigger events* will include such life events as graduation and anniversaries, as well as product browsing and search requests. Together this data will be more complete, more accurate, and more timely than anything presently available—or that can ever be available under existing information capture and use paradigms.

The infomediary's client information profile will help marketers figure out who the best prospects are, when they're ready to purchase, where they can be reached, and what it will take to convert them to customers. It will give marketers access to a set of potential transactions to which they had, at best, indirect and high-cost access in the past. And it will drive customer acquisition costs lower, reduce churn, and increase the vendor's cross-selling opportunities.

Client information profiles are the heart of the infomediary's value proposition to both consumers and vendors. Clients will benefit from reduced search costs and lower purchase prices. Vendors will benefit by reaching prospects more cheaply than ever before, and with more certainty of converting them to customers.

Increasing returns and economies of scope

Aspiring infomediaries must think carefully through the sequence of actions that will best help them build client information profiles and get their business under way. This sequence must take into account the increasing returns to scale that characterize infomediation. Businesses characterized by increasing returns to scale typically experience slow initial growth followed by gathering momentum. Aspiring infomediaries will therefore need time to build trust with customers and demonstrate value to them. Once the powerful interplay between trust and value gains momentum, however, the infomediary will be able to build a critical mass of customers (and vendors) and begin offering them a full range of revenue- and profit-generating services. Done right, these services will also generate significant economies of scope.

Three primary effects

Three forms of increasing returns are particularly important to the infomediary:

- **Network effects** increase the value of a product or service to future users as the number of other users adopting the product or service grows.
- **Amortization effects** reduce the average cost to develop, produce, or deliver a product as the number of customers expands.
- **Learning effects** drive down operating costs as businesses over time discover new ways to operate at lower cost.

A simple example illustrates the way *network effects* occur. Owning a telephone isn't very useful if you're the only one who owns one. Who can you call? As soon as another person owns a phone, however, your phone suddenly is worth more. The more people who buy phones, the more people you can call. The value increases with the number of people connected. Another business driven by network effects is the transportation or logistics business, where the number of pickup and drop-off points expands with the number of users who join the system. Computer operating system software also generates network effects. The number of Windows users heavily influences the investments made by application developers to develop application software compatible with that operating system.

As we will discuss in more detail later in this chapter, this form of increasing returns tends to exhibit inflection points. The growth in value to the customer and to the vendor is not linear; at certain levels of penetration, it tends to rise even more rapidly. In the case of the telephone, a minimum level of installed base must be in place to make the phone truly useful. Once the network of users achieves critical mass, the penetration accelerates more rapidly. Similarly, in operating systems, once a critical mass of application software becomes available, it is much easier to persuade new users to adopt the operating system. Understanding where these inflection points are likely to occur and how to accelerate penetration to reach them is a critical management challenge.

Amortization effects represent a second form of increasing returns dynamic. Where are these likely to occur? Look for businesses that combine a significant up-front investment before any product or service can be sold with a relatively low incremental production cost for each unit of the product or service. Software businesses and pharmaceutical businesses have these characteristics. Software businesses require a significant initial investment to design, program, and test the software, but the incremental cost to produce each new unit of the software is quite modest.

Infomediaries must carefully sequence their entry strategies

Learning effects represent a third form of increasing returns dynamic. Most businesses discover that, with each doubling of cumulative production in the industry, operating costs decline by a relatively constant percentage. This decline in operating costs is the cumulative effect of many efforts to experiment with better ways to produce or deliver products to customers and the dispersion of these best practices throughout the industry. Of course, in very mature industries, the time required for cumulative production to double could be decades, whereas, in new industries with very high growth rates, cumulative production could double every year or so. The learning effects within these newer, high-growth industries will therefore have a much more profound impact than in more mature industries. Learning effects in newer, high-growth industries tend to have greater strategic value because the time required to disseminate these learning effects throughout the industry is typically longer than the time required to generate the next wave of learning effects through the next doubling of cumulative production. The information asymmetries among providers in the industry thus become a significant source of advantage.

Why they benefit the infomediary

Infomediaries will benefit from all three forms of increasing returns. Network effects are likely to be the most significant. The value of the infomediary heavily depends on the number of clients and vendors who participate in their service.

Clients will find more value as the reach of the infomediary expands to include more vendors, and, similarly, vendors will find more value as infomediaries offer them the ability to reach more clients. Stock markets provide a classic example of this phenomenon. Traders tend to gather in stock markets like the New York Stock Exchange or American Stock Exchange because these exchanges have a critical mass of companies listed. The presence of more traders in turn encourages new companies to list their stocks in these markets.

Infomediaries will also benefit from amortization effects at two levels. First, the investment in the systems platform required to operate an infomediary business is significant. Infomediaries will require sophisticated information capture, storage, and management systems and will need to install and deploy complex billing systems early on. Although additional scaling of these systems will be required as the infomediary grows, the initial acquisition and development investment in systems will be amortized as more clients and vendors join the infomediary business. Perhaps more significant is the cost of storing and managing a rapidly expanding set of client profiles. The more the infomediary amortizes this cost through an expanding range of services, the better the economic performance of the infomediary will be.

Learning effects will also be significant for infomediaries. Infomediation is an emerging business with no operating history. While infomediaries can draw on the experience of analogous kinds of businesses from the outset, they themselves must learn about what works and what doesn't work in the infomediary business. Although this learning will eventually disperse throughout the industry, the early entrants who aggressively build a critical mass of clients and vendors will be in the best position to leverage early learning to achieve operating efficiencies and improved effectiveness in serving clients.

The advantages of scope

As they sequence their entry strategies, aspiring infomediaries will also need to trade off the near-term benefits of focus in a particular product category, geography, or customer segment with longer-term benefits from economies of scope. Two main economies of scope will arise.

First, infomediaries with large, diverse customer bases will enjoy an advantage over those with narrower customer bases, thanks to collaborative filtering technology now available in network environments. This technology identifies clusters of customers who display similar needs and interests. When certain customers within a cluster buy a particular product or service, the collaborative filter suggests to other customers within that cluster that they might also like the product or service. The broader the sample set of customers, the more accurate the clusters are likely to be, and the more valid the recommendations made by the collaborative filter.

The second economy of scope that infomediaries with large, diverse customer bases will enjoy will be the insight derived from building a customer profile that encompasses many product and service categories. Early customer-oriented infomediaries are most likely to emerge *within* particular product and service categories, but they will soon find that they can deliver more value by expanding their reach *across* product and service categories. A book buyer who purchases travel guides to Bali is probably intending to spend a holiday there, for instance, and a couple who starts asking for information about baby food may soon trade in their sports car for a roomier family model. In this way, product- or geography-focused infomediaries will eventually give way to broad-based infomediaries serving the full range of their customers' product and service needs.

Accelerating entry

In increasing returns businesses, first movers that build a critical mass of participants become increasingly difficult to overtake, because the value of the product or service in question depends so much on the number of participants that use it. This has singular implications for entrants into the infomediary business. To become one of the long-term players, an aspiring firm must not only enter early, but also pursue an aggressive, preemptive strategy.

Preemptive strategies help preserve the economic value of early entry over time against other aggressive entrants. Because these kinds of businesses tend to evolve into highly concentrated markets with above-average profitability, substantial economic value is at stake. While not necessarily a "winner takes all" business, these are certainly "winner takes most" businesses, so the economic incentive to win is considerable.

This has a number of implications for entry strategies. As we asserted in the previous chapter, this will tend to favor entrants that are already established companies over start-ups. Established companies bring existing customer relationships and low-cost vehicles for reaching these customers. For example, they may already have a salesforce in place to deliver the marketing message to customers and regular billing of customers, where inserts can be used to promote the infomediary service. In contrast, start-ups will struggle to accelerate their entry, unless they choose to ally with an established company.

The fact that infomediation is a "winner takes most" business also underscores the importance of infomediary webs as a strategy for accelerating entry into the business. As we will discuss in Chapter 6, infomediary webs represent a powerful vehicle for mobilizing other players (such as vendors, technology providers, analytic services, support service providers) to contribute resources and innovation

Infomediation is a "winner takes most" business

capability. By focusing on the economic incentives necessary to mobilize these players, an aspiring infomediary can move much more quickly than more conventional players who focus exclusively on traditional joint venture or alliance mechanisms to leverage the resources of others.

Beyond simply accelerating growth, aspiring infomediaries must focus on the existence of inflection points where revenue and profitability tend to accelerate once a critical mass of clients and vendors comes together. The inflection point for an aggressive infomediary will occur somewhere in the fourth or fifth year of business growth. The long, slow ramp-up in revenue and profitability before the business reaches this inflection point represents one of the most significant challenges confronting any increasing returns business. This is typically a period of heavy investment, with proportionately limited impact in terms of revenue and profitability. Anything that can be done to compress this period and reach the inflection point sooner significantly increases the overall economic attractiveness of the business. Once the business reaches this inflection point, the process of industry concentration begins to take root, thereby opening up other growth options through acquisition.

Increasing returns make the infomediary business especially attractive in the long run but also present some unique challenges in the near term, as aggressive entrants struggle to acquire clients and vendors preemptively. Those who reach the inflection point in growth and profitability soonest can best exploit the long-term benefits of increasing returns businesses: high margins, high concentration, and high barriers to entry.

Managing the inflection points

Inflection points occur where the accumulation of a critical mass of clients, client trust, and client information profiles crosses a threshold in terms of perceived value to current and potential clients and vendors. At this point, revenue and profitability take off as the value of the service becomes compelling to a larger and larger market.

For the aspiring infomediary, inflection points will occur as different economic thresholds are reached. All of these will take time to achieve:

- Acquiring a critical mass of clients.
- Accumulating sufficiently rich profiles of these clients to generate higher revenues.
- Building a robust network of appropriate vendors to maximize the value of the profiles.

The focus in stage one of the infomediary's entry strategy should be on acquiring a critical mass of customers and on building an initial profile of those customers, as shown in Figure 5-1.

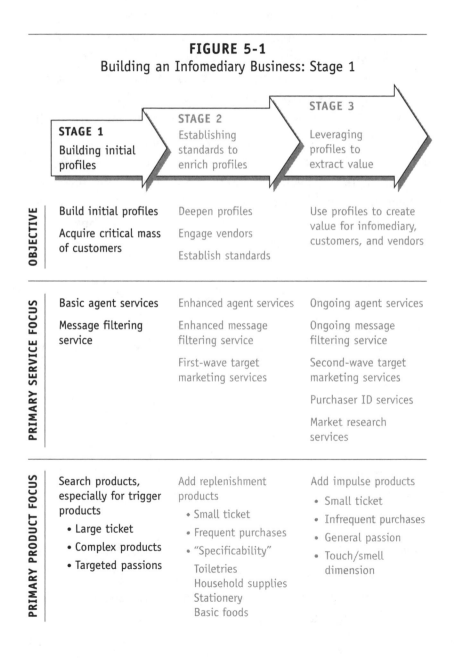

FIGURE 5-1
Building an Infomediary Business: Stage 1

	STAGE 1 Building initial profiles	STAGE 2 Establishing standards to enrich profiles	STAGE 3 Leveraging profiles to extract value
OBJECTIVE	Build initial profiles Acquire critical mass of customers	Deepen profiles Engage vendors Establish standards	Use profiles to create value for infomediary, customers, and vendors
PRIMARY SERVICE FOCUS	Basic agent services Message filtering service	Enhanced agent services Enhanced message filtering service First-wave target marketing services	Ongoing agent services Ongoing message filtering service Second-wave target marketing services Purchaser ID services Market research services
PRIMARY PRODUCT FOCUS	Search products, especially for trigger products • Large ticket • Complex products • Targeted passions	Add replenishment products • Small ticket • Frequent purchases • "Specificability" Toiletries Household supplies Stationery Basic foods	Add impulse products • Small ticket • Infrequent purchases • General passion • Touch/smell dimension

Acquiring a critical mass of customers

An infomediary with no clients will have a hard time convincing the first client to entrust it with information. Trust isn't something infomediaries can manufacture or produce; they'll have to earn it. No matter how sincere the infomediary is regarding privacy, no matter how many processes it puts in place to protect privacy, and no matter what it says about being loyal to clients ahead of vendors, the proof of the infomediary's trustworthiness will be in its track record. This track record will accumulate over time, client by client. The more clients an infomediary has and the longer it has served those clients, the more each client is likely to trust the infomediary to do the right thing.

To a limited extent, the infomediary may use endorsements by companies that already have a track record and trust with customers to reduce concern regarding its own lack of a track record. This is one reason why smaller, entrepreneurial companies targeting the infomediary opportunity will seek to pair up with larger, established companies that already have a track record and trust. Nevertheless, this form of "trust transfer" has only limited value for most customers and must be quickly supplanted by the infomediary's own track record.

Powerful network effects, resulting from the interplay between trust and value delivered to the client, characterize this challenge. The increasing value a consumer receives from an infomediary that understands not just that particular individual, but also others with similar tastes and habits, reinforces trust. The more interaction an infomediary has with consumers, the more insight it gains into their needs, and the more proactive and precise it can be in delivering agent and filter services. The information profiles of consumers that it can subsequently offer to vendors in turn become more compelling and thus generate larger revenues. As consumers see the value of the infomediary's understanding, their trust grows deeper.

Everyone has experienced this phenomenon in a limited form when visiting a new doctor. At first, a patient may be somewhat hesitant about sharing intimate information with a doctor. This often limits the doctor's effectiveness in offering advice and treatment. On the other hand, doctors with many years of experience can quickly take limited information from patients and turn it around into valuable advice or treatment, thus rapidly building trust with patients and a willingness to share even more information about themselves. Less experienced doctors can have trouble soliciting enough information about the patient to be able to deliver services that build trust.

The interplay between trust and value also serves to build barriers to entry. As with most cases of increasing returns, a business that at the outset is relatively easy to enter becomes more difficult and costly to enter over time. Imagine trying to compete as a new entrant with a well-established and trusted infomediary. No matter how compelling your service offering may be, you will find it difficult to persuade clients to switch from their established relationship. Trust locks customers into a

Trust locks in customers

particular infomediary. The costs of client acquisition rise prohibitively for latecomers, provided that privacy is important to consumers and price isn't powerful enough to overcome privacy concerns. For this reason, infomediaries are likely to focus quickly on product or service categories like financial investment and health care, where privacy concerns are likely to be paramount and barriers to entry correspondingly higher.

The process of accumulating information profiles that are deep and broad enough to create substantial value for clients will also demonstrate network effects—the accumulation will be slow in the beginning before gathering steam. As more clients join and more value is generated by the infomediary on clients' behalf, infomediaries will have a progressively easier time convincing the next client to join.

The value of "value exchanges"

The infomediary will set these network effects in motion through a series of "value exchanges." Value exchanges are interactions between consumers and infomediaries in which consumers will try out the infomediary's agent services—most likely by sharing information in the context of a planned purchase—and then seeing if the infomediary makes it worth their while to have done so.

Imagine, for instance, that a new infomediary client wants to buy a home computer. The client wants to get the savings—both from the reduced time and money required for the search and from finding the appropriate product at the lowest possible price—that the infomediary's agent services promise to deliver. (These savings would likely be in the range of 5 to 15 percent—not an insignificant amount on a purchase that currently averages close to $1,500.) To educate the agent—the key to an effective search—the new client would answer some basic descriptive questions about himself, such as how he planned to use the computer (for basic word processing, Quicken, to help the kids with homework), and the infomediary would then take a first pass at recommending a model, perhaps with a discussion of why the client might want to consider starting off with more memory than he'd need immediately. Alternatively, if the client were going to run a consulting business from his home, needed a shared printer, and expected to be creating and transferring large graphics files using Illustrator and Painter, the infomediary would recommend a different computer.

The infomediary would turn the search agent loose on the client's behalf, and the agent would find the home computer that best meets his specifications at the best possible price and then offer to execute the transaction. The client would then compare the ease of shopping for a complex product through the infomediary with the difficulty of shopping for complex products in the past and decide whether it was worth it.

Clients will get further proof of the benefits of infomedia-tion in the weeks following their purchase. They *won't* receive junk mail, spam, or annoying telemarketing calls from the legion of salespeople hawking computer magazines, peripher-als, CD-ROMs, computer games, and on-line services that would inevitably have inundated them had they not channeled their purchase through the infomediary. (Infomediaries will want to remind their clients of this benefit, which may become easy to take for granted.)

Value exchanges thus let the infomediary and the client get to know each other. Clients venture to surrender a bit of infor-mation about themselves, and the infomediary's agent services deliver tangible value in return. Both sides go away happy. The client saves money on a purchase (and avoids a slew of subse-quent direct-marketing and telemarketing messages), and the infomediary earns a measure of trust and valuable information for its client profile.

Primary service focus: agent services

Why focus on agent services rather than on the targeted mar-keting or purchaser identification services that we described in Chapter 2? The simple answer is that the infomediary will have difficulty providing other services until it has first accumulated client profiles. Agent services will allow the infomediary to offer savings to clients and demonstrate that it's capable of delivering value for information. They'll also be essential to building high-value profiles.

You'll recall from early in this chapter that the information the infomediary obtains about clients comes in four different types: descriptive data, transaction history, direct preference measures, and trigger events (see Table 5-1). The infomediary doesn't need *all* of this data to be sophisticated about its clients, but the more data it has, the more sophisticated it will be. The infomediary will use the data it has to draw inferences about its clients and then to rank, on a scale of 1 to 100, their propensity to buy a given product or service. This ranking will in turn have considerable benefits to vendors trying to figure out to whom to send their advertisements.

Let's say a 34-year-old married client engages the infomediary's search agent to look for a real estate broker in his area. (As we'll discuss later in the book, infomediaries may well end up ranking real estate brokers, physicians, even au pairs according to their service performance.) With just this information the infomediary might be able to infer that this client will soon be in the market for a home mortgage. It could then rank this client as having a higher "propensity score" for home mortgages than other clients who haven't searched for a real estate broker or tipped their hand in some other way. (Similarly, the infomediary might be able to infer from a client's searching automobile Web sites that the client might have a high propensity to buy either an automobile or auto insurance, or both.)

Of course, until it has a reasonably in-depth understanding of a particular client's wants, likes, needs, and values, the infomediary will need to move cautiously when ranking each client's propensity to buy a given product or service. That's why the infomediary will offer only search agent and filtering services in this stage of its development, not targeted marketing services. The risk of sending clients undesirable advertisements and marketing offers (thereby failing to shield them from the very intrusions they had signed up with the infomediary to avoid) is simply too high.

Agent services have a number of advantages for the early-stage infomediary. The first advantage is the information about clients that these transactions will generate for the infomediary at a time when it has few other avenues for gathering such information. Agent services also provide the best opportunity to deliver savings to clients, because they're typically used for big-ticket, complex purchases such as computers, automobiles, appliances, health club memberships, life insurance, and home equity loans—products that represent a substantial expenditure for clients and for which clients are likely to invest considerable time and effort to research the best value possible. Because they offer the prospect of substantial savings to the client, agent services also provide an incentive for clients to volunteer substantial information about themselves and their preferences.

The wise infomediary will want to focus its early-stage agent services on products that trigger the purchase of related products and services. These trigger products are particularly valuable for constructing a client profile quickly. In the case of the home computer, for example, the purchaser will also be likely to purchase software, peripherals, consumables, and computer books or magazines, either at the same time or shortly after the computer is purchased. Ditto for someone who has recently bought a house—this purchase will trigger other purchases, from insurance to contracting.

By focusing on big-ticket, trigger products and by working with clients ready to embark on a specific product search, the infomediary can begin to accumulate transaction and preference profiles for product clusters that represent a significant share of total spending within any target entry market segment. Rough estimates of spending by the average household suggest that between 50 and 60 percent of total spending is in search-related product or service categories.

Look for purchases that trigger other purchases

Filter services will also contribute to the early accumulation of client profiles. In order for the filter service to operate, the infomediary will need to request guidance from the client: Does the client wish to receive unsolicited commercial e-mail messages in certain product categories or from specific vendors?

Many clients at the outset may request a blanket filter of all messages. Those who request a more selective filter will be providing valuable preference data for the infomediary.

What the profile looks like

The client profile will now have information derived from two types of transactions: those made under the auspices of the infomediary's agent services and those made without the help of the infomediary's search agent.

Figure 5-2 illustrates what a client profile might look like at this stage of development for a client who has engaged the infomediary's search agent services to look for a new car. From this search the infomediary will be able to glean some valuable information about the client: her descriptive personal data (name, address, demographics, and income); her specific search category (automotive) and items searched within that category (Honda Accord and Audi wagons); and her interest in receiving related offers. Additionally, the infomediary will know the client's preferences and exclusions related to the infomediary's filter service; she may, for example, want to receive unsolicited marketing messages related to ski vacations and outdoor goods, but be unwilling to receive messages related to financial services.

At this stage, the infomediary knows general descriptive information about the client and has come to understand some of the client's broad preferences. As we said earlier, this knowledge will probably *not* be enough to enable the infomediary to make reliable inferences about the client's propensity to buy certain categories of products or services. But the infomediary does know (and doesn't have to infer) that the client is in the market for a car—the client has said so by engaging the infomediary's search agent services. The infomediary also knows the client is leaning toward buying a station wagon—probably either a Honda or an Audi. So the infomediary now has information that would be of significant value to auto dealers in the client's geographic area. Thus we see that transactions involving "search products" yield valuable information for the infomediary's client profile.

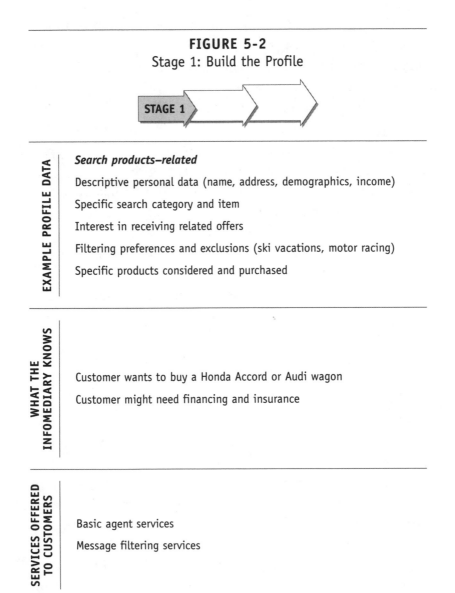

FIGURE 5-2
Stage 1: Build the Profile

STAGE 1

EXAMPLE PROFILE DATA

Search products–related

Descriptive personal data (name, address, demographics, income)

Specific search category and item

Interest in receiving related offers

Filtering preferences and exclusions (ski vacations, motor racing)

Specific products considered and purchased

WHAT THE INFOMEDIARY KNOWS

Customer wants to buy a Honda Accord or Audi wagon

Customer might need financing and insurance

SERVICES OFFERED TO CUSTOMERS

Basic agent services

Message filtering services

But what about transactions that clients make without the help of the infomediary's search agent? In these transactions, the infomediary can at best see that its client has made a transaction, where the client made it, the date it was made, the SIC code, and the amount of the transaction—little more than credit card companies can see today. And this presents a problem. Was the $500 paid to Sears spent on a washing machine or a suit? a fancy new camera or a set of tires for the minivan?

Early limits to the profile

These transactions made without the help of the infomediary's search agent reveal the principal limitation infomediaries will encounter in their early stage of development: they simply can't "see" much information on the majority of what their clients do and buy on-line. By analyzing the click-stream data (the series of URLs, or Web site addresses, that a client "clicks" through with the mouse while on-line), the infomediary will know which Web sites the client visited and how long the client spent at each Web site, but it won't have much useful information about what the client did at each Web site. For example, the infomediary won't be able to discern whether a client made a purchase or whether the client filled out an on-site form for more information regarding a particular product.

Let's say that an infomediary client goes on-line to purchase a book at one of the on-line booksellers. The infomediary will know that the client has accessed the on-line retailer through the profiling tools installed on the client's computer. But once the client accesses the retailer's Web site, the infomediary will have little idea what he or she does thereafter. Although Web sites today have a standardized way of displaying content, no standardized way yet exists to indicate the content of the Web pages themselves. Consequently, click-stream data reveal the URL of where the client has gone, but not what he or she has looked at. There is the further complication that, once a client enters "secure mode" in order to execute a transaction (secure mode makes information provided by the customer secure through the use of cryptographic technology and customer software), the infomediary is unable to track actions due to the encryption enabled by the secure mode. As a result, an infomediary will know that a purchase *may* have been made, but not that one actually has been made. If the client pays with an infomediary credit card, the infomediary will know, through charge card transaction records, that the client made a purchase from an on-line bookseller, which has an SIC code indicating books. The infomediary can overcome this lack of information if it spends the time to index a site and match URLs to content areas. More directly, an infomediary could set up an agreement with a Web site whereby the site could share log data with the infomediary as soon as the client went into the secure area. An agreement like this would allow the infomediary to monitor secure transactions as well.

Unless the infomediary can obtain information relating to all consumer transactions (and not just those taking place through its search agent services), the infomediary will have an extremely difficult time creating an integrated profile of all its clients' purchases, preferences, and behavior. *Integrated profiles*—profiles that reflect purchases from all three product and service categories (search, replenishment, and impulse)— are essential to generating economies of scope for the infomediary and to generating true value for vendors and clients. Because integrated profiles reflect a broad cross-section of purchase categories for a diverse base of clients, they enable the infomediary to engage in collaborative filtering and to maximize its revenues per customer.

Our next chapter examines how infomediaries might position themselves to create truly integrated profiles by persuading vendors to adopt a standardized format for how they represent their Web content and product information on-line. Without such standards, infomediaries that want to integrate their profiles will have to catalog and index each and every Web site their clients might browse through or make a purchase at—a straightforward, but impossibly time-consuming and expensive task.

C H A P T E R

stage two: spinning a web

ALMOST EVERYBODY PUBLISHING CONTENT today on the World Wide Web writes in a programming language called Hypertext Markup Language, or HTML. HTML has the wonderful ability to display text and graphics in a way that Web browsers, like those made by Netscape and Microsoft, can read. But HTML is a display language only—it has no "intelligence" regarding what it displays. As a result, each Web site maintains its own database of product definitions and pricing formats, all of which are proprietary and unavailable to the general public.

Consequently, the only way an infomediary will be able to search a Web site written in HTML, to determine its content (and thus discern what its clients are doing on-line), will be to do a text-based search of the site. Because Web sites follow no standardized way of organizing their content or naming their products, a search for a laptop computer, for example, would involve at least four searches, including "computer," "laptop," "notebook," and "portable." Distilling the results of such text-based searches into a meaningful data set for the infomediary would involve an impractical amount of manual work.

Help is on the way, in the form of a new programming language called eXtensible Markup Language, or XML, which will "tag" the content of Web sites in a standardized format. A group called the World Wide Web Consortium (W3C), the main standards-setting group on the Internet, is driving this language forward and intends to provide the impetus for various industry groups to get together and develop industry-specific tags for their products. Tags in the computer industry, for example, would indicate features such as style (notebook or desktop), price, amount of RAM, and so on, which would enable the infomediary search agent to key on these tags while searching for products.

But the adoption and deployment of XML won't be fully present on the Internet until sometime after the next millennium. That's why the fastest way for an infomediary to take advantage of the new XML technology will be to develop its own set of tags and to persuade vendors to adopt them, not just for product information but for other content presentation as well.

Until the majority of Web sites adopts this standardized format for representing data on the Web, the infomediary will have difficulty creating integrated profiles of its clients. Integrated profiles demand compatible data. Without compatible data, infomediaries can't track the on-line behavior of their clients.

Convincing vendors to adopt a standard data format for their Web sites will be an essential challenge for the infomediary—although, as we'll see, the benefits of standardization will extend to vendors as well. The second stage of the infomediary's development focuses on the challenge of persuading vendors to adopt these standardized tags.

Accelerating adoption of the standards

As they think about ways to persuade vendors to adopt standard data formats, infomediaries can learn much from the emergence of a new form of industrial structure called "economic webs." Economic webs represent a more specific concept than the popular notion of ecosystems and value networks. These popular notions tend to highlight the important theme of interdependence among business enterprises and the value of leveraging the resources of others. Webs are consistent with these broader notions but focus on the strategic issue of how to create the economic incentives that drive participants to join webs and contribute to their expansion. For this reason, web-based strategies focus on the attributes a shaping platform needs in order to generate sufficient economic incentives for web creation and growth. Rather than simply describing interdependent behaviors, web-based perspectives concentrate on the specific mechanisms required to drive and shape interdependent behaviors.

A web that supports rather than traps

Economic webs occur when groups of customers and companies collaborate around a particular "platform" of mutual interest. Typically that platform has been a technology standard. In the computer industry, for example, companies have self-organized around technology standards owned by Microsoft and Intel. But the platform of mutual interest doesn't necessarily have to be a technology standard—it can be any standard that creates collaboration among otherwise unallied competitors. In the case of the infomediary, for example, the platform could be the client information profile. In much the same way that "technology webs" like those in the computer industry are organized around standardized technology components, like an operating system or a microprocessor, infomediaries will organize "infomediary webs" around standardized client information profiles.

The essence of economic webs

Why do economic webs matter? Economic webs create market incentives to mobilize a much larger and more diverse group of companies than joint ventures or alliances, with their cumbersome legal arrangements, could hope to mobilize. The companies in a web act independently in response to these economic incentives but reinforce each other by adding value to the overall web, both for customers and for web participants. Companies can freely join webs whenever it is in their economic interest and leave webs whenever the web ceases to deliver enough value. "Joining" a web means adopting a common architecture, design, or set of standards that provides a common platform for a variety of companies to do business. For example, companies in the computer industry can join the Microsoft/Intel web simply by adopting the PC architecture as the basis of their product or service business. Neither Microsoft nor Intel could even name all the companies participating in their web.

A "shaping platform" owned by the web shaper generates the economic incentives for companies to join the web. While patents or copyrights often protect the ownership rights of the web shaper in the shaping platform, the most significant protection is the ongoing effort by the web shaper to enhance the functionality of the shaping platform over time. This functionality makes it very difficult and expensive for anyone seeking to "reverse-engineer" the platform.

Increasing returns dynamics make the incentives created by the shaping platform even more powerful over time by increasing the value of web participation as more companies join the web. The more companies and customers that join in, the stronger the web gets. For example, the more customers who buy Microsoft's Windows software, the more attractive it becomes for software developers to write for Windows. And the more software written for Windows, the more attractive Windows is to customers.

In the case of the infomediary, the information profiles of clients represent a powerful shaping platform. The ability to access these profiles has substantial economic value to vendors, creating strong economic incentive for vendors to adopt profile presentation standards and to provide information consistent with these standards. As vendors adopt standards, infomediaries will integrate their profiles of clients, thus making profiles more compelling to vendors.

Economic incentives drive all markets, of course, but in webs the shaper wields these incentives in a deliberate effort to enhance cooperation and to dampen competition within the web itself. The invisible hand of the market is assisted by the deliberate actions of an aspiring web shaper.

The benefits of economic webs

Deploying a web-based strategy will have a number of benefits for the infomediary:

- The economic incentives generated by the web are better vehicles for convincing vendors to adopt standards than legal agreements would be.

- Webs give infomediaries a "beachhead strategy" in which they focus on one narrow element of the total value received by the client; other web participants will deliver the remaining elements.

- Webs help the infomediary manage risk associated with moral hazard and asymmetrical information.

Reliance on *economic incentives*, rather than on legal agreements, substantially accelerates the standards adoption process. Legal agreements take time to negotiate. The more parties are required to join the legal agreement, and the more diverse their interests, the more time it takes to negotiate the agreement, and the more fragile the agreement becomes. For this reason, most joint ventures or alliances tend to involve relatively few companies with similar interests. In contrast, standard data formats must be adopted by a very broad and diverse group of vendors, in addition to such specialized businesses as providers of profiling and privacy technology tools and analytic service providers delivering consulting services to infomediaries and vendors. Economic incentives can provide a much more powerful mechanism than legal agreements for quickly reaching out to such a diverse group of companies and motivating them to adopt specific standards.

A web-based strategy also allows infomediaries to establish a *beachhead* in which they focus on one narrow element of the total value received by the client. This helps the infomediary to enter markets faster than vertically integrated companies, which must build all the necessary elements required by the customer. The infomediary needs only capture information on behalf of clients and deliver specialized services based on this information. Then the profiles themselves, functioning as a shaping platform, help engage the specialized resources of a broad range of other players to support the infomediary's role.

Beachhead strategies minimize risk

Vendors free the infomediary from developing or delivering products. The infomediary facilitates connections between vendors and customers, but it does not own inventory. Instead, it will enlist specialized order fulfillment and payment services companies to provide many of the services necessary to support the purchase and delivery of products. Infomediaries will incentivize technology companies to create innovative privacy and profiling technology tools compatible with the open technology architectures defined by the infomediaries. Professional services firms might find attractive niches helping vendors and the info-mediaries themselves to interpret profile data captured by info-mediaries. Other companies will help customers compare vendor offerings and ensure the best possible purchase given their individual needs.

By creating the incentives and standards to facilitate looser business relationships, economic webs also help to *manage risk*. Webs tend to emerge in markets characterized by significant uncertainty because of their ability to manage risk. Of course, all new ventures face significant uncertainty and risk, but technological or regulatory discontinuities like those in the computer or banking industries compound these risks. In these industries, the very rules of the game are uncertain. What are the sources of advantage? What will the structure of the industry look like? What kinds of economic returns are likely? In these industries, entrepreneurs not only don't know their ability to play by the rules; they don't even know what the rules are. Compare the uncertainty experienced by an entrepreneur opening a car wash to that of an entrepreneur introducing a new software product on the Internet using Java technology. Which seems to be higher risk?

Infomediaries will arise in response to the increasing uncertainties resulting from the tension between growing information capture capabilities made possible by electronic commerce and privacy concerns. These uncertainties cover a broad range of issues: sources of advantage, industry structure and performance, and regulatory policy. Who will be in the best position to capture information about customers? If new players capture information about customers, will this lead to more or less industry concentration? Will it erode profitability or enhance profitability for other industry participants? What are the risks of a privacy backlash? Who would be most adversely affected by such a backlash?

Webs help to manage risk by leveraging the resources of other companies, thereby sharing investment risk, rather than requiring a single company to make all the investment required to deliver specific offerings in the marketplace. To enter one of these markets, a vertically integrated company must truly bet the company to develop the capabilities it needs to serve customers. A web-based company, in contrast, can invest a much smaller amount and focus on the areas where it excels, because it can count on other companies in the web to supply the remaining elements of value that the customer requires. In the computer industry, Apple could enter the market literally from a garage because it needed only to develop and market a relatively small component of the total assembled system that most customers needed.

Key roles within economic webs

Companies can play a number of roles within economic webs:

- Web shaper
- Adapter
- Influencer
- Hedger
- Disciple
- Key player

Web shaper. Only one or two companies within each web can play the role of web shaper. The *web shaper* owns the shaping platform that creates the economic incentives for other participants to join the web. At the outset, the web shaper assumes primary responsibility for driving others' adoption of the shaping platform, to ensure that it becomes a de facto standard. In later stages of web development, the web shaper focuses on enhancing the functionality of the shaping platform and encouraging new applications to sustain the growth of the overall web. For example, both Intel and Microsoft are aggressively investing to encourage new applications for the desktop computer in order to realize additional penetration and growth. While these investments clearly benefit the investors, they also benefit all web participants by steadily expanding the available market.

In the case of infomediary webs, the infomediary plays the role of web shaper. It plays this role by virtue of its privileged access to the customer profiles that serve as the shaping platform. Only the infomediary can generate the economic incentives for collaboration that are necessary for the formation of a customer web.

Adapter. Adapter is the second basic role within a web. *Adapters* are companies that adopt the shaping platform and enhance the value of that platform by delivering additional products or services tailored to the platform. They create value by remaining alert to new opportunities for innovation or cost reduction around the basic platform and by moving quickly to address those opportunities before anyone else spots them.

Influencer. Within the adapter role, many subroles can be identified. Perhaps most important is the *influencer,* an adapter that possesses assets or capabilities that can significantly influence the success of one shaping platform relative to competing shaping platforms. These assets or capabilities might be a brand, a large installed base of customers, superior distribution capability, or an innovative and widely needed new product. Influencers create value for themselves and the web by moving quickly in the early stages of web formation. They bet big by committing their assets or capabilities exclusively to an emerging shaping platform and thereby help to build critical momentum for the emerging shaping platform, both in reality and in perception.

An example of an influencer in the computer industry was Lotus, a software company that developed an enhanced spreadsheet application and then decided to make that application available only on the newly introduced personal computers developed by the IBM web. Because Lotus had a superior implementation of a widely demanded application, this decision materially helped to drive the success of this web relative to the competing Apple web. Compaq played a similar influencer role within the IBM (and later Microsoft/Intel) web by introducing an innovative new form factor for a personal computer—the portable—and offering this form factor only within the IBM web.

In infomediary webs, several kinds of companies might play the role of influencer. Any company that possesses a large database of customer profiles could provide a substantial accelerator by allying with an infomediary and helping to populate customer profiles at the outset with rich data accumulated in other contexts. These companies would include large credit or marketing database companies like Experian or Acxiom. Similarly, any company with well-established trust-based relationships with customers and frequent interactions with customers could be attractive to infomediaries as a way to build a large client base quickly. Thus vendors in the financial services industry might be natural candidates for the role of influencer in an infomediary web.

Hedger. Another subrole within the adapter category is the *hedger*, a company that participates across multiple webs by developing its products or services to support multiple shaping platforms. The hedger tends to be risk averse and tries to spread its bets across multiple shaping platforms until it is more certain which shaping platform will be most successful. At this point, it prunes support for multiple web platforms until, in the end, it may support only the dominant standard.

Disciple. Once an adapter commits exclusively to one web, it becomes a *disciple*. In contrast to influencers, disciples are risk averse and commit to only one web either because they don't have the resources to support multiple platforms or because the uncertainty has diminished so much that it is clear which web will prevail. A key goal of the web shaper is to reduce perceived risk so much that hedgers quickly evolve into disciples in order to maximize the investment and differentiation of their web relative to other webs. In the application software business, many companies played a hedger role, developing their software for both the Macintosh and the Microsoft/Intel platforms. In recent years, there has been an accelerating trend to "decommit" on the Macintosh platform and to focus exclusively on the Microsoft/Intel platform, thereby increasing the perceived value of the latter platform.

Key player. Finally, another adapter subrole is the *key player*, which might be viewed as the "arms merchant" developing key technology essential for multiple shaping platforms and maintaining compatibility across competing shaping platforms.

Arms merchants supply competing platforms

In this category, one could cite Hewlett-Packard in the laser printer business or Verity in the search engine business. These companies are not particularly risk averse. Instead, their focus is on maximizing value by developing compelling technology and then maximizing the accessible market by providing this technology across all webs. These adapters are agnostic as to who wins. They incur little cost in supporting multiple platforms and seek to maximize revenue and profits by supplying all sides.

In infomediary webs, specialized technology companies that develop the privacy and profiling tools for use by infomediaries might assume the key player role. Infomediaries would be naturally interested in developing exclusive relationships with these companies, to provide differentiation in the tool kit offered to their clients. On the other hand, technology vendors may decide that they can maximize value for themselves by playing the "arms merchant" role, selling their technology tools to a broad range of infomediaries. Infomediaries themselves may help to promote this kind of behavior by adopting open architectures for tools integration.

Some basic misconceptions often arise regarding the relative attractiveness and availability of the two roles of shaper and adapter. Do shapers create more value than adapters? Participants are often quick to conclude that the shaper necessarily creates more value as an enterprise than the adapter and that, therefore, wherever possible, one should choose to play the role of shaper rather than of adapter. This conclusion is not warranted.

You don't have to be big to shape a web

Adapters can often create significant value, provided they understand the implications of choosing the role of adapter and aggressively focus on building the capabilities required to be successful in this role. Compaq provides an example of a company that has created enormous value as an adapter within the Microsoft/Intel web.

Can only large firms succeed as shapers? In fact, large companies are disadvantaged in playing a shaping role relative to smaller, more nimble players. Shapers must routinely make large bets relative to the size of the company. They need to be able to move quickly and to consistently communicate a compelling vision to other potential web participants. These are all attributes that large companies often lack.

Building a robust shaping platform

What attributes help maximize incentives for adoption and determine the relative success of the infomediary in the second stage of evolution? If the infomediary can create sufficiently powerful incentives for vendors to adopt specific data presentation standards and to provide information to the infomediary consistent with these standards, it will be able to generate much richer information profiles than can competing infomediaries. In short, its "standard" format for presenting data will win out.

Robust shaping platforms in the early stages of web formation display the following attributes:

- Significant functionality
- Opportunity for a broad range of value creation roles
- Simple but powerful early adoption driver
- Low-cost access

Significant functionality. Significant functionality shapes the incentive to adopt. Shaping platforms that fulfill an important function for a potential web participant are more likely to be adopted quickly. Client information profiles meet this test. They provide vendors with a resource that has substantial economic value and a broad range of applications. For example, these profiles not only help vendors to connect more efficiently with appropriate customers, they also help refocus product development based on a deeper understanding of customer needs and preferences. Much as the microprocessor and operating system provide the core functionality necessary to define the architecture of a personal computer in technology webs, client information profiles provide similar functionality to define the architecture of a vendor's relationship with its customers.

Broad range of value creation roles. Robust shaping platforms also make available a broad range of value creation roles. This increases economic incentives to adopt the platform by expanding the opportunity to create value while minimizing the risk of direct competition with other web participants. Client information profiles provide the basis for a rich set of value creation roles. Vendors covering diverse product categories can make use of the profiles without competing directly with each other. Even within product categories, rich information profiles help vendors avoid direct price competition by focusing on the customers who most value their distinctive product attributes. As discussed earlier in this chapter, other value creation roles supported by client information profiles include specialized order fulfillment and payment services companies; technology tool companies; and professional services firms working with infomediaries, vendors, and clients to enhance the value of the information available in the profiles.

Powerful early adoption driver. Simple but powerful early adoption drivers help the most successful shaping platforms. Spreadsheets played that role for desktop computer webs, printer sharing played that role for local area networks, and desktop publishing played that role for Adobe's printer font web. These powerful applications help kick-start the increasing returns dynamics by quickly bringing together a critical mass of web participants and customers. They also require limited infrastructure deployment to generate value for the user. For example, some of the early efforts to create webs around personal digital assistant technology foundered on the limited availability of wireless data networks. As this chapter suggests later, the simple but powerful "beachhead" driver for the info-mediary shaping platform will be the first wave of targeted marketing services to leverage the information profiles captured in the previous stage of infomediary evolution.

Low-cost access. The shaping platform must also provide low-cost access to potential web participants. In technology webs, *low cost* refers to both licensing fees and the ability of open and well-documented interfaces to reduce the investment required to develop complementary products. These interfaces enhance the incentive for potential web participants to adopt the plat-form rather than investing to duplicate the functionality or committing to a competing platform. For infomediary webs, low cost refers to the targeted marketing service fees the info-mediary charges vendors. It also suggests that infomediaries should invest in strong documentation of profile presentation standards to make it as easy as possible for vendors to imple-ment these standards in their own information systems.

Of course, the ability of the infomediary to provide access to client information profiles at all hinges on client willingness to authorize such access. Establishing trust is essential for infome-diaries to leverage the potential value of the shaping platform. Infomediaries that establish trust will offer vendors a broader range of information sooner than infomediaries that are still working to establish trust.

We'll have more to say about the shaping platform in our next chapter, when we examine the challenges of maintaining client profiles as a robust shaping platform in a later stage of infomediary development.

Deploying a web-based strategy

Now that we've reviewed the general case for economic webs, and their application to the particular circumstances of the infomediary, we can turn our attention to how infomediaries will use a web-based strategy to accelerate adoption of standards. Figure 6-1 reviews the primary objectives and service focus of this second stage of the infomediary's entry strategy.

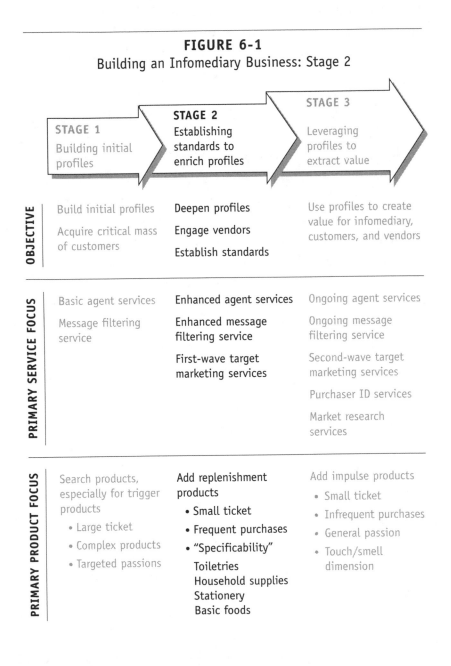

FIGURE 6-1
Building an Infomediary Business: Stage 2

	STAGE 1 Building initial profiles	STAGE 2 Establishing standards to enrich profiles	STAGE 3 Leveraging profiles to extract value
OBJECTIVE	Build initial profiles Acquire critical mass of customers	Deepen profiles Engage vendors Establish standards	Use profiles to create value for infomediary, customers, and vendors
PRIMARY SERVICE FOCUS	Basic agent services Message filtering service	Enhanced agent services Enhanced message filtering service First-wave target marketing services	Ongoing agent services Ongoing message filtering service Second-wave target marketing services Purchaser ID services Market research services

PRIMARY PRODUCT FOCUS	Search products, especially for trigger products
	• Large ticket
	• Complex products
	• Targeted passions
		Add replenishment products
		• Small ticket
		• Frequent purchases
		• "Specificability"
		  Toiletries
		  Household supplies
		  Stationery
		  Basic foods
			Add impulse products
			• Small ticket
			• Infrequent purchases
			• General passion
			• Touch/smell dimension

The first wave of targeted marketing services

The infomediary's primary lever when convincing vendors to adopt standard data formats will be its targeted marketing services. This service allows vendors to send advertisements and other marketing messages through the infomediary to customers who meet certain profile criteria. An adventure travel company, for instance, might be interested in sending an ad to all customers between the ages of 18 and 35 who own mountain bikes and have purchased flights within the last 12 months. Or the marketer of a theme park might want to target all parents of young children who have taken those children on vacation in the last year or two.

The infomediary's clients will now more readily acccpt these targeted marketing messages because the infomediary has

Using the carrot and the stick proven its ability, through stage-one value exchanges, to deliver immediate and tangible value in return for personal information from clients. (The infomediary will now be able to more confidently offer these services as well, because its client profiles will be yielding ever more accurate inferences, as described below.)

The ability to specify in advance how many messages they wish to receive, and from what kinds of vendors or product categories, will further increase client willingness to receive messages. Setting up the rules in this way will help clients to ensure that their privacy is protected and at the same time help the infomediary to ensure that the targeted marketing messages are truly relevant for the client. As clients gain more experience with the value of targeted marketing messages, they will be willing to expand both the number of messages they are willing to receive and the range of vendors or product categories covered by the service.

The infomediary can use access to its client profiles as a bargaining chip to persuade vendors to adopt certain standards specified by the infomediary, as well as to provide information to the infomediary that is consistent with these standards. The infomediary could approach vendors and offer to help them find customers who meet certain profile criteria. In addition to paying the targeted marketing service fees, the vendor would have to adopt prescribed standards on its Web site (and eventually in bricks-and-mortar retail establishments) in return for using these services. For example, an infomediary could approach BMW, Audi, and Mercedes and inform them that it has 100,000 customers with incomes over $100,000 who will declare themselves in the market for a new car in the next 12 months. To make their products available to this group of customers, the automakers would have to conform to standards for tagging their product information so that clients could more easily search across the three brands for the car that best met their needs.

In this second stage, the infomediary might also begin offering to get lower prices for its clients on replenishment products. These are typically small-ticket items when purchased individually, but can add up to a significant amount in aggregate—representing roughly 25 percent of the average household's spending. For most households, the purchase of these products is a chore. The infomediary could aggregate these purchases—not just for an individual client, but for all its clients—and then solicit bids to get the best possible price for these products. In the process of providing this service, the infomediary can capture valuable transaction, preference, descriptive, and "trigger-events" data for a wide range of products. For example, the infomediary could approach Procter & Gamble with the news that the infomediary has 1 million customers, all of whom regularly buy toothpaste and sundry products. In exchange for putting together special pricing or special services, the infomediary would make P&G products available to its client base.

By carefully targeting agent services at specific products, the infomediary may be able to gain insight into life events that are likely to have a broad impact on client purchase behavior. For example, helping clients to find the best baby carriage or baby crib will signal the likely birth of a child.

Two standards

The standards that the infomediary would propose to vendors would cover both information presentation and purchaser identification standards.

Information presentation standards would prescribe a set of "tags" the vendor would use to identify categories of information provided about the vendor and the products or services sold by the vendor. These tags would be invisible to the user of the Web site. As a result, they would not interfere with each vendor's ability to adopt a distinctive look and feel in presentation of information to users, but they would help the infomediary to collect and compare information across vendors, as well as more precisely track clients' usage preferences. The specific content of the tags would vary depending on the product category, but they could help identify important attributes of each product, including size, color, performance measures, and specific features. These tags would also help the infomediary classify the content contained on each page of the Web site, to allow the infomediary to track in more detail where clients spend their time on-line.

Purchaser identification standards would specify procedures for determining whether a client is willing to reveal basic descriptive information such as name and address at the time of purchase, specifying whether the vendor wishes to purchase this information *from the client* if it is available, and arranging for payment and delivery of information. All of these standards need to be implemented in advance to minimize inconvenience at the time of purchase by making the information transaction as transparent as possible to the client (assuming the client has preauthorized this transaction).

The adoption of these standards by vendors would significantly expand the revenue generation opportunities for infomediaries. With these standards, infomediaries can also be more helpful to clients in maximizing the value of their information profiles. The full potential of targeted marketing services and purchaser identification services will depend on the widespread adoption of the standards. For this reason, the infomediary will want to require vendors to adopt these standards as a condition for gaining access to the first wave of the infomediary's targeted marketing services.

Vendors will have strong economic incentives to accept this requirement. At this point, the infomediary will have valuable profiles of its clients in terms of transaction histories and preference profiles for major search products. Vendors will gradually become less and less able to find much of this information through any other source. In particular, the integrated profiles of purchases across vendors within a product category and the trigger event of a search request provide vendors with valuable information regarding the potential life cycle value of customers and their readiness to purchase. Infomediaries will likely offer the first wave of targeted marketing services at low prices to reinforce vendors' incentive to adopt the specified data standards. Vendor incentives will be particularly strong if vendors can implement the standards at a relatively low cost and if the vendors don't have to compromise on the distinctive look and feel of their Web site presentations to visitors.

What the profile looks like

During this second stage, the infomediary's client information profile gains considerable depth, as shown in Figure 6-2. Standardized data formats will allow the infomediary to glean more

FIGURE 6-2
Stage 2: Establish Standards

EXAMPLE PROFILE DATA

Search products–related

Descriptive personal data (name, address, demographics, income)

Specific search category and item

Interest in receiving related offers

Filtering preferences and exclusions (ski vacations, motor racing)

Specific products considered and purchased

+

History of searches and outcomes by category and product

Measure of auto site usage

Replenishment products–related

Purchase detail for multiple categories (food products, beverages, household supplies)

Categorical spending levels and frequency

Life event data (move, new child, new job)

Frequency, extent of on-line usage

WHAT THE INFOMEDIARY KNOWS

Customer wants to buy a Honda Accord or Audi wagon

Customer might need financing and insurance

+

Customer likes high-end products, has a five-year-old child, clicks through ski vacation and outdoor ads, and has an older, fully paid automobile

Customer a good prospect for a SUV or station wagon

SERVICES OFFERED TO CUSTOMERS

Enhanced agent services

Enhanced message filtering services

+

Early target marketing services (e.g., from SUV manufacturers)

data from transactions that take place without the help of the infomediary's search agent services. The client profile will broaden accordingly. Comparing Figure 6-2 with our example profile from Chapter 5 (Figure 5-2), we now see that the infomediary is able to piece together a much better picture of its client. The history of her searches (and the outcome of these searches) by category and product are now available, as well as purchase details for multiple replenishment-type goods and services, including food products, beverages, and household supplies. The infomediary will also be able to gather more life event data about the client, as well as information about the frequency and extent of her on-line usage.

As a result, the infomediary now knows the client likes high-end products, has a five-year-old, "clicks through" on-line banners for ski vacations and outdoor ads (but ignores mortgage ads), and has an older, fully paid automobile. This information will support sending targeted messages to this client, consistent with her privacy preferences, from sport-utility vehicle manufacturers (on the assumption that, if she's searching for a station wagon, she'll also be interested in sport-utility vehicles), and from vendors of products and services for children.

As the infomediary begins to promote its first wave of targeted marketing services, these services will in turn begin to enrich its profile information, particularly in the area of preference data. The mere act of authorizing the infomediary to solicit targeted marketing messages in specific product categories or from specific vendors will provide useful insights into client preferences. Once the infomediary delivers the message, the client's response will provide additional insight. The infomediary will know to send similar messages when the client asks for more information or makes a purchase. The infomediary will know that different messages are required when the client ignores the message it sends. As the infomediary aggregates similar responses for one client and across groups of clients, it will gain significant insight into product and marketing preferences.

In our next chapter, we'll see how the client profile expands even further as the full range of infomediary services gets up and running.

C H A P T E R

stage three:
playing the
spider's role

ONCE THE INFOMEDIARY HAS BUILT AN initial client profile and has convinced vendors to adopt a standardized format for their Web sites, the infomediary will begin reaping the advantages that accrue to a powerful web shaper. As we'll see in this chapter, the infomediary may soon dominate its own web the way Microsoft and Intel dominate theirs.

In this stage of its development, the infomediary's client information profile—and its use of that profile to match consumers and vendors—will increase in sophistication and robustness so that the infomediary can unfold the full range of client and vendor services described in Chapter 2 (Figure 7-1). As it does so, the infomediary will begin to enjoy economies of scope and powerful increasing returns to scale. Its position as the holder of valuable client profiles will enable it to lock in the customers and vendors that depend more on the increasing ease—and lower cost—with which they can find each other. The "spider's" position at the center of a burgeoning web will give the infomediary considerable market power across many different product and service categories.

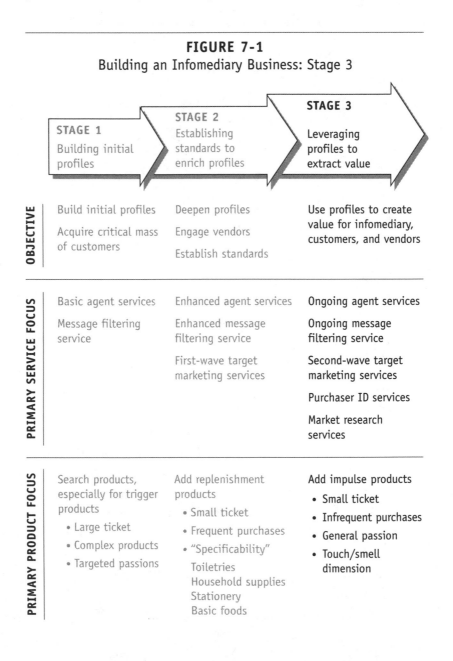

FIGURE 7-1
Building an Infomediary Business: Stage 3

	STAGE 1 Building initial profiles	STAGE 2 Establishing standards to enrich profiles	STAGE 3 Leveraging profiles to extract value
OBJECTIVE	Build initial profiles Acquire critical mass of customers	Deepen profiles Engage vendors Establish standards	Use profiles to create value for infomediary, customers, and vendors
PRIMARY SERVICE FOCUS	Basic agent services Message filtering service	Enhanced agent services Enhanced message filtering service First-wave target marketing services	Ongoing agent services Ongoing message filtering service Second-wave target marketing services Purchaser ID services Market research services
PRIMARY PRODUCT FOCUS	Search products, especially for trigger products • Large ticket • Complex products • Targeted passions	Add replenishment products • Small ticket • Frequent purchases • "Specificability" Toiletries Household supplies Stationery Basic foods	Add impulse products • Small ticket • Infrequent purchases • General passion • Touch/smell dimension

This chapter examines the client information profile as it becomes increasingly populated with valuable customer data. It describes the next wave of targeted marketing services (and the other services to customers and vendors) that the infomediary will be able to launch as a result of this enriched client profile. And it examines the increasing returns dynamics that the infomediary will set in motion as customers and vendors are gradually locked into the services it provides.

What the profile looks like

As the infomediary persuades vendors to adopt data format standards, the client profile managed by the infomediary becomes a much more valuable asset. In addition to basic descriptive data, the profile will contain

- Detailed transaction histories, including itemized data on frequency of purchase and amount spent for individual products and services. These histories will help vendors to identify high-revenue potential customers.

- Detailed preference information, including which vendors the client chooses and the attributes of the products or services purchased. This information will help vendors determine what they need to offer customers in order to win their business.

- Detailed media usage profiles, including on-line information (Web sites visited, content accessed at those sites) and magazine and newspaper subscriptions. These profiles will help vendors determine where and how to best present a targeted marketing message to specific customer prospects.

- Valuable trigger information—life events, information searches, search requests, and trigger product purchases— that will provide insight into the likely timing of the next purchase.

In contrast to the customer profiles that marketers have today, in which much of the preference information is inferred with limited accuracy from generalized descriptive or behavioral data, the profiles of the third-stage infomediary will contain demonstrated preference data based on the specific behavior of individual clients. For example, an infomediary might know that a client living in Baltimore likes river rafting, fishing, California wines, and jazz - and might therefore "market" that profile to a travel adviser offering highly tailored vacation packages to the West Coast.

Going beyond generalized customer data

By this time, the client profile we discussed in the first two stages of entry is coming into much sharper focus. From tracking her on-line behavior via standardized data formats, the infomediary will now know that the client often visits the California Winter Weather page on the World Wide Web from November to May, that she gets regular snow reports through Yahoo!, that she recently purchased a new pair of skis on-line, and that she periodically buys gasoline at filling stations near Lake Tahoe, California. Based on this information, the infomediary might send her marketing messages for a time-share condominium at Squaw Valley (a ski resort near Lake Tahoe), suggest to her a Ford Explorer, Eddie Bauer model, instead of a two-wheel-drive station wagon, and winter clothing for her son from L.L. Bean and other qualified vendors.

Figure 7-2 shows the client profile's increasing sophistication. The infomediary now begins weaving a web in which the client is connected to a wide range of vendors that will catch her interest. Becaue the client is a skier, the infomediary contacts hotels and restaurants near Lake Tahoe that will be interested in paying to send their messages to her. Because she has a five-year-old, the infomediary connects her to retailers that sell bicycles for children. And so forth.

Of course, the infomediary uses the profile consistent with

the client's privacy preferences. At no time does the vendor know the identity of the client (unless the client decides to make her identity known). As the infomediary builds trust with clients and demonstrates the ability to connect them with appropriate vendors in ways that protect clients' privacy, clients will allow selective use of their profile to facilitate these infomediary services. Paradoxically, by protecting the client's privacy, the infomediary will enable vendors to leverage more detailed information about customers and deliver correspondingly tailored and valuable offers.

The second wave of targeted marketing services

The ability to make these kind of inferences about its clients will enable the infomediary to launch its second, most rewarding wave of targeted marketing services. The infomediary's targeted marketing services in this stage will differ from the first wave of targeted marketing services on a number of significant dimensions. The infomediary will be able to target clients on the basis of

- Search and replenishment products purchased through agent services.

- Impulse products that depend on inference for targeting.

- Smaller-ticket items, purchased on an infrequent or sporadic basis.

- Products or services in which touch or smell is important (for example, fashion clothing or perfume), so that search is less effective in determining an appropriate product (unless it is a repurchase of an item already sampled).

- Products within a category the client likes—for example, a jazz fan may always be on the lookout for interesting new jazz groups.

FIGURE 7-2
Stage 3: Leverage the Profile

EXAMPLE PROFILE DATA

Search products–related

Descriptive personal data (name, address, demographics, income)

Specific search category and item

Interest in receiving related offers

Filtering preferences and exclusions (ski vacations, motor racing)

Specific products considered and purchased

+

History of searches and outcomes by category and product

Measure of auto site usage

+

Searched for realtors in North Lake Tahoe area

Replenishment products–related

Purchase detail for multiple categories (food products, beverages, household supplies)

Categorical spending levels and frequency

Life event data (move, new child, new job)

Frequency, extent of on-line usage

+

Gasoline purchase history, including locations

Browsing products–related

Regularly visits Lake Tahoe weather pages in November to May time frame

Reviews Yahoo! snow reports

Purchased new skis on-line

Frequent purchaser of classic rock 'n' roll music

Regular visitor to AFL-CIO home page

Customer can save $370 on auto insurance with new carrier

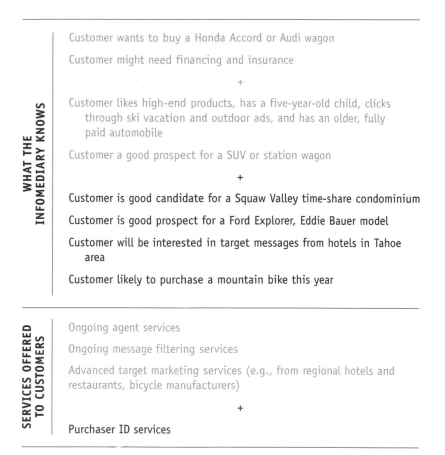

Information presentation standards will enable the infomediary to capture much more detailed transaction and preference profiles on all products purchased through the infomediary payment mechanism, including impulse purchase products.

Relevant products

Given more detailed preference profiles, the second wave of targeted marketing services will focus much more specifically on helping to connect vendors with appropriate customers, given the match between the vendor offerings and the preferences that clients demonstrate through purchases of related products. Collaborative filtering technology (the leading vendor of which is currently Net Perceptions) will help the infomediary compare preference patterns across clusters of clients. These comparisons will identify products or services that clients might enjoy given the preference clusters in which they participate. In addition, the accumulated experience of the infomediary in presenting targeted marketing messages in the second stage will help it to make better inferences about which vendors and products will appeal to which customers.

Good timing

Infomediaries will also help vendors reach customers when it matters—at the time they are about to make a purchase. In the earlier stages of infomediary development, agent services helped the infomediary to determine when clients were looking to buy a specific product. Now the infomediary will be even more effective in identifying client needs, as client searches give early indications that the client is considering a purchase.

Infomediaries will also help vendors understand the key drivers of customer loyalty and potential triggers for switching behavior. For example, when the infomediary observes that one client purchases repeatedly from vendors that offer customer loyalty discounts, whereas another client tends to stay with vendors that offer substantial advice and help following a purchase, the infomediary will advise vendors to tailor their offerings accordingly. Clients will also benefit as vendors offer products and services that more closely match their buying needs and preferences. Similarly, the infomediary will know when a client who was previously loyal to one vendor is now starting to research other vendor offerings in the same category. This information could help the original vendor focus on winning back the loyalty of the

Reaching customers when they're ready to buy

customer before she switches to another vendor. Clients will of course control whether the infomediary can disclose this information to vendors, but most will not object—their interests are served by alerting vendors to changes in their buying needs or preferences.

The right context

Infomediaries will also help vendors place targeted marketing messages in a relevant context. The first wave of targeted marketing messages will be launched directly to the client via e-mail. As the infomediary gains additional insight into how its clients use media, the infomediary will also be able to help vendors deliver these messages in an appropriate environment on a third-party Web site. An infomediary might realize that a car buff regularly visits a specific car racing site and could help a car dealer or manufacturer position a targeted marketing message on that Web site.

By this time, the infomediary will have a track record, and clients will be more trusting of its ability to anticipate their needs and preferences. As a result, they will be more likely to increase the number and range of targeted marketing messages they're willing to receive through the infomediary. Each new targeted marketing message delivered to a client, acted on or not, further enhances the client profile and the infomediary's understanding of the needs and preferences of that client.

At this stage, the infomediary will also offer a broad range of market research services to vendors. These services will enable the infomediary to leverage the scope of profiles collected to help vendors understand broad purchase patterns and trends. Rather than focusing on individual profiles, these services will aggregate data to reveal broader market opportunities.

Vendors today, especially those that reach their end customers through distributors and retailers, have only limited information about market opportunities. At best, they get sampled data or very basic summaries of "sell-through" data (for instance, how many units of each product were sold in a given month). In the case of sampled data like the Nielsen ratings, many vendors question the accuracy of the data because of concerns over the sampling techniques. Sell-through data provide little insight regarding who bought which products and what drove the purchase decisions. Even retailers and distributors who capture the sell-through data have limited ability to track purchases down to the level of the individual customer. Efforts to do this through customer loyalty programs have met with limited success.

Infomediaries will overcome these limitations and provide more detailed information for vendors. The infomediary will gather information for a broad cross-section of the market and reduce concerns about sampling error. Because clients will be far less concerned about sharing their data once combined with data from other clients, the infomediary will be able to provide significant insight about purchase patterns—and tie purchase activity to specific demographic or buying preference information—without revealing the identities of its clients. An infomediary could inform a consumer electronics vendor that its latest VCR is being outsold by a competitor's product and provide true insight regarding the causes. Perhaps buyers are putting more emphasis on the quality of instructions and customer support than on the product features themselves. A product review publication like *Consumer Reports* may draw attention to deficiencies in these areas, but the vendor needs to know to what extent these deficiencies really drive customer purchase behavior.

Insight into the reasons consumers buy or don't buy has enormous potential value for vendors in all aspects of their business. It would help them redesign products and services and identify new product or service opportunities. It would refocus marketing efforts by identifying segments of customers who purchase the product but are currently unaware of its features or functionality. Infomediaries are likely to become significant channels for test-marketing products and services, to fine-tune both product design and positioning.

Customer concerns about timeliness of delivery might drive a reconfiguration of logistics operations, including location of distribution facilities and inventory-stocking policies. Customer need for increased advice and support might lead the vendor to develop alliances or joint ventures with companies that are better able to provide this advice and support. Infomediary-supplied market research might indicate that salespeople are not sufficiently knowledgeable about the product or its uses and might lead to changes in recruiting or training programs to address these deficiencies. Companies might rely on infomediary-supplied market research to raise capital on more favorable terms.

Why do customers quit buying your product?

Both the targeted marketing services and the market research services will, of course, be offered only to vendors who agree to adopt the information presentation and purchaser identification standards defined by the infomediary. These two services will continue to create a powerful incentive for broader adoption of these standards, which will in turn increase the value of these services as the standards deepen the client profiles available through the infomediary.

Purchaser identification services—in which clients earn a small fee from vendors every time they choose, during an on-line session or a purchase with an infomediary credit card, to reveal who they are or what their e-mail address is—will now be much more broadly deployed, given the adoption of relevant transaction standards. Clients will specify their privacy preferences with regard to specific vendors or product categories in advance, or they'll simply adjust their disclosure decision case by case. In either case, the actual purchaser identification transaction will be as seamless for clients at participating vendors as the shipping charge or sales tax is in today's purchase process.

Other infomediary services

As infomediaries deploy the full range of their services, agent services will begin to cover a broader range of vendor products and services, including all relevant search and replenishment products. The infomediary will monitor in detail impulse purchase product transactions by each client. This information will help the infomediary to create tailored "push" browsing environments for each client through the infomediary's targeted marketing services. Although clients will still go out to their favorite vendor locations to browse for interesting products or services, they will find their infomediary becoming more and more insightful about the products and services they browse. Each day, as they open their e-mail box, they'll find an attractive set of targeted offers that match their browsing profile.

Clients will also spend less time "shopping." The time they do spend will have a higher yield, both in terms of products and services tailored to their individual needs and preferences and in terms of price. Beyond these less quantifiable benefits, clients will also be paid for the selective sharing of their information profile with appropriate vendors through the targeted marketing service and purchaser identification service programs.

As clients develop confidence in the infomediary, the infomediary's services might extend beyond commercial transactions and privacy protection to provide broader analytic or monitoring services for clients. One might imagine the infomediary providing parents with reports on their children's usage of computers and the Internet. Was Doug really doing his home-

work, or was he playing Doom with his friends on-line? Infomediaries might arrange to deliver preprogrammed tutorials for
children experiencing difficulties with certain subjects in
school. They might even deliver programming to occupy children while parents are out doing errands. Infomediaries might
also provide advice on preventive maintenance of household
fixtures—when to replace batteries in smoke alarms or when to
replace the filter in the home fax machine.

Some vendors, meanwhile, will significantly reduce marketing expenses as they connect with high-potential customers
through the infomediary's agent and targeted marketing services. Vendors skilled in using the information profiles accessible through the infomediary will also improve their revenues by
tailoring their products and services to clients' demonstrated
preferences and more accurately target the most receptive segments of the market.

The more you sell, the more you sell

In Chapter 5 we described a number of increasing returns
dynamics that the aspiring infomediary would attempt to set in
motion. The most important of these are network effects. *Network effects* mean that the more clients and vendors an infomediary affiliates with its service, the more attractive the infomediary becomes to subsequent clients and vendors—and the
easier it becomes to attract still more clients and vendors to the
web. This virtuous circle demonstrates the truth of the observa-
tion that "nothing succeeds like success."

The infomediary's attractiveness to clients . . .

The attractiveness of the infomediary's services to clients will
increase as the infomediary expands its number of affiliated
vendors (Figure 7-3). The more vendor relationships the info-

FIGURE 7-3
Attractiveness to Clients and Vendors

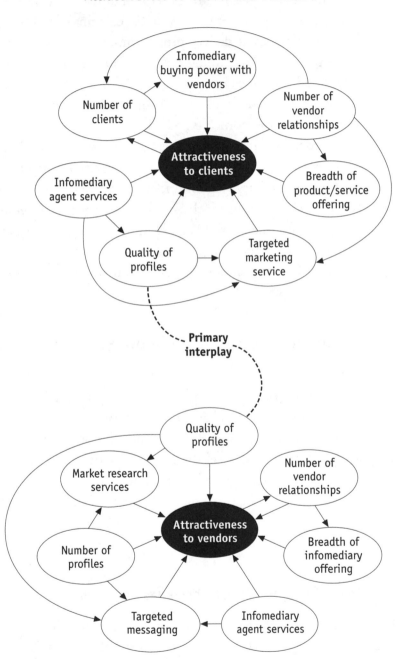

mediary has, the more selection it can offer to clients. This dynamic applies particularly to targeted marketing services and purchaser identification services. (The infomediary's search agent services would, of course, search for the best possible product and price regardless of whether or not a vendor is affiliated with the infomediary.)

The more clients an infomediary has, the more attractive the financial rewards for the client are likely to be. The bargaining **"Nothing** power of an infomediary on behalf of **succeeds like** its clients will increase with regard to **success"** vendor fees and pricing discounts as the infomediary gathers a critical mass of clients within specific market segments. This will apply not only to consumer markets, but also to a variety of business-to-business markets. General Electric's TPN Register service, for example, is mobilizing large corporate purchasers to increase their buying power relative to suppliers.

The increasing returns dynamics of the infomediary's attractiveness to clients combine to make the infomediary ever more effective at acquiring clients over time. Aside from increasing the value of the infomediary for each client, the growth in clients also helps drive word-of-mouth reference selling. As clients experience growing value from the infomediary, they start to promote the infomediary to their friends and acquaintances.

. . . and to vendors

The attractiveness of the infomediary to vendors will also increase as the infomediary expands its number of clients and vendors (see Figure 7-3). Vendors will flock to the number of clients and the quality of their profiles. At the outset, they may reluctantly participate so that the infomediary won't come between them and their customers or charge for previously free information.

Two events will overcome this reluctance. First, the initial focus of the infomediary on agent services in stage one of its development will generate a substantial stream of qualified buyers for vendors with superior products and services (the vendors selected by the infomediary's search agent). Second, the vendors will realize (as the infomediary markets its services to them) that member clients match the profiles of the vendors' ideal prospects.

Vendors will flock to the infomediary

The more of these clients (and their profiles) that the infomediary signs up, the more incentive for vendors to participate in the infomediary web.

The vendors most likely to sign up early for the infomediary's targeted marketing services are the small vendors or new entrants into a market that have relatively few existing customers. These vendors have relatively little to lose and a lot to gain by leveraging the profiles accumulated by the infomediary. For example, not only will infomediaries reduce vendors' need to build expensive bricks-and-mortar retail distribution, they will also provide highly flexible supply chain capability. Relying on specialized web participants that are focused on elements of the supply chain, infomediaries will configure tailored supply chains for each client and vendor, as and when needed.

As smaller vendors join the infomediary service and begin to experience positive results, the larger vendors will have additional incentive to participate as well. If the larger vendors don't participate, they'll risk erosion in market share to those vendors who can access more integrated profiles of target customers. The tangible impact of increased sales for smaller vendors will also help strengthen the incentive to join.

As more clients and vendors join an infomediary's service, the range and value of services to vendors will increase. For example, the market research services of the infomediary become more valuable as more clients join. Concerns about sampling error diminish as the size of the sample increases. Test-marketing programs develop for narrowly defined segments. If a vendor wishes to test the appeal of a product with teenagers from midwestern farming communities, a larger infomediary can more readily gather a set of clients meeting this profile than can a smaller infomediary with few, or even no, clients who meet this profile.

Scope effects

A third set of increasing returns dynamics sets in motion crucial economies of scope that increase the economic value of clients and vendors to the infomediary. Simply put, the infomediary will generate more revenue from each client and vendor relationship as the number of clients and vendors grows.

How? Recall from Chapter 5 that infomediaries will employ collaborative filtering technology to identify clusters of customers who display similar needs and interests. When certain customers within a cluster buy a particular product or service, the collaborative filter suggests to other customers within that cluster that they might also like the product or service. The more clients an infomediary has, the more effective it's likely to be in deriving insight from the profile of each client. By looking "across" a number of client profiles, for example, the infomediary can suggest new products that might interest individual clients, even if those individuals had not previously been aware of them. By using this collaborative filtering technique, the infomediary can, for example, cluster clients with similar tastes in movies and then suggest movies to individual clients who may not have seen them but are highly likely to enjoy them. The more clients

Delivering more than eyeballs

an infomediary has and the more detailed the profiles of each client, the more finely tuned the clusters can become, and the more accurate and valuable each client's suggestions can become.

The infomediary will also generate economies of scope through its targeted marketing services, which have the potential to become a significant source of revenue over time (exact revenues generated by each line of the infomediary's business will be discussed in the following chapter). As the infomediary learns to target ads to customers according to their needs and preferences, client response rates will go up as clients increasingly tolerate and even invite more ads. The number of targeted ad opportunities per client will increase.

The infomediary will also be able to charge more for each ad delivered. As the infomediary accumulates more detailed profiles and is able to cross-reference profiles against each other, it will be able to assure vendors not only click-through rates but also purchase rates from the advertising. This positions the infomediary as more than just an advertising medium— now it is a distribution channel able to charge rates consistent with delivering buyers to vendors, rather than simply eyeballs to vendors.

Agent services will also generate growing revenues per client over time as a result of similar kinds of increasing returns dynamics. As the infomediary gains more clients, it is likely to become increasingly effective in delivering the best product available at the best price through agent searches. As the effectiveness of agency searches increases, clients will be motivated to divert more of their search-oriented purchases to the infomediary service to ensure the best value possible.

Generating more revenue per client is a key driver of infomediary growth and profitability. The first two sets of increasing returns dynamics discussed above help the infomediary to acquire new clients much more cost-effectively over time, providing a first layer of growth and improved profitability. This third set of increasing returns dynamics—and the economies of scope they create—ensure that each client, once acquired, generates an increasing amount of revenue, providing a second layer of growth and improved profitability. In any service business, the opportunity to acquire new customers at rapidly decreasing costs, combined with the ability to generate an increasing amount of revenue per customer, amounts to a very compelling business proposition.

Barriers to entry

The increasing returns dynamics that characterize the infomediary business will have yet more beneficial effects for the infomediary. These dynamics have to do with the high levels of industry concentration that represent a natural outcome for any increasing returns business. These levels of concentration stem from two related forces unleashed by increasing returns dynamics. First, barriers to entry tend to rise rapidly; late entrants can't carve out a significant market position. Second, the growth and profitability advantages derived from larger aggregations of clients tend to squeeze out marginal players over time and increase the incentives for leading players to acquire smaller players as a way to accelerate growth further.

How do barriers to entry rise rapidly in increasing returns markets? Consider the difficulty today unseating Microsoft as the vendor of the leading desktop operating system. With its large installed base, Microsoft can generate an enormous web of complementary product and service providers to add value around the core operating system. Enticing these providers away to a competing operating system, or even convincing them to straddle both operating systems (which is what Apple has tried to do), would be extremely difficult and—even if feasible—would require huge expenditures by the new entrant.

New entrants competing with well-entrenched package delivery service providers or airlines that have built broad networks of nodes and routes would face similar difficulties.

Comparable barriers to entry will confront anyone arriving to the infomediary business after the first few years. Potential clients won't trust a new entrant relative to established players who have proven their ability to represent their clients' interests effectively. Established players will offer a broad range of infomediary services based on the aggregated profiles of their clients and developed vendor relationships which a new entrant won't be able to match given more limited profiles and vendor relationships.

Barring some major set of technology innovations that existing infomediaries couldn't integrate into their service offering, late entrants would need to spend heavily to catch up with existing competitors. Because they won't be able to "buy" higher-quality service levels—given the dependence of service quality on the availability of aggregated profiles—late entrants could only lower prices to "buy" new client and vendor relationships. The entry investment could increase by an order of magnitude after the industry's early years have passed, with the risks of failure increasing proportionately as well.

Bad news for the late entrant becomes very good news for the early entrants. Higher barriers to entry mean high levels of profitability over extended periods of time.

Increasing returns dynamics also tend to produce highly concentrated markets with one dominant player and, at most, a few other large players. The economic model presented in the next chapter suggests that the dominant infomediary may have as many as 16 million clients and generate revenues of almost $5 billion within ten years. The significant advantages accruing to larger providers relative to smaller players tend to produce this concentration. As indicated above, larger infomediaries will acquire new clients and vendor relationships more cost effec-

tively than smaller infomediaries. At the same time, larger infomediaries will be able to generate more revenue from existing
client relationships than will smaller infomediaries. These two

Late entrants will need to spend heavily to catch up

advantages combine to put increasing
economic pressure on smaller infomediaries. Over time, smaller infomediaries either need to search out
defensible niches where they might
be able to develop specialized exper-
tise to serve their clients or need to position themselves for
acquisition by larger infomediaries.

This is also good news for aggressive early entrants. Two
sources of growth become available as the market evolves and
matures: growth from new clients joining an infomediary for
the first time and growth from acquisition of smaller, less
aggressive infomediaries experiencing intensifying economic
pressure. The earnings multiples accruing to aggressive early
entrants will help them to fund growth by acquisition and
thereby accelerate the concentration trend in the market.

Taking the "spider's" role: the late-stage shaping platform

The beauty of rapidly rising entry barriers is that customers and
vendors will gradually be "locked in" to the infomediary's service. (*Lock-in* refers to the high switching costs that vendors
and clients experience as time passes. Clients, for example, will
come to trust the infomediary to safeguard their information
against abuse. Should the infomediary itself abuse this trust,
then obviously clients would experience much less reason to
stay with the infomediary. Switching costs would therefore
decline, and the client would no longer be locked into the infomediary.) Creating lock-in with clients and vendors will require
infomediaries to be very shrewd at managing their shaping

platform through this later stage of the infomediary's development. In Chapter 6, we defined the early stage shaping platform as having the following attributes:

- Significant functionality
- Opportunity for a broad range of value creation roles
- Simple but powerful early adoption driver
- Low-cost access

In later stages, the infomediary will imbue its platform with different characteristics.

As in Chapter 5, it's best first to review the general case for economic webs. Recall that economic webs occur when groups of customers and companies collaborate around a particular "platform" of mutual interest. Typically, that platform has been a technology standard. In the computer industry, for example, companies have self-organized around technology standards owned by Microsoft and Intel. But the platform of mutual interest doesn't necessarily have to be a technology standard—it can be any standard that creates collaboration among otherwise unallied competitors. In the case of the infomediary, for example, the platform could be the client information profile. In much the same way that "technology webs" like those in the computer industry are organized around standardized technology components, such as an operating system or a microprocessor, infomediaries will organize "infomediary webs" around standardized client information profiles.

In the general case for economic webs, the shaping platform needs to change and develop as the web develops and matures. As webs mature, web participants become motivated by the prospect of continued growth while the owner of the shaping platform becomes motivated by the prospect of capturing an increasing share of the value within the web. The ability to continually enhance the functionality of the shaping platform is essential to serving both needs.

At this point, a robust shaping platform continues to evolve in functionality. This evolution means expanding the range of potential applications of the shaping platform, thereby generating more revenue growth opportunities for web participants and more value to customers. From the infomediary's or web shaper's perspective, the evolution of functionality in the shaping platform helps in many ways. First, other web participants

Enhancing the shaping platform

must invest in the capabilities and skills required by the new functionality. This helps the owner of the shaping platform to create switching barriers for other web participants. The more incremental investment web participants must make in complementary capabilities and skills to keep up with the enhancements in the shaping platform, the more difficult it will be for participants to shift to a competing platform.

Second, it generates a continuing revenue stream for the owner of the shaping platform. Each time the web shaper significantly enhances the shaping platform, it creates new incentives for web participants to access the shaping platform, providing opportunities for the web shaper to charge for access.

Finally, the evolution of the shaping platform creates economic incentives for all web participants to interact with the owner of the shaping platform. Web participants interact with the owner of the shaping platform because they want to try to influence its evolution in areas that benefit them. At a minimum, they seek to gain insight into the direction of future enhancements to the shaping platform so that they can modify their own product and business strategy accordingly. In return for discussing enhancement plans for the shaping platform, the shaper receives information about future product and business plans of web participants. The shaper thus occupies a privileged position in terms of information flows within the web. Although a rich network of information flows typically emerges within webs, these information flows tend to be highly fragmented. The shaper in effect becomes a significant concentration node for information flows within the web, giving the shaper a unique ability to anticipate moves throughout the web. Just as all roads led to Rome, all roads in the Microsoft/Intel web lead to Redmond and Santa Clara, as web participants make the pilgrimage to discuss product plans. In any market characterized by high uncertainty, the concentration point for information flows has enormous strategic value.

The infomediary's client information profiles certainly meet this attribute of a shaping platform. In the early stages, the infomediary will enhance the profile by adding new information categories as the range of infomediary services expands. For example, when the infomediary promotes the first wave of its targeted marketing service, this service will generate a whole new category of response history. What was the response of clients as the infomediary presented targeted marketing messages to them? Did they ignore the message, or did they request more information? In either case, important new information is added to the profile. The functionality of the profiles will increase further as the infomediary gathers longer histories of each client and as the number of clients expands. In later stages, as the number and the depth of their client information profiles expand, infomediaries will be able to move from targeted marketing services to market research services analyzing broader purchase trends and the evolution of needs and preferences across clusters of clients.

With each new enhancement to the client information profiles, vendors will want to invest in a new wave of capabilities and skills to exploit the value of the new information. For example, vendors today focus primarily on mass-marketing skills, whereas direct-marketing skills will be required to exploit detailed client information profiles. Rather than focusing on compelling images that grab the attention of large audiences, the vendor will need to develop the analytic skills required to identify the most likely purchasers and the marketing skills to tailor messages to these prospects to increase probability of purchase. Throughout the vendor organization, the ability to move quickly from information profiles to action plans will determine competitive success. If customers are demanding improved delivery times, the first vendor to acquire appropriate logistics facilities will capture the most value from this information. As infomediaries become more prominent, information about customers will become more widely available to all vendors. Competitive advantage will shift from privileged information access to analytic insight and speed of implementation.

A continuing stream of new value creation opportunities will flow for vendors as the infomediary enhances the profiles. The infomediary will be able to charge more on behalf of clients as the value of the profiles increases. Major vendors will have ideas about additional information that might be captured in the profiles and seek to influence the profile enhancement plans of infomediaries. The resulting interactions will position infomediaries at the crossroads of a rich set of information flows regarding new product and service opportunities.

The spider cometh

Thus, by the end of the third stage of its development, the infomediary will find itself at the center of a growing web in which the shaping platform of information profiles will provide compelling economic incentives for both clients and vendors to stay within—and continue to invest in—the infomediary web.

The shaper's advantages

In fact, the successful infomediary may now dominate its own web as Microsoft and Intel dominate theirs. Increasing-returns industries tend to consolidate as they mature—as customers and companies become increasingly locked into the shaper's shaping platform. Consolidation will also take place in the infomediary industry as successful infomediaries go beyond persuading vendors to adopt a standardized format for data presentation to creating a shaping platform that is in itself the standard for how customers and vendors find each other and interact. The infomediary's dominance will manifest itself in three ways:

1. Through the infomediary's ability to extract value from markets by controlling functionality of the shaping platform.

2. Through its ability to use that platform to influence the behavior of other participants by generating compelling economic incentives.

3. Through its ability to gain superior insight into rapidly evolving and uncertain markets by concentrating information flows among web participants.

In computing technology architectures, the operating system and the microprocessor "shaping platform" embody *functionality* that all web participants depend on for value creation. In the "Wintel" technology web, for example, all participants have at least tacitly agreed to adopt Windows as their operating system of choice, or "standard." This functionality is now what they depend on for their own products to work. All of the software written for Windows, for example, conforms to the software protocols standardized in Windows. Similarly, in infomediary markets, the customer profile provides the functionality required to connect customers with the appropriate vendors—a functionality on which both customers and vendors will increasingly come to depend.

Infomediaries will also be able to use the shaping platform to *influence* the behavior of others in the web—for instance, by reducing the price of targeted marketing services to encourage adoption of product information presentation standards. Infomediaries will also use access to client information profiles to influence the privacy policies of vendors themselves. Vendors would have to contractually commit not to share this information with any other company. Because no company will be able to access this information without dealing directly with the infomediary, this contractual restriction preserves the privacy of clients, at the same time increasing the value of the infomediary services.

Infomediaries will also have the ability to gain superior insight into rapidly evolving and uncertain markets by concentrating *information* flows among web participants. This will occur naturally as infomediaries become gateways for all interactions between clients and vendors, and because infomediaries will be the owners of an evolving standard regarding which other web participants will want to keep in close contact. In their role as gateway, infomediaries will anticipate new product

Shapers are *not* monopolists

introductions because vendors will rely on infomediaries to do much of the market research and test-marketing of new products. As the owner of an evolving standard, infomediaries will have unique insight into the most valuable information for vendors and what analytic techniques and tools are available to maximize the value of this information. Leading-edge vendors will try to persuade infomediaries to capture certain kinds of information or to present the information in certain formats to facilitate analysis.

Sources of the shaper's advantage

Becoming the owner of the shaping platform on which other web participants depend is a position of considerable power, from which web shapers can reap enormous rewards. The source of this wealth differs from that of traditional monopolist returns, however, which derive from economies of scale at the firm level. Monopolist strategies include an important focus on maximizing profits at volume levels below those of the competition, and employing predatory pricing to inhibit entry and to discipline would-be competitors. In contrast, as we've seen, shapers strive to catalyze and accelerate increasing returns dynamics at the web level.

As we've explained throughout Part II of this book, the sources of advantage for the infomediary as web shaper include

- Strong, trust-based relationships with a broad and diverse range of clients, which are sustained by a continuing stream of valuable services.

- Privileged access to detailed and integrated profiles of these clients.

- Continuing refreshment of profiles based on services offered to clients and vendors.

- Widespread adoption of standards defined by, and over time enhanced by, the infomediary, including standards for client profile presentation, product presentation, purchaser identification, and the technology architecture behind privacy and profiling tool kits.

- Powerful economic incentives that both "lock in" and encourage vendors to continue to use client profiles actively.

- Growing barriers to entry driven by increasing returns economics which make it difficult for new entrants to unseat well-established infomediaries.

One other source of advantage is a rich network of relationships with specialized third parties focused on enhancing the value of the standards, including

- Specialized analytic consultants focused on extracting value from the information captured in client profiles on behalf of clients, vendors, and infomediaries.

- Specialized data-mining and analytic tool vendors focused on helping analytic consultants extract value from profiles.

- Third-party evaluators helping clients and infomediaries to evaluate vendor performance based on captured transaction and vendor information profiles.

- Technology companies innovating new tools to be included in the client privacy and profiling tool kit.

Greed isn't always good

The infomediary's role as shaper of its web will require it to balance its own self-interest and that of its web as a whole. That balancing act involves a shift in mind-set from maximizing value for the shaper to maximizing value for the web. If the web doesn't maximize value, then neither can the shaper within it.

Consider what happened to Apple when it focused on near-term profitability in the late 1980s and early 1990s. Other participants in the web either shifted to straddle the Macintosh and PC webs, thus eroding the difference between them, or migrated completely to the PC web. By not licensing its Macintosh operating system, Apple captured the lion's share of the revenues in its web, but the web itself—at least in terms of market share—began to shrink. For example, in 1993, Apple captured an estimated 83 percent of the hardware and software revenues available in the Macintosh web, whereas, in contrast, Microsoft and Intel captured only 11 percent of the revenues in their web. This is one reason why the PC web generated $66 billion in hardware and software revenues in 1993, whereas the Macintosh web remained much smaller, at about $10 billion in revenue. Striking the right balance between maximizing value for the web and for the shaper is one of the main strategic challenges that will face the infomediary with an emerging dominant position.

The web shaper must be certain to continue providing value creation and capture opportunities for other participants in the web, rather than trying to capture all of these opportunities itself. Participants will otherwise eventually be drawn to competing webs instead. For the infomediary, this will mean never abandoning their clients' interests, but at the same time not squeezing vendors too hard on behalf of consumers. Either path might maximize revenues for the infomediary in the short term, but would undermine the infomediary's web longer term as participants lose their economic incentive to stay in the web.

The infomediary that succeeds at playing this shaping role will be in a position of considerable economic advantage, a position made all the stronger by the industry's inevitable consolidation. As certain shaping platforms for connecting customers and vendors win out over others, only a few dominant infomediaries will be left by the time the industry is fully mature.

In our next chapter, we assemble an economic portrait of the infomediary, in which it becomes clear that infomediation—at least for those who successfully stick around long enough for the industry to consolidate—will be a very profitable business indeed.

the economics
of infomediation

INFOMEDIARIES WILL PROTECT THE PRIVACY
of their clients and provide new ways for customers
and vendors to find each other. They will also create
considerable wealth for the infomediary's investors.
A dominant infomediary will generate as much as
$700 million in revenue by its fifth year of existence
and command over $20 billion in shareholder value
by its tenth. This success won't come cheaply: cumulative investment along the way will total as much as
$210 million.

In this chapter, we describe the economic model
of the infomediary—its revenues, costs, cash flows,
and potential market value. We then examine and
put a value on the economic drivers of infomediary
performance.

Context for the economic model

The exact nature of infomediary economics will vary greatly depending on its starting point (traditional business or start-up), its product or service focus, its service offerings, and its entry strategy. In this model, we assume that the infomediary will start through an alliance of traditional businesses with well-established customer relationships and trust. This new venture would offer the basic services of an info-

A market value of $20 billion

mediary—such as agent services, filtering, and targeted marketing services— outlined in Chapter 2. A key assumption is that, although the infomediary would focus initially on Internet transaction activity, its services would quickly include the traditional market transactions described in Chapters 5–7.

At the outset, targeting a substantial segment of household spending, such as housing, cars, or personal financial management, the infomediary in our model would, over a ten-year period, expand its services to cover all the major categories of household spending. We also assume that the infomediary modeled here

- Focuses exclusively on the U.S. market over the entire ten-year period, although infomediaries could easily address opportunities in other countries and markets as well.

- Pursues an aggressive, preemptive entry strategy and grows to become the leading infomediary in the United States by the tenth year, representing about 50 percent of the total market. This is consistent with other increasing returns businesses. In fact, it may be somewhat conservative. Microsoft has captured a 90 percent share of the market in the United States and has managed to well exceed 50 percent market share ten years immediately following the introduction of its first DOS operating system product.

- Makes no acquisitions, although that option might well accelerate growth and increase profitability.

Our model focuses specifically on the economic performance and characteristics of the infomediary itself. We do not attempt to explicitly model either the economics of the broader web of participants that help to accelerate infomediary entry and growth or the economics of the rivalry among competing infomediaries. Obviously we'll need to make important assumptions, as we go along, about both of these broader economic environments in order to properly model the infomediary's economics.

Economic profile of the infomediary

An aggressive infomediary could grow into a sizable business over a ten-year period. As Figure 8-1 indicates, revenue by the second year could approach $100 million, growing to about

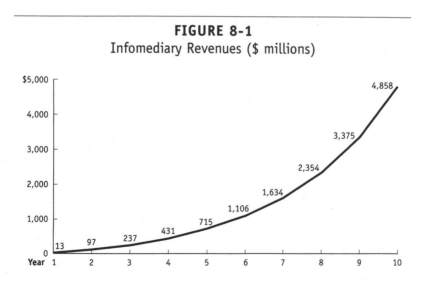

FIGURE 8-1
Infomediary Revenues ($ millions)

$700 million by the fifth year and reaching as much as $4.9 billion by the tenth year. This represents an extremely rapid trajectory relative to most start-ups, especially in the first several years. To put the infomediary's growth in context, Amazon.com, one of the fastest-growing Internet businesses, generated $148 million in revenue in its second full year of operation. Our economic model assumes that the infomediary is not a pure start-up, but instead leverages the existing brand and customer relationship assets of a larger, well-established company. Under these conditions, the revenue ramp-up reflected in the economic model is more reasonable than for a pure start-up.

Two key variables drive this revenue growth: number of clients and revenue generated per client. To generate this level of revenue growth, the infomediary must aggressively recruit clients—roughly 1 million by the end of the second year, 3.4 million by the fifth year, and 16 million by the tenth year. In comparison, Amazon.com took 27 months to acquire 1 million customers and then took only 6 months to acquire the next 2 million customers. With the help of the brand and established customer relationships of a larger, well-established company, an infomediary should at least match this level of customer acquisition performance.

The infomediary will need 16 million customers

To put these numbers in context, American Express has 29.6 million cardholders, and Citicorp, the largest retail bank, has approximately 100 million consumer accounts. The American Airlines AAdvantage program for frequent fliers has 29 million members. America Online, as the largest on-line business, has 12 million subscribers. Cendant provides purchasing services to 73 million consumer households. The infomediary can certainly acquire 16 million clients in the U.S. consumer market, but it must be aggressive to do so, especially over a ten-year period.

The infomediary will require so many clients because each client generates a relatively small revenue stream. In the second year, the infomediary will generate only about $130 in revenue per client. Although the revenue per client increases over time, reaching roughly $250 in the fifth year and as much as $345 in the tenth year, this business clearly requires large numbers of clients to reach significant scale.

Revenue components and sources

Not only does revenue per client increase over time, but the composition of this revenue shifts as well, as indicated in Figure 8-2. In the early years, agent services represent between 70 and 80 percent of the revenue of the infomediary, with targeted marketing services accounting for most of the rest of the revenue.

The assumption is that agent services depend less on the accumulation of client profiles than on targeted marketing services. Because explicit client requests can drive agent services

---

FIGURE 8-2

Composition of Infomediary Revenues ($ millions)

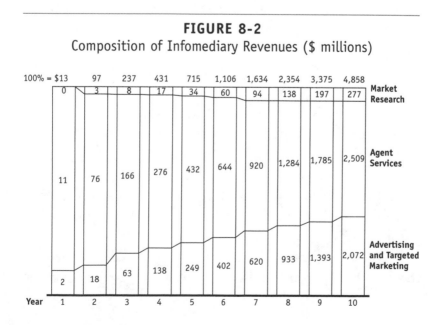

("I'm looking for a new computer. Can you help me find one that meets my application needs and offers good value?"), they can be quickly promoted by the infomediary. In fact, agent services promise to deepen the infomediary's client profile—each agent search will provide significant learning about the needs and preferences of the client.

In the early stages, the infomediary will focus on delivering ads that the client requested ("I'm an avid gardener and would welcome ads about new gardening tools, especially if they're from the following vendors"). Infomediaries won't be likely to target marketing services until they've built considerable trust and knowledge about the client to avoid exposing the client to irrelevant ads.

By the tenth year, as much as 43 percent of the infomediary's revenues will come from targeted marketing services, while agent services will provide roughly another 52 percent of the revenue, with market research services generating the remaining 5 percent.

This longer-term revenue split suggests that infomediaries will be valuable to clients and advertisers by virtue of their deep understanding of the clients' needs and preferences. Infomediaries will estimate the likely receptivity of clients to specific advertising messages and, given this understanding, will deliver higher response rates to advertisers. Accumulating client profiles and growing skill in interpreting these profiles will increase the infomediary's willingness to deliver targeted advertising to clients while increasing the client's willingness to receive the advertising.

In terms of revenue sources, the infomediary will draw 48 percent of its revenue by its tenth year from fees charged to vendors for targeted marketing services and market research. The remaining 52 percent of revenues will come from client payments for agent services. In the first two years, clients will generate about 80 percent of the fees received by the infomediary, given the heavy dependence on agent services. This heavy dependence on client-generated fees in the early years ensures that the infomediary tightly focuses on client needs. It also builds the trust with clients that is essential to generating fees from other services over time.

Operating expense components of the infomediary

As might be expected, the operating expense structure of the infomediary represented in Figure 8-3 evolves significantly over the ten-year period. In the early years, marketing expenditures, both to enlist clients and to sign up vendors, represent a substantial operating expense, constituting 70 percent of the cost structure in the first year and still accounting for about 25 percent of the cost structure by the third year. Infrastructure and account support costs represent another 30 to 60 percent of the operating expense in the first several years of operation.

FIGURE 8-3
Composition of Infomediary Expenses ($ millions)

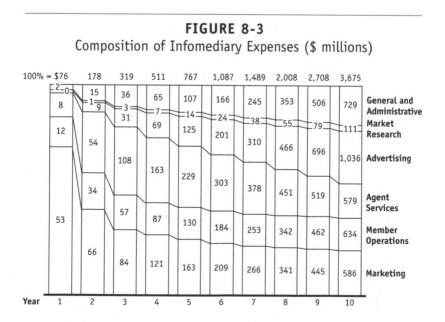

This operating expense structure highlights two key aspects of the infomediary business. First, the economic model assumes an aggressive entrant pursuing a preemptive strategy to acquire clients. As a result, marketing expenditures remain high in absolute terms over the course of the ten years, but are particularly prominent as a percentage of operating expense in the early years.

The infomediary must spend heavily to acquire new clients. Acquisition costs per new member are likely to start at the $80 level. This assumes an infomediary closely linked to an existing enterprise with well-established customer relationships and cost-effective ways to market the new infomediary's services to these customers. A start-up without the benefit of these customer relationships and low-cost access to customers would likely encounter much higher acquisition costs, making this business venture very difficult, if not impossible, to undertake.

Second, the model also assumes relatively low churn rates. In any service business with recurring revenue streams from the client, churn—or the percentage of clients who leave the service in any year—determines growth and profitability. The model assumes that churn rates start at 19 percent in the first year and decline to 13 percent in the tenth year.

The most difficult challenge will be to acquire the client, given the high level of trust necessary. This level of trust will likely exceed what consumers need today in order to sign up with a bank, brokerage firm, or credit card company. Once the infomediary acquires a client, the relative "stickiness" of the profile-learning process will limit incentives to switch to another infomediary. In other words, even if the client can transfer his or her profile to another infomediary, the new infomediary will take time to learn from the profile that has been transferred.

Clients who do switch will find that messages from their new infomediary are less relevant and helpful than those from their previous infomediary—at least at the start. Each infomediary will have its own standards for capturing, storing, and presenting data, which will make it difficult and potentially expensive for a new infomediary to convert the profile of a client accumulated by a prior infomediary and may lead to potential loss of information value. Adapting to a new infomediary's approach to capturing and presenting information will inconvenience clients. For all these reasons, few clients, once acquired, will switch from one infomediary to another, unless their infomediary somehow violates or abuses their trust.

This operating expense structure highlights a second aspect of the infomediary business: the high initial cost of building the appropriate systems infrastructure and account support capability. As we mentioned in Chapter 5, an infomediary will require sophisticated information capture, storage, and management systems and will need to develop and install complex billing systems as well. Even assuming that much of this capability can be outsourced, a minimum systems investment of $10 million is likely to be required in this part of the business. Account support will also be a significant operating expense, especially in the early years when most of the clients and vendor accounts are relatively new to the infomediary.

The infomediary must spend heavily for new clients

Over time, the operating expense structure shifts significantly. Marketing expense will likely decline to about 15 percent of total operating expense, and much of this operating expense will likely relate to specific services the infomediary delivers. The delivery of targeted marketing services to infomediary clients could account for as much as 30 percent of the operating expense, while supporting agent, purchaser identification, and market research services could account for another 20 percent.

Infrastructure and account support expense would likely represent almost another 30 percent of operating expense. This cost remains a large portion of the operating expense. Full-service infomediaries can share this operating expense across multiple service lines. In contrast, more focused services, which concentrate exclusively, for example, on either agent services or targeted marketing services, will have to bear the full burden of this operating expense. As a result, the economics of the infomediary business favor full-service infomediaries over more focused players.

Cash flow profile of the infomediary

Infomediaries require significant investment to build, but they also have the potential to become very profitable over time. As Figure 8-4 indicates, an infomediary will consume almost $380 million in cash cumulatively over a five-year period before turning cash flow positive. An established company owning an info-

---

FIGURE 8-4
Cumulative After-Tax Cash Flows ($ millions)

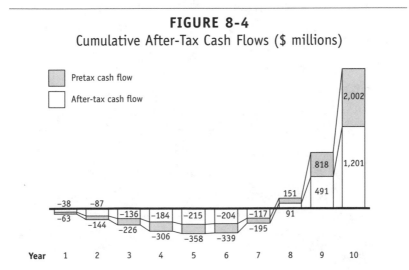

mediary could convert some of the operating losses into a tax benefit applied against operating profits in the core business. Such an opportunity reduces net cumulative cash consumption to roughly $210 million.

Once again, the economic model assumes that the infomediary is closely linked to (or starts out from an alliance with) an established business with privileged access to customers, to substantially reduce customer acquisition cost. A "greenfield" start-up with no privileged access to customers would encounter substantially higher customer acquisition costs, would probably take longer to accumulate a critical mass of clients and vendor relationships, and would likely generate proportionately less revenue per client in the early years due to more limited client trust. All of these factors would contribute to a significant increase in the cumulative cash investment required to start the business. Even $380 million in cash investment begins to put this kind of business beyond the reach of most venture capital firms; a multiple of that figure would make this a nonstarter for virtually any venture capitalist.

By the tenth year, however, the cash flow picture changes dramatically. Figure 8-4 indicates that an aggressive and successful infomediary could be generating as much as $1.2 billion in positive, pretax operating cash flow annually. Generating this level of cash flow assumes a high level of pretax operating profitability, rising to roughly 24 percent by the tenth year. This cash flow growth assumes that the infomediary has successfully set in motion the increasing returns dynamics and economies of scope we've described in Part II.

Given this profile of operating cash flow, an infomediary could generate very large shareholder value. Both growth potential and profitability potential shape shareholder value. On both counts, a successful infomediary is likely to be quite attractive. The economic model suggests that the revenue growth of the infomediary in the tenth year would still be over

40 percent per year, while pretax operating profits would be growing even faster, at about 75 percent per year. Assuming a P/E multiple of 30 on after-tax operating profits, the leading infomediary in the business could command a shareholder value of over $20 billion by the tenth year.

The infomediary's cash flow profile by its tenth year will be attractive by any company's standards, but well-established companies looking to form infomediaries may have difficulty navigating the early years. The senior managers of established companies focus on near-term earnings performance. They're

Navigating the difficult early years

reluctant to undertake an initiative that requires many years of increased operating expense before profits kick in—no matter how substantial those profits promise to be. Because so much of the increased operating expense is in the form of marketing and support spending, large companies will find it difficult to capitalize this expense the same way they might for long-term R&D spending. These difficulties provide more reasons why large companies are unlikely to spawn infomediaries within their current operations. They may instead spin out this investment within a partnership with one or more small, entrepreneurial companies. This spinout will likely result in a minority investment for the larger company in the near term (to avoid consolidating its operating results on the income statement), with the option to acquire a larger interest once the business reaches certain revenue or market capitalization thresholds. Aside from the benefits of accessing different skills and cultures (as discussed in Chapter 4), this approach allows the larger company to fund the initiative without adversely affecting its income statement in the near term. As the next chapter discusses, this spinout also provides an opportunity for the larger company to begin unbundling and aggressively building the customer relationship portions of its business.

Economic drivers of infomediary performance

Senior managers who understand the economic model of the infomediary, however, are only partway toward understanding what drives the performance of the infomediary. As we've explained in Part II, the successful infomediary will harness the power of increasing returns to lock clients and vendors into an ever-expanding infomediary web. We don't review these dynamics in detail in the sections that follow, except to quantify them in terms of their effect on the economics of the infomediary.

As we explained in Chapters 5 and 7, the infomediary business model displays three primary network effects that shape its economic performance:

1. Attractiveness to clients

2. Attractiveness to vendors

3. Interplay between clients and vendors

The more clients and vendors the infomediary has affiliated with its service, the more attractive the infomediary becomes to each client. This *attractiveness to clients* manifests itself in lower acquisition costs for each new client. Acquisition cost for each new client declines about 20 percent from $83 in the first year to $67 by the tenth year (note that for both credit card companies and Internet service providers, acquisition costs per customer run between $50 and $100 per account).

These figures actually understate the impact on acquisition cost, at least in the early years, because a certain percentage of the clients acquired by the infomediary will come from established businesses with whom the infomediary is affiliated. These are likely to have a lower acquisition cost than clients acquired from the broader market.

Not only can the successful infomediary grow more rapidly while spending less per new client over time, but it can reduce churn rates as well. The more value clients receive and perceive from the infomediary relationship, the less likely they will change to another infomediary service. Given the high cost of client acquisition in the first place, even relatively modest declines in churn rates deeply affect infomediary profitability and growth potential. As a result of these increasing returns dynamics, the model assumes that the average client churn declines from 19 percent in the first year to about 13 percent in the tenth year. Once again, the shift in mix over time, from clients acquired through affiliated businesses to clients acquired from the broader markets, dampens the effect that attractiveness to clients has on churn rates. Churn rates for the infomediary are expected to track closely to churn rates in the overall credit card industry, which currently average 13 percent annually.

In terms of *attractiveness to vendors,* increasing returns dynamics will produce similar effects to the client-focused increasing returns dynamics above. They will significantly reduce the expense and effort of getting new vendors over time. The infomediary can either spend less to aggregate comparable vendors or, as will be more likely in the infomediary's early years, spend the same amount, but with much greater impact in terms of vendor response rates. Amazon.com provides an analogue. Amazon is building on its success in the book business by expanding into other entertainment categories (music and videos) and by reinvesting its growing revenue into expanding relationships with more vendors in adjacent product categories. Similarly, American Airlines and United Airlines have made significant strides in expanding their frequent flyer programs to include credit card purchases, telephone service agreements, restaurants, and even mortgage financing.

Finally, the *interplay between clients and vendors* means that the infomediary will be able to generate more revenue from each client and vendor relationship as the number of clients and vendors grows. As we discussed in the previous chapter, the infomediary will be able to use its detailed profiles to position itself to vendors as a distribution channel able to charge rates consistent with delivering buyers to vendors, rather than simply eyeballs to vendors. Executive recruiters provide one analogy for the highly targeted "connection services" that an infomediary would provide. Successful executive recruiters build their business on a deep understanding of the needs and culture of the company seeking an executive, and on a broad network of relationships with potential candidates. The infomediary will use its highly targeted "connection" expertise to move from $27 CPM rates in the early years to CPM equivalent rates exceeding $350 by the tenth year.

Thus will the dominant infomediary create significant economic value as it develops. The assumptions embedded in this model are as conservative as possible, but the infomediary's ability to deliver this level of value will ultimately depend on how effectively it manages the challenges laid out in Chapters 5 through 7.

Our next chapter broadens the discussion in order to consider the implications of infomediation for businesses that decide not to pursue the infomediary opportunity themselves. We then discuss, at the close of the book, the ways the infomediary might contribute to the growing power of the consumer.

P A R T

T H E
I N F O M E D I A T I O N
O F   M A R K E T S

the unraveling
of the firm

WHAT ARE THE CONSEQUENCES FOR COMPANIES
as the global economy becomes increasingly "frictionless"? If the history of the computer industry is
any indication, the markets in which they compete
may rapidly restructure.

In 1978 Apple Computer entered the market with
the Apple II, a new kind of computer with an open
architecture. This open architecture significantly
reduced interaction costs (defined as the costs of
searching, coordinating, and monitoring that consumers and companies incur when they exchange
goods, services, and ideas) and increased economic
incentives for highly focused companies to introduce
complementary products and services. The technology webs that emerged in response radically

transformed the computer industry. In a brief period of time, companies leveraged the microprocessor technology and the Web-based strategy pioneered by Apple to compete with large, vertically integrated computer vendors like IBM.

Fast-forward seven years to a massive shift in value creation. Between 1985 and 1990, the entrenched, vertically integrated mainframe and minicomputer vendors like IBM, Burroughs, Digital Equipment, and Data General lost nearly $35 billion in market value, an amount equaling roughly one-third of the shareholder value of the entire computer industry in 1985. At the same time, challengers operating within technology webs, such as Apple, Sun, Novell, Microsoft, Intel, and Adobe, were creating $23 billion in shareholder value. Subtract the $35 billion lost from the $23 billion created, and you get a net gain for the computer-buying customer of $12 billion.

Rapid restructuring of industries and markets

The moral of the story? Once web-based strategies and information technology systematically reduce interaction costs, the impact on a given market can be rapid and dramatic. Only seven years elapsed from the time the first web-based competitor entered the computer industry to the time a massive shift in economic value had taken place.

As infomediary webs take hold, infomediaries will catalyze and accelerate a vast change in the structure of many consumer-oriented industries. They will in fact force the "unbundling" of traditional organizational structures into three distinct businesses:

1. Customer relationship businesses (of which Yahoo! might be an early example)

2. Product innovation and commercialization businesses (of which Inktomi provides an early glimpse)

3. Infrastructure management businesses (of which US Web is a good example)

By seizing control of customer relationships, infomediaries will force all companies to ask the most basic question about their business: What business am I *really* in? In the infomediated world, successful companies will redefine their business in ways once seemingly impossible.

Infomediaries won't change the landscape alone. The infomediary will harness much broader forces on the Internet and other electronic networks—forces that are lowering interaction costs. This chapter will sketch the profound changes catalyzed by the infomediary and describe the role the infomediary plays in driving these changes.

The unnatural bundle

What does your company do, *really?* Chances are it represents a "bundle" of three distinct kinds of businesses.

One business finds customers, builds relationships with them, develops a deeper understanding of their needs, and consequently tailors a range of products and services. These activities could be called a *customer relationship business.* In a bank or retailing business, for example, the marketing function focuses on drawing people into the branch bank or retail establishment. Once the customers are there, another set of employees builds a personal relationship with the customers—maybe it's the loan officer in a bank or a salesperson on the floor of a retail outlet. Other employees respond to questions ("Why isn't my latest deposit showing up on my bank statement?") or complaints and product returns. All of these activities focus on interactions with customers; few tailor the service to the individual customer.

Within the same company, another kind of business likely conceives of innovative new products and services, and figures out how to bring them to market. These activities could be called a *product innovation and commercialization business.* In a bank, for example, this often happens within various product units or in the business development function. These employees research new product offers like reverse mortgages and ensure that the back-office operations of the bank can handle rapid roll-outs of new products. In retailing businesses, buyers and merchandisers perform this role, constantly searching for interesting new products and ways of presenting them to the customer.

Yet a third part of the firm builds and manages facilities for high-volume, routine business operations such as logistics and storage, manufacturing, and communications networks—essentially an *infrastructure management business.* In a bank, this business extends from construction services, to building new branch banks (and the facilities support services required to keep a branch bank operating), to the back-office services needed to process enormous volumes of deposits and withdrawals and to present regular statements to the customer. Similarly, in the retailing business, infrastructure management businesses construct new outlets (and facilities support for existing outlets) and complex logistics networks designed to ensure that each store has the right product offering at the lowest possible cost.

What does your company do, *really?*

These "businesses" may not map neatly onto the functional boundaries of your corporation. For example, your product innovation and commercialization business likely surpasses the boundaries of product development to include such activities as market research, qualifying suppliers to provide key components for the new products, training the salesforce, designing marketing materials, and training field support. These activities, which today cross the functional organizations of a typical company, are all essential to the broader process of designing and successfully marketing new products and services.

Instead, these "businesses"—customer relationship management, product innovation and commercialization, and infrastructure management—really correspond to the basic core operating processes that define most corporations. No matter what industry or national market your corporation operates in, its operations usually consist of these three core processes that extend throughout the enterprise from suppliers to customers.

Compare a newspaper and a specialized steel products manufacturer. Both of these companies find customers, manage relationships with those customers over time, and seek to increase sales over time. In the case of the newspaper, two distinct sets of customers exist—the reader and the advertiser. Both of these companies seek to develop and commercialize new products and services. For the newspaper, the new products might be specialized regional editions or new sections to attract different readers or advertisers. Finally, both companies operate large, high-volume facilities—the printing press and delivery fleet in the case of the newspaper, and the smelter, rolling mill, and logistics facilities in the case of the specialized steel manufacturer.

In the past five years, senior management of large companies has focused on operational performance improvement by redesigning all core processes using the latest information technology to reduce such inefficiencies as handoffs (in which errors are often made as the product or document moves from one work station to another) and wait time (in which the product or document sits idly waiting for the next action to take place). Such fundamental rethinking of the core operating processes of a company can often yield impressive performance breakthroughs, resulting in both more value to the customer and dramatic cost and time savings for the company.

Management talks about its key activities as "core processes" rather than "businesses" because, with rare exceptions, few managers question whether these three core processes ought to coexist within the same company. Conventional thinking suggests that these core processes must coexist within the same company because the costs of coordinating the activities embodied within these core processes across companies would simply be too great relative to the benefits.

But these core processes represent very different kinds of businesses, each with unique economic and organizational characteristics. Bundling them together into a single corporation inevitably forces management to suboptimize the performance of each business in ways that no amount of core process redesign can overcome. Ronald Coase, in his seminal economic work on the nature of the firm in the late 1930s, explained why transaction costs made bundling of these diverse activities into a single firm the most rational economic choice, even though the performance of the individual activities might be suboptimized.

Much of this suboptimization has to do with the different economics that drive each of these "businesses." Take customer relationship businesses, for example. Economies of scope drive these businesses, which usually spend a considerable amount to find and develop a relationship with a customer. Once the business finds the customer, profitability hinges on extending the relationship for as long as possible and generating as much revenue as possible from each customer. Share of wallet is thus a key determinant of profitability. These businesses seek to offer as many products and services as possible to maximize the selection for the customer and to tailor bundles of products and services to capture a larger share of wallet.

Businesses driven by scope, speed, or scale

These distinctive economies of scope also shape a distinctive culture. Customer relationship businesses tend to be service oriented, tailoring products and services wherever possible to increase value to the customer. When a customer calls, the organization seeks to respond to the customer's needs. These businesses understand the value of marketing, they spend a lot of time interacting with customers, and they develop a sophisticated "feel" for the customer's needs and preferences.

Contrast this kind of business with product innovation and commercialization businesses. Speed drives the economics of these businesses. Once the business invests the resources necessary to develop a product or service, the faster a product moves from the development shop to the market, and the more money the business makes. Early entry into the market and accelerated adoption increase the likelihood of being able to capture a premium price on the product. For this reason, product innovation and commercialization businesses use any and all distribution channels to reach the customer faster than competing product companies.

What is the culture of these product innovation and commercialization businesses? These companies do whatever they can to attract and retain the creative talent required to come up with the latest product or service. The creative talent are the "stars." These businesses reward breakthrough innovation and seek to minimize administrative distractions that might frustrate or slow down the creative talent. Smaller organizations usually provide both a receptive home for creative talent and ensure that the output of this talent quickly moves into the market. While customer relationship businesses tailor their operations to better serve the needs of customers, product innovation and commercialization businesses tailor their operations to better serve the needs of the creative talent.

Economies of scale drive the third kind of business—the infrastructure management business. These businesses typically require capital-intensive facilities to operate. The high fixed costs generated by these capital-intensive facilities create strong scale economies. Pumping as many products or activities as possible through these facilities is essential for profitability, and bigger facilities are usually lower cost on a per-unit basis than smaller facilities. Operating labor skilled in performing repetitive, high-volume tasks quickly and efficiently represents the other major cost in these businesses. Typically, large-scale businesses best develop the appropriate skills in the labor force to operate these facilities at the lowest possible cost. Because these businesses tend to commoditize over time, achieving low-cost operating position is a key business imperative.

The culture of these businesses couldn't differ more from the other two types of businesses. Infrastructure management businesses abhor tailoring to anyone's needs. These businesses achieve low operating costs by standardizing activities and making them as predictable as possible. They account for every penny and frown on anything that doesn't directly contribute to efficiency of operations.

All too many of today's corporations bundle together these three very different businesses under one roof as "core processes." While management seeks to squeeze out every possible operating efficiency from each of these core processes through intensive and laborious core process redesign projects, they often miss the cost of keeping these core processes bundled together.

Thus none of these divergent processes (Table 9-1) gets optimized. Few organizations have even a single manager responsible for the entire range of activities performed in *one* of these core processes. The typical company splits the customer relationship business between sales and marketing, with others performing customer relationship activities in the customer support, the finance, and even the manufacturing functions. It's hardly surprising that this fragmented approach rarely yields integrated measurement systems capable of tracking the operating performance of even one of these processes.

As a result, scope, speed, and scale are routinely sacrificed to accommodate the divergent needs of three bundled processes.

For example, a company will often limit the opportunity for economies of scope by prohibiting its customer relationship core process from selling another company's products or services. In part, the need to promote economies of scale in the company's infrastructure management core process drives this kind of restriction. Yet opportunities to achieve economies of scale in the company's infrastructure management core process run afoul of the requirement, for example, that the company's manufacturing and logistics operations handle only the products developed and commercialized by the company. This restriction often occurs because management is concerned about limiting potential sales of its own products by providing competitors with access to low-cost manufacturing or logistics facilities.

The Regional Bell Operating Companies (RBOCs)—the local telephone carriers in the Uunited States—provide a current example of this kind of tension, often expressed as the conflict between "retail" and "wholesale" business opportunities. The retail telephone business within the RBOC is a customer

---

TABLE 9-1
Unbundled Businesses

	Customer relationship management	Product innovation and commercialization	Infrastructure management
Driver	Economies of scope	Speed of development	Economies of scale
Determinant of profitability	Share of wallet	Number and quality of distribution channels	Utilization of facilities and low-cost operations
Culture	Customer service focused	Employee focused	Cost reduction and standardization
Examples	Cendant, Auto-by-Tel, Yahoo!	AP Wire service, Inktomi	First Data Corp, UPS, McKesson, Solectron

relationship business that acquires and builds relationships with customers. The wholesale telephone business corresponds to the infrastructure management business—it manages the RBOC's physical communications facilities, as well as its specialized support services, such as network management. If it weren't for concern over intensifying competition within the retail phone business, these wholesale facilities could be leased to specialized telephone service resellers who focus on the customer relationship business. As a result, the RBOCs have limited the growth potential and economic performance of the infrastructure management business in order to protect the customer relationship business. This decision has encouraged entry by more focused infrastructure management businesses operating fiber optic telecommunication facilities in dense metropolitan areas.

Most senior managers compromise because they believe, or assume, that they have no other option. The emergence of infomediaries will fundamentally challenge this misconception. In the process, infomediaries will catalyze a systematic unbundling of core processes into distinct businesses that will survive and, for the first time, thrive as independent companies.

The infomediary as catalyst

Infomediaries have no products of their own, nor do they even take ownership of the products and services of others, as a retailer or wholesaler might. They are pure customer relationship businesses. They develop relationships with customers by understanding the needs and preferences of these customers, connecting them with appropriate vendors, and protecting their privacy. Virtually all of the labor force of the infomediary focuses on customer relationship management tasks.

As infomediaries capture and manage the customer relationship, other companies will have increasing incentive to focus exclusively on the development of innovative products and services. These companies will concede to the infomediary a comparative advantage in managing the customer relationship

Customer relationship companies will concede comparative advantage to the infomediary

and in capturing related profiles, because the infomediary will have an economic incentive to share that information with them. This is very unlike today's retailers and distributors, most of which jealously guard customer information as the source of bargaining power with product vendors. They will also face increasing pressure to perform in terms of product innovation and commercialization under the harsh spotlight directed by the infomediary on behalf of its clients. They will either respond or lose their relationship with the infomediary—and their access to the infomediary's clients. Most will optimize their business in innovation and speed.

These companies will also align with any business that can help improve their agility and cost-effectiveness. For this reason, they will aggressively seek scale infrastructure management businesses that can help reduce their routine costs of operation and increase their flexibility. By shedding the infrastructure management components of their business, product and service vendors will be able to develop a more focused culture designed to attract and retain the creative talent so critical to their success.

By assuming the tasks of customer relationship management, creating incentives for customers to share information about themselves with appropriate vendors, and pressuring vendors to satisfy their clients, infomediaries will play two key roles in catalyzing the unbundling of traditional businesses. First, infomediaries will free other businesses to focus on either product innovation and commercialization or on infrastructure management. Second, they will create strong incentives for other businesses to choose between product innovation and commercialization or infrastructure management and to optimize their business accordingly.

The unbundling is already under way

This unbundling has already started to occur in markets and industries like media, credit cards, specialized wholesale banking services, computers, and telecommunications. It will likely become even more prominent as electronic commerce begins to surge on digital networks.

Look at the newspaper industry. In the first half of this century, the newspaper business tightly integrated all three core processes. The newspaper took full responsibility for finding readers and advertisers. It developed most, if not all, of the news stories presented in the paper, to the extent of sending its own reporters to distant parts of the globe. It also printed the newspaper in its own printing press facilities and distributed the newspaper with a fleet of its own trucks.

Now more of the product component of the newspaper business—the news content itself—is outsourced to specialized news services. The average metropolitan newspaper today depends heavily on wire services, syndicated columnists, syndicated cartoons, and specialty magazine insert publishers to provide much of the content in the newspaper. On the other side of the business, many newspapers are shedding their scale-intensive printing facilities and relying on specialized printing operations to produce the newspaper each day. In many cases, the newspaper business is concentrating more and more on the customer relationship portion of the business—helping to connect readers and advertisers, while letting other specialized companies focus on the other core processes of the traditional business. The cumulative effect of this unbundling makes the economics of the newspaper business much less capital intensive, while focusing operating expenses on the marketing side (for example, circulation and advertising) of the business.

With their strong brands and restructured economics, newspapers will be in a better position to evolve into the infomediary role. As indicated in Chapter 4, newspapers will need to develop much more sophisticated targeted marketing skills and broaden the trust relationship with their audience. Would readers trust newspapers to manage their personal profiles effectively and provide unbiased product and vendor information? At a more fundamental level, senior management of newspapers must expand its commitment to on-line environments and move from simply delivering advertising messages to providing more robust, infomediary-like services connecting customers directly with vendors.

Certain portions of the banking industry are experiencing a similar unbundling. Credit cards, for example, began as a product offering of banks, and the business operated as a tightly integrated bundle of activities. Each bank **Companies** designed and introduced its own credit **are already** cards, acquired and maintained customer **unraveling** relationships, and handled all the back-office processing to support a credit card transaction. Today, specialized players are beginning to focus on each of these activities. Affinity groups—everyone from the AARP to airlines—are assuming the responsibility for finding customers and maintaining relationships with them. Specialized credit card companies focus on driving product innovation in terms of new features and pricing of credit cards. Certain firms focused on delivering back-office and other scale-driven services have begun to specialize in processing credit card transactions and managing call centers to support credit cardholders. Firms like First Data Corporation now process more than half the credit card transactions in the United States.

Specialized product innovation and commercialization

companies have also begun to reshape the pharmaceutical industry and promote at least a limited form of unbundling. For example, some biotech companies like Genentech, Amgen, and Myriad Genetics focus on specific techniques, such as understanding genes, whereas others focus on specific diseases or specialties (Medicis Pharmaceuticals specializes in dermatology while Bausch & Lomb focuses on eye care). This specialization in specific medical technologies creates an opportunity to develop expertise that reduces the risk and cost of developing successful diagnostic and therapeutic products.

Larger drug companies are taking equity stakes in or allying with these niche players to leverage their focused expertise in certain technologies or product categories. Roche Holdings, for example, has purchased over 67 percent of Genentech and has the right to purchase the remaining 33 percent at a predetermined price if it desires. Alternatively, Merck & Co. has entered into a collaborative research and licensing agreement with Aurora Biosciences Corp. Under the agreement, Aurora will receive up to $33 million in committed research funding, license fees, and delivery payments in exchange for access to several of Merck's key technologies. The larger drug companies have also begun to outsource the planning and conduct of trials to contract research organizations (CROs) like Quantum, which often conduct these trials more effectively and efficiently. These CROs have specialized expertise in designing a trial to yield the required information at the lowest cost.

Distribution companies have begun to expand into the outsourcing business for logistics management as other companies have begun to appreciate the economies of scale of specialized infrastructure management businesses. In an increasing number of cases, companies like UPS and Federal Express contract to store product inventories of other companies in their own warehouses and deliver these products on demand on behalf of the other companies.

- In the pharmaceutical industry, the top four wholesale distributors (McKesson, Cardinal, Bergen Brunswick, and Amerisource) have over 60 percent market share with sales of almost $50 billion. Each has built a nationwide distribution network of warehouses, distribution centers, and delivery vehicles, enabling them to supply thousands of retail pharmacies, physician offices, and hospitals on a weekly or even daily basis. These distributors have focused on the infrastructure management and, to a lesser degree, the customer relationship dimension of the pharmaceutical business, helping the pharmaceutical companies to focus on the product side of the business.

- In the computer industry, SCI Systems, Solectron, and Jabil have built successful businesses as contract manufacturers providing manufacturing facilities and services for electronics companies. Their services include circuit design, systems assembly, subassembly manufacturing, software duplication, warehousing, and distribution. Companies such as Cisco, Dell Computer, and Hewlett-Packard use contract manufacturers to save money and improve production times.

Mixed models

Many of the companies on the Internet today have "mixed" business models that represent hybrid bundles of the three distinct businesses discussed earlier. In some cases, this is the result of the early stage of Internet development, in which companies have been forced to play many roles. In others, it is the result of a company's implementing a business model based on an analogy to a traditional business. Excite, for example, although principally a customer relationship business, has acquired several product innovation companies, including Jango and

Classifieds2000, in order to quickly offer new on-line services to its customers.

Yet there are also signs of unbundling in evidence on the Internet today. Amazon.com pioneered affiliate programs that provide a commission to other Web sites that generate book purchases. These programs encourage some companies to focus on customer relationship management, while companies like Amazon.com provide the infrastructure management capabilities required to process the transaction and deliver the product to the customer. Portal businesses like Yahoo! focus tightly on customer relationship management while leveraging the resources of other companies to provide specific products and services as well as some of the scale-intensive infrastructure management functions. For example, the string of partnerships between Internet access providers and portal businesses allows the access provider to focus on the infrastructure management part of the business and to contract out the customer acquisition and management service to the portal business. To this end, AT&T has partnered with both Excite and Lycos, and MCI Internet has partnered with Yahoo!.

Auto retailing provides an excellent example of specialized customer relationship management businesses emerging on the Internet. Entrepreneurial companies like Auto-by-Tel and Autoweb.com are providing specialized customer acquisition services to generate qualified leads for automobile dealers. These companies provide a broad range of information about new car models and pricing for customers considering a car purchase. These companies refer purchase-ready customers to a relevant automobile dealer to close the sale. In 1997 qualified leads generated as much as 2 percent of all nonfleet new-car sales. Although 2 percent is a small percentage, it represents 300,000 cars, or $6 billion in revenue. According to J. D. Power & Associates (www.jdpower.com), one-third of all new car buyers will buy cars through the Web by the year 2000.

These new customer relationship intermediaries will force automobile companies to rethink the role of the traditional automobile dealer. Perhaps automobile dealers will focus much

Rethinking the role of the car dealer more narrowly on the management of automobile showrooms and service facilities. They could become specialized infrastructure management companies providing complementary services to the customer relationship intermediaries who would take over the role of acquiring and managing customer relationships.

Over time, these "new game" customer relationship intermediaries might develop into more full-fledged infomediaries focusing on the automotive product and service category. For example, by developing a deeper understanding of each customer, these intermediaries might suggest specific automobile attributes or even automobile models to consider given customers' specific needs and preferences.

In fact, these customer relationship intermediaries could fulfill virtually all of the customer's car-related needs by evolving into a full-fledged infomediary. They could

- Help customers find the best rate on an auto loan and determine the best term of loan for each customer.

- Provide insurance quotes for the various cars customers are considering—taking into account customers' age, driving record, location, usage (business/pleasure, miles driven each year), and so on.

- Help customers get the best rate possible and determine the most cost-effective trade-offs regarding premiums and deductibles.

- Give customers a list of qualified repair and maintenance shops, detailers, and road/towing service companies (like AAA) in their area.

- Provide customers with a list of quality car phone companies and help customers find the best price and service package.
- Prompt customers for service/maintenance checkups and then record that information for the customers' records.

Auto manufacturers would love to access all this valuable information. Moreover, they couldn't obtain it as efficiently or effectively themselves, as they lack the scope and customer database management skills to do so. Instead, they could unbundle their businesses—outsourcing the primary customer relationship management role to the infomediary and focusing on product innovation and commercialization. Who knows? Automobile manufacturers already outsource a significant portion of subassembly manufacturing—perhaps some day they might outsource all of manufacturing to specialized infrastructure management businesses.

In financial services, Microsoft, Intuit, and E*Trade are using the Internet to evolve into specialized customer relationship businesses, and they may ultimately evolve into full-fledged infomediaries. This evolution may in turn precipitate a series of spin-offs in larger, more traditional financial services businesses, as they seek to unbundle and restructure in response to the competitive challenge posed by specialized customer relationship businesses.

Players like Microsoft (through its Money product) and Intuit (through its Quicken product) have already begun to assume the role of specialized customer relationship business on-line. They are bringing together a broad range of financial services providers to enable their customers to find and select the best provider for each product in a one-stop shopping environment. Logging onto the Quicken web site, customers are presented with a variety of financial services information to help them find the best rates on CDs, loans, mortgages, and checking or savings accounts. They can get tips on tax, financial, and retirement planning. Through Quicken, they can also access providers like Charles Schwab and Ameritrade for on-line trading.

But neither Microsoft nor Intuit has yet taken on the full role of an infomediary. An infomediary would

- Build a more complete profile of customers.

- Help anticipate customers' needs, assess the customers' specific situation, and help find the best set of financial providers to meet those needs.

- Track the customers' financial situation over time and apprise customers of new financial services products or services relevant to their financial situation.

For example, the infomediary could notify customers if it determined that mortgage rates had dropped enough to make refinancing worthwhile. Based on the customer's credit card usage, it might recommend a card with a higher annual fee but a lower APR as a better alternative for the customer. It would have a complete understanding of the customers' financial needs and factors that affect those needs (for example, birth of a baby, marriage, divorce, purchase of a new car or new home, relocation, new job).

If companies like Microsoft or Intuit were to evolve into a full-fledged infomediary role, traditional banks might find a very different kind of customer relationship business coming between them and their customers. Traditional banks could carve out of their current operations a similar kind of customer relationship business. However, such a business would face significant challenges. Most banks have proven reluctant to resell the products or services of other institutions (except in limited cases in which the banks in question offer no products or services in that category). Customers would likely prefer an infomediary that offers a broader range of products and services from a variety of financial institutions. They might suspect banks of systematic bias where they have products and services of their own. Even more fundamentally, most banks still struggle with the systems integration challenge of integrating their account profiles into a single customer account. The integrated customer view still eludes them.

Given these challenges, many banks might ultimately choose to concede the role of customer relationship manager to specialized infomediaries. Some of these banks might choose instead to focus on developing best-of-breed product and service portfolios that could be marketed through infomediaries and, over time, could evolve into specialized product businesses. Others might choose to concentrate on scale-intensive back-office processing operations and provide processing support for the products like credit cards, loans, and investment products offered for sale by other financial institutions. In the end, these specialized infrastructure management businesses could become quite large.

Strategic challenges and options

What will this unbundling mean for today's corporations? First, they must either compete or cooperate with new and increasingly powerful players to reach their core customers. Second, they themselves must unbundle their corporation and decide which existing "business" they will focus on: customer relationship management, innovation and commercialization, or infrastructure management.

Traditional corporations may be more vulnerable than they realize. Many traditional business models are economically unstable in the face of the loss of even a small fraction of their best business. In banking, for example, where 20 percent of the customers typically generate 80 percent of the profits, the loss of any significant fraction of these most attractive customers will seriously affect the economics of the whole operation. The same is true for ad agencies with major accounts, or shipping, or defense, or virtually any large, contracted business.

Option A: transition

To capitalize on the fundamental forces at work, rather than being squeezed by them, traditional businesses should think proactively about a transition or migration path to facilitate and leverage the unbundling of the corporation. Unbundling into the three distinct businesses doesn't mean that industries will fragment into a structure characterized by large numbers of small businesses competing on a level playing field with low barriers to entry.

Of the three businesses that are likely to emerge, only one is likely to remain fragmented. Economies of scope drive customer relationship businesses. The infomediary business exemplifies pure customer relationship business and, as we've seen, these businesses have a strong tendency to concentrate over time. Similarly, economies of scale drive infrastructure management businesses, creating irresistible pressures toward large, focused enterprises. Product innovation and commercialization businesses are the only category likely to remain fragmented. The need to provide a fertile environment for creativity and innovation tends to favor smaller organizations. The need for speed and agility in bringing products to market also tends to favor this bias toward smaller organizations. Even here, large-scale conglomerates of focused product businesses like Canon and 3M can organize around specific technology competencies.

Traditional corporations are more vulnerable than they realize

Option B: M&A

By using focused merger and acquisition programs to restructure their industries today, traditional businesses may be able to create significant value. Of course, industries around the world are currently experiencing substantial merger and acquisition activity. Responding to increasing competitive intensity, corporations are moving quickly to build scale in an effort to reduce operating costs. While understandable, this wave of merger and acquisition activity is quite different from, and may even complicate, later efforts to use mergers and acquisitions to anticipate business unbundling. By merging existing companies, those unnatural bundles of three very different businesses, senior management may only be creating larger unnatural bundles. While generating near-term operating cost savings, these mega-mergers may make subsequent restructuring through unbundling and rebundling more difficult.

Option C: divestiture

An alternative approach might be, first, to unbundle an existing company into its three component businesses. Senior management of large companies has rarely pursued systematic divestiture programs, except in the case of conglomerates that sought to acquire companies in highly diverse industries and discovered that expected synergies never materialized. Even the highly publicized AT&T divestiture of its computer and telecommunications equipment businesses falls more into this category than into the divestiture program proposed, in which a company in a single industry like banking or newspapers divests two of its three component businesses. A limited form of this divestiture occurs when companies announce new "outsourcing" relationships in areas typically involving infrastructure management activities such as logistics or manufacturing operations. Companies in markets experiencing major technological or regulatory discontinuities are likely to initiate such divestiture programs first, because management must confront a significant perceived threat before undertaking such radical surgery on its core business. In this context, computer, telecommunications, media, and banking businesses are all promising candidates for divestiture.

Having undertaken this kind of divestiture, management would then be in a better position to launch a systematic merger and acquisition program designed to build scope in relevant customer relationship businesses, scale in infrastructure management businesses, and speed in technology-based portfolios of product companies. Each company acquired would likely have to go through a similar process of unbundling, with unneeded businesses spun out to help fund the next wave of acquisition, and relevant businesses realigned into their appropriate business clusters. By pursuing such a strategy, farsighted management may leverage the unbundling process ahead in ways that yield large-scale rebundled businesses capable of generating sustainable value.

Senior management of traditional businesses will face difficult choices as they decide which elements of their current bundle of businesses to focus on for advantage and how to deal with the wrenching changes likely to occur as other elements of the existing bundle are shut down or spun out. Difficult as these choices may be, there may not be much time available in which to make them. When interaction costs are systematically reduced, the ensuing restructuring of an industry can happen very quickly—as we saw at the beginning of this chapter with the story of Apple and the computer industry.

As challenging as the unbundling of companies and industries will be, this unbundling poses a further set of challenges

for senior management. Moving beyond restructuring impera-
tives, these challenges will call for new management approaches
in competitive strategy and marketing. The next chapter
explores some of these challenges in more detail.

reverse markets

AS CUSTOMERS ASSERT OWNERSHIP OF THEIR
information profiles, a profound shift in the basis of
competition will occur. Today, competitive advantage
in many businesses lies in the ability to capture
unique information about customers—information
that is not accessible to other vendors. For example,
airlines develop frequent-flyer profiles that are not
accessible to other airlines. Banks use information
about balances and individual funds flows to market
various financial products to their customers. Even
grocers create loyalty card programs in order to build
and act on proprietary profiles of their customers.

In infomediated markets, infomediaries will hold
these customer profiles on behalf of the customer
and, subject to the customer's privacy preferences,

make them available to appropriate vendors willing to pay to access them. Profiles will no longer be limited to individual vendors, but instead will be integrated across all vendors in relevant product categories. The frequent-flyer profile that captures the passenger's travel on a specific airline but is silent about the passenger's travel on other airlines will be replaced by a profile that records in great detail the passenger's travel on all airlines. In infomediated markets, proprietary access to information will become harder and harder to sustain (except, of course, by the infomediaries—but even these businesses will have only conditional access to the profiles).

Upending conventional markets

What will this mean for vendors? Most markets today are "vendor-centric"—they help vendors target and sell consumers an ever-increasing quantity of products and services. Vendors benefit in vendor-centric markets by setting uniform prices and creating a variety of "selling" channels (such as retail stores, branch offices, or agents) to find appropriate customers. They benefit when customers invest time to educate the vendor regarding specific customer needs, as with health care or financial services purchases, or even at the hair salon or pet supply store. This investment typically increases switching costs, thereby locking customers into subsequent purchases of the same product or service. Vendors also benefit from the fact that many of the "replenishment" items consumers buy—such as household products, stationery, and groceries—do not warrant the consumer's time to search repeatedly for the best deal. Consumers instead buy familiar brands at familiar outlets.

By helping consumers capture and leverage their own infor-

Even grocers have loyalty programs

mation profiles, infomediaries will upend conventional markets. Through the mechanism of their profiling and agency services, infomediaries will "announce" their clients' purchase intent (like brokers issuing a "buy" order on behalf of a client) and then organize the bidding environments to ensure that appropriate vendors compete for the client's business. In contrast to vendor-centric conventional markets, infomediated markets will shift advantage to consumers by

- Reducing consumers' search costs
- Connecting consumers with the most relevant vendors in a timely fashion
- Extracting as much value for consumers as possible from vendors

Markets in which power shifts to the consumer might be called "reverse markets"—these are markets in which customers seek out and extract value from vendors, rather than the other way around. In reverse markets, consumers can easily switch vendors—the new vendor can readily download the necessary information about the customer's needs and preferences from the infomediary, without the customer's providing it again. Consumers will also have much more information to evaluate the performance of specific vendors, data that will help overcome the moral hazard and information asymmetries that plague so many consumer markets today. The perceived risk of switching vendors will therefore decline. As a result, relationship purchases will evolve into event-specific purchases in which the customer can switch vendors based on the unique needs of each purchase event or new information about better vendors.

Similarly, infomediaries will create mechanisms for consumers to aggregate purchases of replenishment products and solicit vendor bids for this business. Given lower interaction costs and aggregated purchases, infomediary clients will comparison shop for replenishment products, and switch from one vendor to another to ensure the greatest value. Vendors of replenishment products that now depend on consumer familiarity and high interaction costs to sustain consumer loyalty will compete much more aggressively for each customer's business. What if, for example, the infomediary bundled the bulk of a family's grocery purchases for a one-year purchase contract to be awarded to the lowest bidder? What if the infomediary bundled a family's grocery purchases with those of 50 other families in the same town?

Even where auction markets are not feasible, reverse markets enabled by infomediaries will force businesses to reassess their approaches to marketing. Today, vendors dedicate the vast bulk of consumer marketing expenditures (about 70 percent) to preemptively capturing the attention of the consumer in advance of the purchase occasion. In reverse markets, customers will shun this kind of intrusive marketing. Successful marketers will learn how to list themselves effectively in search environments, how to engage the consumer at the time of purchase, and how to tailor products and services in ways that reduce incentives for switching to other vendors. While a crude analogy, think of yellow pages advertising as an early form of reverse market advertising in contrast to traditional mass-market advertising on television or in the print media.

In the process of redefining marketing, reverse markets will also force vendors to rethink the role of brands and to redeploy marketing spending. This redeployment will have profound effects on a broad range of businesses that depend on advertising and promotion expenditures from product and service vendors, including television, radio, newspapers, and magazines, as well as sports franchises, retailers, and agents who represent celebrity talent.

Reengineering brands

By leveraging the capabilities of electronic networks, infomediaries will help undermine the value of brands in conventional markets. They'll do so by removing the two constraints that make brands viable today, both of which have to do with scarce resources:

1. Limited information about vendors.

2. Limited "shelf space" for access to products or services.

In the process, they will undermine the two basic planks of a conventional marketer's power base—control over information and presence—and force marketers to find new sources of economic power. Marketers can either evolve into infomediaries and regain privileged access to information, or they can focus on product innovation and commercialization by developing the skills needed to deliver tangible value back to customers more quickly than anyone else can.

For example, when customers lack detailed information about the full range of vendors or the functionality and pricing of their products, brand becomes a proxy for imperfect information. Rather than overinvest in collecting difficult-to-find

The death of conventional brands information, customers rely on brands to assure them of a predictable product experience. McDonald's may not offer the best meal experience, but it does offer a predictable meal experience relative to a no-name restaurant where the consumer may experience either a gourmet treat or food poisoning.

Brands play a similar role with regard to limited shelf space. From a vendor's viewpoint, brands help "pull" customers into retail stores. In the process, they help the vendor persuade the retailer to dedicate some of its scarce shelf space to the vendor's products. Similarly, retail brands help customers decide which retail stores to frequent. Given the limited selection that scarce shelf space affords, customers look to brands for assurance that the limited selection will be consistent with their buying preferences. If the customer's primary consideration is fashion and he isn't sensitive to price, he may frequent an upscale men's clothing boutique. On the other hand, if he's looking for durable work clothes at a low price, he's more likely to frequent a well-known discount mass merchant.

Infomediaries will help remove shelf space constraints by providing access to an essentially unlimited range of products and services in an on-line environment. On-line vendors like Amazon.com exploit the economics of networks to offer customers access to any book published (including out-of-print books that have traditionally been the most difficult to find). Infomediaries carry this process one step further—they will enable the customer to search across multiple book vendors, maximizing selection based on such factors as price and shipping lead times.

At the same time, infomediaries will help clients access detailed information about individual products or services through their profiling and agency services. Not only will customers be able to access information from vendors, they will also be able to examine detailed product reviews and evaluations by third-party firms. Infomediaries will also be able to generate information of their own. For example, a client might want to find out how many other clients of the infomediary have bought a particular brand of computer, how many of these computers were returned as defective, and how many of the clients repurchased the same brand of computer. The infomediary's profiling database could readily provide this information.

As reverse markets erode shelf space and information constraints, does this trend mean that brands will disappear? Not at all. It does mean that the role of brand is likely to change and that, in the process, ownership of the most meaningful brands may change. Once again, infomediaries will play a key role in this redefinition of brand.

In an environment of unlimited selection and access to information, the scarce resource becomes customer attention. Customers still face one unyielding constraint: they still have only 24 hours a day. Where and how they choose to use this time will have enormous economic consequences. With limited time and unlimited choice, customers will likely focus their attention on providers that best understand their needs and can, as a result, maximize their return on attention by delivering highly tailored bundles of products and services.

Today, brands are largely product-centric—they are statements about the vendor or the products offered by the vendor. Brands say: Buy this product because the vendor has a reputation for high-quality products or excellent service or because the product itself is a reliable or low-cost product. In an environment where return on attention becomes the key measure of performance, a new kind of brand will emerge—a customer-centric brand. Customer-centric brands have two components—they assure the customer that the vendor knows and understands that individual customer better than anyone else does, and they promise the customer that the vendor can tailor products and services to meet that individual customer's needs better than anyone else can. These brands thereby assure customers that they will receive a very high return on any attention they focus on the owner of the brand. They also offer the promise of increasing returns—the more attention the customer gives to a brand, the more the brand owner will learn about the customer, and the stronger the value of the brand becomes to the customer.

Some brands today have moved partway in this direction. These brands speak to customers as members of a specific market segment. They urge customers to buy their products or services by claiming that the vendor understands the needs of that segment better than anyone else does. For example, Disney has been successful in the past by developing a brand addressing the concerns of parents with small children. Nike did the same for urban youths. But none of these brands says anything about knowing the customer as an individual with unique needs and preferences. This is the challenge and opportunity for customer-centric brands.

Who will deliver on the promises implicit in a customer-centric brand? Certainly infomediaries will have a natural claim to knowing the customer better than anyone else and could tailor bundles of products and services to meet the needs of the individual customer. For this reason, infomediaries will develop very strong customer-centric brands.

Specialized intermediaries might also build strong customer-centric brands by developing expertise working with customer profiles to configure tailored bundles of products or services to meet the needs of the customer. These "personal shopper" intermediaries might become junior partners of the broader-based infomediary to offer customers expertise in specific product categories. For example, specialized "clothing consultants" might take on the role of a personal shopper in on-line environments, building unique skills to match the individual fashion preferences of a customer with a deep understanding of evolving fashion trends and to suggest wardrobes tailored for the customer. Clients who want help deciding which products are right for them might seek out these specialized intermediaries. If, as in the case of today's personal shopper or personal banker, these intermediaries demonstrate their commitment to and skill in tailoring offers to an individual customer's needs, they, too, might develop customer-centric brands. Unlike personal shoppers or personal bankers today, these "personal shopper" intermediaries wouldn't be pushing the products of their employer. Instead, they would operate as consultants, collecting fees from the client and perhaps a surcharge on products purchased as a result of their recommendations (much as interior decorators do today).

Certain vendors who invest deeply in the skills necessary to convert customer information into deliverable value to the customer would also build strong customer-centric brands. In general, vendors who offer information-intensive products like newsletters or knowledge-intensive services like medical care will have the greatest success in building customer-centric products by tailoring these products or services to the needs of individual customers.

Building trust through value exchange is the best way to establish a customer-centric brand. A customer-centric brand can't be built without information from customers about their needs and preferences—information they often provide reluctantly. In the end, customer-centric brands require an intensely personal relationship between the business and the customer. We may not think of them as owners of customer-centric brands, but the traditional family doctor or the local financial adviser exemplifies the kind of relationship required. These relationships begin with a limited request for information from the customer; in exchange, the doctor or adviser quickly turns that information into helpful advice. The doctor or adviser thus rewards the customer for providing personal information and, in the process, begins to build the trust required to solicit even more information. Ideally, a series of value exchanges creates deep bonds of trust that deliver on the customer-centric brand promise: I know more about you than anyone else and can be trusted to use this information and insight in your interest.

The shift from customer-centric brand positioning to vendor-centric brand positioning may be one of the reasons the medical profession is experiencing bad press these days. As individual and small-group general-practice physicians merge together in HMOs and other large enterprises, the public perceives a loss of tailored, personal service. Instead, the brand becomes the institution, and the brand promise becomes much more vendor-centric: You can trust us to deliver reliable, low-cost medical care.

Customer-centric brands aren't restricted to individuals in professional and personal service occupations. Rich information capture and analysis capabilities and the ability to tailor offerings cost-effectively for individual customers make it possible for large institutions to develop customer-centric brands. Although still at a very early stage of development, Amazon. com is building a customer-centric brand based on its ability to track book purchases by individual customers and to use this information to offer tailored suggestions of other books that customers might enjoy. Now a global company can play the role the local neighborhood bookseller plays—building a powerful customer-centric brand in the process—by using the Internet and related information capture and analysis technologies.

Redeployment of marketing spending

Reverse markets enabled by infomediaries will shift the relative impact of different kinds of marketing programs, driving vendors to redeploy their marketing spending. This redeployment will present new challenges for businesses that depend on a product vendor's advertising and promotion expenditures.

Given the opportunity to connect with new customers in a low-cost manner, marketers will shift spending from less-targeted image- or brand-building advertising to more targeted forms of marketing to leverage the infomediary's accumulated profiles. Marketers will find that this more focused spending generates higher returns than conventional mass-market advertising.

In contrast to today's direct-marketing programs, the infomediary's marketing services will provide more detailed profiles of relevant customers and the opportunity to more quickly adjust the targeting and tailoring of messages. The agent services of the infomediary will ensure that search and replenishment products or services are visible to the customer at the time of purchase. Targeted marketing services will provide vendors with the opportunity to reach relevant customers at an appropriate time for browsing or impulse-type product purchases.

Vendors will also develop new approaches to marketing designed to respond to the more demanding environments of reverse markets. For example, marketers will move beyond conventional direct-marketing approaches, which use transaction histories to target and tailor marketing messages, and which often intrude on the privacy of the "targets." Instead, marketers will begin to put in practice *collaboration marketing*, a term we've developed to describe techniques that address the unique challenges presented by the Internet and reverse markets. Three basic principles shape these techniques:

Infomediaries come between vendors and customers

1. Vendors will focus on drawing people to them, rather than intrusively reaching out for them.

2. Vendors will maximize the value customers receive from the purchase and use of their products and services, by providing tailored help in purchasing and using those products and services

3. Vendors will mobilize the resources of third parties and focus on assembling and packaging these resources to meet the needs of each individual.

Schwab is one of the pioneers of what we're calling "collaboration marketing." On its Web site, Schwab has assembled a broad range of third-party resources designed to be helpful to stock investors. Schwab's Advisor Source connects investors with over 5,000 independent investment managers to provide them with detailed advice on their investment strategies. The Analyst Center assembles a broad range of third-party information services relative to stock investment, delivered by companies like Dow Jones, Standard & Poor's, and First Call Corporation. Automated analytic tools like Schwab's IRA Analyzer help investors develop tailored investment strategies. And Schwab's One Source service offers investors a broad selection of over 800 mutual fund products from a variety of third parties. While third parties provide much of the help delivered to the customer, Schwab

- Becomes the architect of tailored service.

- Develops detailed profiles of the needs and preferences of each customer.

- Builds strong, trust-based relationships with its investors.

Through collaboration marketing, Schwab attracts new investors to its site and learns much more about these investors than a conventional discount broker ever would.

Of course, such efforts to be helpful may to some degree replicate the services offered by an infomediary. If they are done well, though, the infomediary might structure relationships with collaboration marketers to leverage its own resources and provide additional value to its clients. In this way, vendors will seek to build trust and customer-centric brands in an effort to increase customer willingness to seek out their offerings over those of other vendors.

For example, an infomediary might collaborate with Schwab to provide tailored investment help for the infomediary's clients. The infomediary would strengthen its broadly based customer-centric brand by helping its clients connect with specialized environments like those being created by Schwab, especially when these environments organize the resources of a broad array of third parties. Schwab would benefit from the references provided by the infomediary and, in the process, help build its own customer-centric brand focused on understanding the investment needs of individual customers. These kinds of relationships between infomediaries and leading collaboration marketers can be very helpful for the client, but they must be carefully structured so that they serve the interests of the client, rather than simply reducing choices for the client by funneling them to "preferred" vendors. Rather than referring the client to one vendor in a category like stock investments, infomediaries might evaluate vendors based on their collaboration marketing skills and provide a rating service to help clients choose which vendor to connect with based on the usefulness of the environments created.

As marketing expenditures are redeployed, many of the businesses now emerging on the Internet are going to feel the effect. Regardless of the Internet business model involved—content aggregators, transaction aggregators, virtual communities, or portal businesses—the economics depend heavily on the assumption that the company will capture unique information about prospects and customers and will leverage this information to generate advertising revenue. If this assumption is challenged by the infomediary, the economics of these business models rapidly deteriorate, and the potential for value destruction increases. What happens when an infomediary comes between these businesses and their customers and then helps the customer to establish his or her own profiles and use them in interactions with other vendors? What happens when marketers shift their marketing expenditures from broad-reach advertising to targeted marketing driven by the profiles accumulated by the infomediary?

Internet business models will have a limited set of choices about how to respond. They can evolve into infomediaries themselves, as discussed in Chapter 4. They can develop privileged relationships with an infomediary as part of an infomedi-

ary web, perhaps by providing a superior environment for plac-
ing targeted marketing messages and for learning more about
the needs and preferences of the infomediary's clients. In return
for creating these environments, they might receive a share of
the infomediary's targeted marketing revenues. Of course, the
infomediary now becomes the source of revenue, rather than
the marketer. The success of these business models will depend
on their ability to create superior environments to engage infomediary clients and to enhance the shopping experience.

For example, these business models could organize large
amounts of information that would help educate infomediary
clients regarding specific kinds of products and services.
Schwab, for example, is developing a transaction aggregator
business model, helping to connect investors with a variety of
investment products on-line. In the process, Schwab is employing collaboration marketing techniques to enhance its helpful-
ness to investors and is building a very rich information environment to maximize returns for investors. Other transaction
aggregators like Auto-by-Tel, CDnow, and Amazon.com are
creating similar kinds of helpful environments for purchasers of
cars, music CDs, and books. Other business models might
develop superior skills in creating environments to merchandise
products that are more likely to be purchased on impulse or as a
result of browsing. A gardening virtual community or content
aggregator might offer a compelling environment to merchandise gardening tools or books on gardening. Whenever possible, the infomediary will seek to build relationships with these
more focused on-line businesses as a way to leverage its own
resources and add value to its clients.

On-line businesses might also shift to other revenue sources,
such as subscription, usage, or transaction fees. In general,
though, these revenue sources typically make it much more difficult to build substantial scale.

This dilemma goes beyond Internet business models. What

about the various forms of traditional media that rely on advertising for support? Newspapers, for example, critically depend on classified advertising revenues for their profitability. What happens to classified advertising employment revenues when prospective employers can, with the help of an infomediary, seek out very specific candidates? For example, an infomediary might help an employer find people who, within a 50-mile radius of their business, possess the right background and skills and have expressed interest in seeing offers of employment from companies fitting the profile of the prospective employer.

Television networks and advertising-supported cable channels like CNN and ESPN have felt somewhat insulated from competition for their advertising revenue because of the importance of video in communicating brand-oriented advertising. Leaving aside the prospect of steadily increasing bandwidth in Internet environments, making video a more feasible format for the Internet, what happens to this advertising revenue when marketers shift an increasing share of their marketing budgets to more targeted marketing formats due to the superior targeting capabilities of the infomediary? This issue is most pronounced in the United States, where advertising-supported television is more fully developed and the Internet is more broadly accessible than in most other countries, but it is relevant to any media company seeking to commercialize new television channels across the globe. To the extent that advertising provides the primary revenue source for commercial television, this medium will face aggressive competition from emerging infomediaries. As video on demand creates the potential for more targeted forms of video advertising, television networks and cable channels might become vehicles for delivering infomediary-generated advertising messages to clients, much like the Internet businesses described earlier.

Nor is this impact limited to traditional, advertising-supported media. What about retail stores that today heavily depend for their profitability on promotional spending by product vendors trying to reach customers at the time of purchase? What happens when the infomediary can use the superior targeting capability embedded in its client purchasing profiles to deliver them only to the most receptive customers purchasing competitor products? What happens when the infomediary downloads promotional offers directly into the smart card that customers will one day use to make their purchases in the retail store? Anyone who depends on advertising or promotional revenue today will feel the effects of the expanding reach of the infomediary.

Shifting sources of advantage

In this environment, competitive advantage shifts from access to information to the skills required to use information to deliver tangible and, increasingly, tailored value back to the customer. Vendors will struggle to master these skills because they require tight integration across the vendor's business system. Information profiles that the marketing organization accesses will need to redirect product development programs, manufacturing and logistics operations, and customer service procedures. Vendors developing these skills will be in the best position to earn a return on the price they will now have to pay for access to the profiles in the first place.

Those who develop these skills early will be hard to overtake. Indeed, vendors that earn a high return on the price of information about customers will be willing and able to pay for more of that information than vendors with fewer information skills. This dynamic has already, in a more limited form, played itself out in the credit card business. In this arena, all lenders can access the same standardized credit bureau profiles, but a small number of more skilled, analytically driven players moved large share from competitors that failed to take full advantage of the available information in terms of refining targeting and product development efforts.

In general, sources of advantage for product innovation and commercialization businesses will shift from marketing capabilities to product design and execution capabilities. In a world where information about customers is more broadly available and where shelf space is no longer a constraint, product vendors will find less opportunity to differentiate based on marketing programs. The more meaningful differentiation will reside in product attributes and performance.

Vendors will struggle to master new skills

Today, many product vendors achieve market success by focusing on developing relationships with distribution channels so that they can gain privileged access to scarce shelf space. Other vendors focus on massive advertising campaigns to promote a specific brand image that will draw people into retail outlets and create a "pull" for their products. Both of these approaches typically require substantial financial resources and thus create barriers to entry for smaller product vendors.

In reverse markets, where virtual shelf space is essentially unlimited, infomediary agent services will relentlessly search out the best products given the individual needs and preferences of the client. Marketing will become much more an exercise in developing superior insight into market needs, so that product attributes and performance can be quickly improved and tailored, rather than creative attempts to overcome limited distribution capacity. The next chapter will develop some of the implications of the infomediary's role in increasing product attribute and performance "visibility" on behalf of customers.

consumer
unbound

NO CONSUMER HAS THE POWER (OR THE TIME) to challenge vendors alone. A particular vendor represents a small slice of consumer spending and warrants a correspondingly small share of customer attention and emotional engagement. (The same holds true for individual shareholders of corporations.) As a result, vendors make the rules about products, price, services, and company policy on any variety of topics, from employment practices, to customer service, even to environmental impact. Customers can basically take it or leave it—and they do, with firms frequently failing to understand just why consumers have made the choices they have made.

As infomediaries aggregate millions of consumers into one voice, they will broadly increase consumer influence in both commercial practices and public policy. Think of trade unions, which exist to combine the power of working men and women relative to management and to influence issues such as wages, working conditions, worker's compensation, and health care coverage. What if infomediaries were to do the same for consumers as unions like the United Auto Workers (UAW) or the teamsters do for workers? What if, in other words, infomediaries were to aggregate the individual voice of the consumer into a "collective will" wielded against vendors on such important consumer issues as product safety, the environment, privacy and information capture, prices, warranties, and customer service, to name just a few? In this kind of scenario, one could imagine consumer advocate Ralph Nader in the role that Jimmy Hoffa used to play for unions, a startling development for a few of today's large corporations.

Such a scenario might play out in three different ways:

1. An increase in information transparency for consumers.
2. Growing consumer influence over commercial practices.
3. Growing consumer influence over government and public policy.

An increase in information transparency for consumers

In Chapter 3 on promising markets for infomediation, we saw how infomediaries will smooth out some of the price distortions at play in many consumer markets. This smoothing will be an important means by which infomediaries will increase information transparency for consumers.

Infomediaries may have even more impact, however, when making transparent for consumers various issues relating to product and service performance. Most car buyers know how J. D. Power ranks the reliability of automobiles. (*Consumer*

Reports evaluates a range of consumer products, from washing machines to health clubs.) J. D. Power is highly influential among car buyers precisely because it stays independent of (and has no commercial relationship with) the automakers whose cars it is evaluating. For this reason J. D. Power is also influential with the automakers themselves.

An independent position is unusual in today's world. For instance, the movie reviewers in most daily newspapers keep an eye on advertising revenues (because both movie studios and

No consumer can challenge vendors alone

theater chains advertise heavily in newspapers) as well as on their critical opinions. So do the writers and editors of the many "Best of" editions of city-oriented magazines like *New York*. Magazines run "service" issues like these precisely because they are popular with advertisers—hardly a prescription for objective reporting. (After all, there aren't many "Worst of" issues published.) Writers who travel to various locales and then "review" them for other travelers are in a similar position: a corporate parent with a vested interest in increased travel revenues owns many of the magazines in which they publish.

The fact that nearly all magazines today clear (or at least show) their copy to advertisers mentioned in an article—particularly if that article says anything to which the advertiser might object—neatly symbolizes the conflict of interest many publications face between their editorial and advertising functions. We're not saying that movie reviewers and travel writers can never be trusted. But they aren't completely objective either. That's why so many investment reporters have now become careful to make disclamatory disclosures regarding their own investments, and that's why J. D. Power employees switch cars every year.

What if the infomediary were to make it its business to fairly and unflinchingly review the performance of various products and services? What if it were to play the role that J. D. Power plays for autos with everything from au pairs to physicians? In the health care industry, for example, one could imagine infomediaries forcing HMOs to publish quality of treatment outcomes data for their patients. Right now, HMOs publish data about how long their customers wait in line or how many physicians they have access to—both of which are important to consumers who value greater convenience when it comes to health care. But HMOs don't publish much information about how well their physicians' care stacks up against the competition's. Do a particular HMO's patients with lung cancer live three years after diagnosis on average? five years? What about those with breast cancer, or diabetes? The infomediary could generate the same quality of treatment outcomes data for hospitals. These are the true measures consumers need in order to make informed choices about HMOs and hospitals, yet these measures are not forthcoming from the industry.

The same holds true for the electricity industry, to name another example. There is surely some segment of consumers, for instance, that would be interested in making its purchases based on the amount of air pollution a particular electric utility generates. In states like California and Rhode Island, consumers already have a choice between various providers of electricity. But they don't have data about who is polluting the air. Will the infomediary collectivize the voice of environmentally minded consumers interested in pressuring General Electric to dredge PCBs from the Hudson River?

Growing consumer influence over commercial practices

Infomediaries will give consumers an equal (or superior) voice not just about their privacy preferences, but also about the ways firms conduct their affairs. How true is the assertion that a particular apparel maker uses unfair labor practices overseas or partners with an inhumane third party? Some consumers may not care. Others may object. Both types of consumers could rely on the infomediary to shed as much nonpartisan light on the subject as possible. In cases in which a clear "collective will" of the consumer existed, the infomediary could then make consumers' preferences known in a way that would "enforce" the desired outcome.

There is precedent for such a role. For years, individual shareholders have had little voice in the companies in which they invested, unless they were big enough shareholders to get management's attention. If company managers made bad strategic or investment decisions, operated poorly, or, even worse, engaged in self-dealing behavior, the individual shareholders could do little about it other than sell their shares in the company. (This was usually an unattractive option, because the actions of management had driven down the value of those shares.) Recognizing this imbalance, the California Public Employees' Retirement System (CalPERS)—which is one of the largest public pension systems in the United States, controlling over $140 billion in investable assets—began to aggregate its investors' interests and economic clout to influence the decisions made by the management of many companies. This activist stance on behalf of investors has changed the rules for the managers of many firms.

Imagine Ralph Nader in the Jimmy Hoffa role

Recently, for instance, it pressured the struggling database software vendor, Sybase, to change its policies and procedures for the election of members of the board of directors. It also took on a Marriott International management proposal that would have created a dual-class stock structure, which CalPERS considered unfairly advantageous to Marriott family shareholders. A quote from Charles P. Valdes, chairman of the CalPERS Investment Committee, illustrates the potential power of this sort of customer aggregation and collective action:

> *We've sent a message to the company and the Marriott family that we refuse to accept a stock structure that is less than hospitable to its shareowners. This action serves as a reminder to the Marriott family that we are the patient long-term capital of the company and part of this "family." We won't be forced into a system that treats family unequally. After all, we've paid for our interests to be represented fairly.*[1]

CalPERS also provides retirement and health benefits to more than 1 million state and local public employees, retirees, and their families, and it has aggregated their purchasing power to pressure big managed-care companies to keep prices down. In a similar way, infomediaries can aggregate and represent the views of customers on matters involving customer service, hiring policies, and treatment of workers just for starters.

Of course, starting an advocacy group is easy enough. The infomediary, however, will have leverage that most advocacy groups can only dream of. First of all, the infomediary will represent a considerable amount of aggregated purchasing power in any one product or service category. Second, the infomediary, because of its detailed profiles of consumers, will be able to alert customers to issues that are important to them. Those customers who want to avoid personal-care products that are tested on animals or who want to avoid foods with nonorganic ingredients will rely on the infomediary to alert them to products they should buy or steer clear of. Similarly, the infomediary can help consumers concerned with global working conditions or the environment to understand how vendors behave in relation to these issues.

Far-thinking firms will recognize this affiliation of customers as a low-cost way to understand the fullest extent of their own value proposition and, where appropriate, to act accordingly to modify that value proposition when it's out of step with what consumers want. This aggregation of customer power may threaten other firms that will seek regulatory or legislative protection from the growing influence of infomediaries and their customers.

Growing consumer influence over government and public policy

Infomediaries may also give consumers greater voice when it comes to influencing government and public policy. The most obvious place this will occur is in issues of privacy. As we discussed in Chapter 1, infomediaries offer the potential for a market-based solution to privacy concerns—issues that have previously seemed addressable only through government regulation. (In fact, in many parts of the world, government regulation of information capture and use has already been put in place.) But infomediaries will influence more than just issues of privacy. The following sections touch on areas the infomediary will have to carefully consider during its launch and as it matures.

Antitrust

Conventional antitrust policy at least nominally tries to protect the consumer against unnaturally high prices as companies consolidate (although much economic and historical scholarship suggests that, from the outset, such policies have had a very different effect—protecting inefficient producers from more efficient competitors and in the process supporting higher prices to the consumer). What happens when infomediaries squeeze companies on behalf of customers? How do regulators deal with concentration in businesses explicitly focused on maximizing value for the customer? Will vendors turn antitrust legislation on its head and argue that infomediary concentration leads to the formation of customer "cartels" that damage vendor interests?

More broadly, infomediaries and infomediary webs have the potential to lead to a dramatic shift in value creation within and across markets. Shifting value

What happens when infomediaries squeeze companies on behalf of consumers?

creation will certainly benefit "new game" players who understand and adapt to the new rules for value creation. What about the "old game" players who today represent enormous shareholder value, but who move too late to protect or grow this shareholder value? Will they seek to use political influence to erect barriers to competition that will at least slow down the growth of "new game" players?

Infomediary liability

By helping customers protect their privacy in a commercial context, will infomediaries make their privacy even more exposed in a governmental context? Consider what an infomediary might do when presented with a subpoena from a government agency. (In some countries, of course, a subpoena isn't necessary to seize information.) The controversy in the United States when a special prosecutor subpoenaed the purchase records of a White House intern at a local bookstore will seem trivial compared to the ability of a special prosecutor (or any other government agency) to subpoena the integrated profile of an individual's purchases, conveniently aggregated by the helpful infomediary. To some extent, existing civil remedies will help to control unauthorized release of this information to government or other third parties. If clients can prove damages as the result of the unauthorized release of the information, they might be able to sue the infomediary for both compensatory and punitive damages.

Concerns over the potential abuse of such sensitive information profiles might also lead courts to create an "infomediary-client" privilege. This privilege might be analogous to the existing "attorney-client" or, in some jurisdictions, the "therapist-client" or spousal privileges recognized by courts today. Like these existing privileges, the infomediary-client privilege might protect the infomediary from government agencies' demands for the release of client information profiles. As with the therapist-client privilege, courts would likely impose certain limits on this privilege. For example, if there is probable cause to believe that the client is about to commit a violent act, law enforcement agencies might be able to access the information profile of the client with appropriate court orders to obtain only the information necessary to prevent the violent act.

Governments will face growing pressure, from clients who value the services of the infomediary, to adopt (and enforce) stricter controls on the ability of government agencies to access this information. Of course, clients and infomediaries will face uncertainties created by the global operations of an infomediary. Governments will certainly differ in their policies regarding government access to customer information profiles. When will these policies apply? For example, will a government be able to access customer information profiles of infomediary clients in other countries? Whose laws and policies will determine constraints on access to this information—the government of the home country of the infomediary? the government of the home country of the client? or the government of the country where the client purchased a specific product leading to an entry in the client information profile?

Differing government policies regarding classes of commercial transactions create an additional level of uncertainty. Some governments prohibit, or tightly regulate, gambling. What's the liability of an infomediary that helps its clients access on-line gambling operations in countries where gambling is more freely available? In some countries, certain kinds of pharmaceuticals are available without prescriptions, whereas other countries may require a prescription. Is the infomediary liable if it helps clients in the latter countries purchase these pharmaceuticals in the former countries? What if it doesn't facilitate the purchase but merely captures a record of the transaction as part of its information profile?

To respond to client concerns about potential abuse of the information profiles, infomediaries may take steps of their own to encrypt or anonymize profiles, making them attachable to an individual only through a special password controlled by the client. Clients may also value a global delete feature that would allow them at their own discretion to erase their own profile and related archived data—especially if they're concerned they might be about to receive a visit from a representative of the special prosecutor.

A global delete feature might foil the special prosecutor

National boundaries

Another important question relates to national boundaries. How will governments react to the prospect of global enterprises managing rich databases of their citizens? What if maximizing value for their clients leads infomediaries to help their clients reduce the impact of local sales taxes or arbitrage product prices across national boundaries, to the disadvantage of national vendors?

Privacy regulation

The varying levels of government regulation of commercial privacy around the world may put up a roadblock to the globaliza-

tion of the infomediary business. If commercial entities are prohibited from capturing information about customers or from
using that information for commercial purposes, even with the
permission of the customer, then presumably infomediaries
could not operate in those countries.

Offshore infomediaries

Yet cyberspace laws are still open to interpretation in many
countries, and infomediaries may still have room to operate offshore. If an infomediary locates its server in a country with
relaxed privacy regulations, will more restrictive countries consider it "offshore"? What if the privacy and profiling software
provided by this offshore infomediary is installed on the client's
computer which is located in a country with restrictive privacy
laws?

Even if a restrictive country considers an infomediary an
offshore business that is exempt from the privacy laws, the
scope of the infomediary's operations could still be severely
constrained. It would have difficulty offering purchaser identification services or even targeted marketing message services to
vendors based in the country with restrictive privacy laws. The
bottom line is that a market-based entity seeking to help customers protect their privacy might be prevented from operating
in countries that have chosen to rely on government regulation
to protect privacy.

Protecting clients

The resolution of these issues won't be entirely exogenous for
infomediaries in democracies. Given their efficient access to
and insight into customers, and their role as agents for their
pecuniary and nonpecuniary interests, infomediaries will be
able to organize a customer response to status-quo defenders'

attempts to circle the wagons. Threats to privacy and the financial benefits of infomediation for customers will likely bring strong reactions from infomediary clients. Although not all customers are likely to share one view, infomediaries can serve as loci for efficient organization and communication of varying views that *are* widely shared, much as they will do for corporate policy.

Infomediaries' ability to influence governments, as customer aggregators, will likely extend beyond defending customers from reactionary attacks on their clients' privacy and economic well-being. By way of profiles, infomediaries will be able to make inferences about the social and public policy issues that are most important to individual clients and, with their permission, create opportunities for them to combine their voices and even financial resources. In large part, this will likely happen because influence "vendors"—political parties, political action committees, and even candidates themselves—will want to organize or otherwise reach the customers of the infomediary.

More broadly, a new type of activism may emerge, as previously apathetic citizens find a new way to exercise their economic and voting power to influence government policies and the outcomes of elections.

The uncertainties created by conflicting government policies affecting key aspects of infomediary operations across the world will certainly require that aspiring infomediaries carefully assess both where they choose to incorporate and where they choose to operate. These choices will significantly shape the protection—and the potential liabilities—that an infomediary might experience as its operations evolve.

Taxation

Tax law is another area in which infomediaries might play an important organizing and influencing role. Perhaps infomediaries will be able to ensure that consumers influence tax law in a way that will truly make these laws simpler. Senior management today carefully evaluates such issues as tax regimes, employment laws, and intellectual property protection before making decisions about where to locate operations globally. The infomediary business raises additional issues regarding commercial privacy laws, government controls on information access by its own agencies, and government policies regulating or prohibiting certain classes of commercial transactions. The global growth of the infomediary business will be shaped by assessments of opportunities and risks along all these dimensions.

The impact of infomediaries and infomediary webs is likely to be profound and widespread. This book has argued that infomediaries can play an extremely valuable market role in reconciling the tension between the growing value of customer information and the growing concern over commercial privacy. Consumers will benefit enormously from their services. Those vendors that understand and anticipate the changing rules of value creation will also benefit. In the process, infomediaries will reshape firms and markets. In doing so, they will unleash broad social changes and call into question many conventional approaches to public policy. Our response to these social and public policy issues will in many respects determine the pace and the ultimate effects of this innovative new business model.

Note

1. CalPERS press release, 20 May 1998.

the technology
tool kit

GETTING THE STRATEGY RIGHT IS THE MOST important first step in building a new business venture. However, getting the technology right is also crucial for any new business—all the more so for those, like the infomediary, that will be unfolding much of their services on-line.

This appendix describes the profiling and privacy tools that the infomediary will provide to each of its clients. It also describes in more detail the technology the infomediary will require to build and maintain client profiles, and to deliver the customer and vendor services described in Chapter 2.

Standards and established technologies will be important drivers of success for the infomediary.

Where standards are not yet established, as will be the case for client profiles, establishing and promoting an open standard will streamline the infomediary's operations and allow it to focus on running the business rather than on building a proprietary technology infrastructure. Standards have the potential to greatly reduce the cost of matching customers with products and services through the intelligent use of profile data.

Technologies that serve and protect: tools for data capture

A combination of existing and emerging technologies will form both the core and supplemental methods of data capture. (See Figure A-1 for a diagram of infomediary profiling and examples of existing technologies.) As we described in Chapter 1, the Internet, with its information-rich on-line environment, provides the most fertile context for the early emergence of infomediaries, because it can leverage existing technologies, including the Web browser and installed base of personal computers. Other emerging network-based technologies, such as television set-top boxes and broadband networks, promise to provide a follow-on capability to further enhance profiles. Adding to this, physical-world data-capture technologies, particularly those involving card-based payment systems (such as those using credit cards and smart cards), will provide powerful complements to data captured on the Internet and other networks.

Complementing these on-line data-capture technologies will be a set of technologies to protect the infomediary client's privacy. These technologies will continue to evolve, but at the outset will include simple tools like reverse cookies, anonymization software, cookie suppressors, e-mail filters, anonymous e-mail, and digital cash.

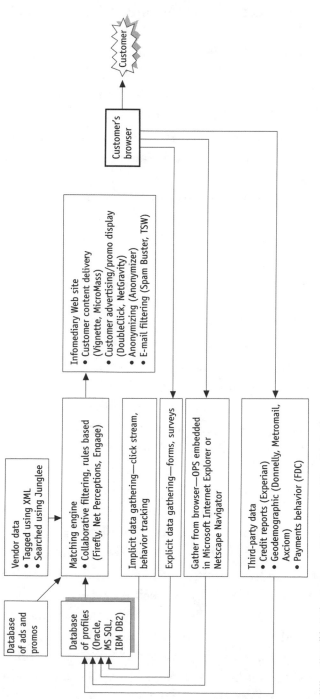

FIGURE A-1 Infomediary Profiling and Examples of Existing Technologies

XML = eXtensible Markup Language; OPS = Open Profiling Standard.

Capturing the data on-line . . .

Customer profiles are nothing more than a database of information with defined fields. To be most effective, this is a relational database (such as Oracle, Informix, Microsoft SQL Server, or IBM DB2) with object extensions that allow real-time feeds from the Internet as well as integration with enterprisewide systems. The profile database should be designed to integrate cleanly with any existing enterprise resource planning (ERP) and customer relationship management (CRM) software, such as those offered by SAP, Baan, or Siebel, so that the profile data can be used by various applications and across departments.

To develop customer profiles, infomediaries will help consumers capture and manage data available from on-line and physical-world environments. On-line data will be readily captured through the consumer's browser as the consumer interacts on the Internet. In the physical world, credit card transaction data, geodemographic data, and other market research data can serve as powerful complements to profile data captured on-line. Infomediaries will need to regularly update profiles with on-line data and periodically add physical-world data.

The infomediary will capture data through both explicit and implicit means. Explicit data collection will mean asking clients directly for the information. Infomediaries are likely to do this sparingly, probably only at the time they first sign up a client. Implicit data capture is the process of monitoring a client's behavior and recording it in some useful manner. It is a more complicated process than explicit data capture. Behavioral data will most likely be collected this way, for instance, which will mean collecting data across all sites on the Internet.

The primary tool for behavioral data capture will be what is referred to as a "reverse cookie." A *cookie* is a common technology used by Web sites to track visitors to the site and to monitor which areas of the Web site visitors are spending their time in. It involves the Web site's putting a piece of data into a specific file on the visitor's hard drive when the individual visits various parts of the Web site, which allows the Web site to track which visitors have gone where on the site.

In contrast to the cookie, the *reverse cookie* is a piece of code in the client's browser that tracks where on the Internet the client has visited. This file of activity could include which sites were visited and which sections a member viewed. Theoretically, it could also track which articles were read, which were printed, which ads were clicked, and what was purchased. Keeping a record of the pages that are viewed and the duration of viewing will accomplish all of this.

Companies today offer products similar to the reverse cookie. RelevantKnowledge (www.relevantknowledge.com), for example, uses a technology that works this way to track Web usage and to develop the RelevantKnowledge Web Report, which tracks traffic on the top visited Web sites (as of mid-1998, approximately 800 sites met RelevantKnowledge's minimum reporting standards). RelevantKnowledge participants download a small piece of software into their browser, and the rest is automated. On a real-time basis, each URL the participant goes to is sent to RelevantKnowledge and stored in a master database. With these data, RelevantKnowledge tracks page views as well as behavioral data, such as order of pages visited and time spent on a site, on the top visited Web sites.

The main difficulty with capturing behavioral data is that, once a participant enters a secure area of a site, all data into and out of that site are encrypted. When a participant purchases something on-line on a secure server, that action is invisible to anyone reading a user's click-stream data. At present, companies collecting user click-stream information are able to track only that a participant entered the secure area of the site and consequently may have purchased something. (As this book was going to press, RelevantKnowledge was developing a new version of its software designed to give greater transparency to the secure click stream of the user.)

This obstacle could be overcome by an infomediary's utilizing the reverse cookie technology, if the infomediary were to set up an agreement with selected sites such that, when one of the infomediary's clients entered secure mode, the site would share "behind-the-firewall" data. For example, an infomediary could set up an agreement with GardenEscape (www.garden.com) whereby, whenever an infomediary member entered the commerce part of its site, GardenEscape would notify the infomediary of the activity and share log files regarding this particular individual.

A second complication of this process for the infomediary will be to keep a record of which page addresses mean what. For example, the infomediary would have to know that a visit to www.amazon.com/exec/obidos/ISBN=1568846444/o/002-1325721-6414437 indicates that a customer was looking at the book *Gardening for Dummies* by Michael MacCaskey at Amazon.com. Again, a relationship with the target site would simplify this process. An infomediary would want to put into place agreements with the top 50 to 100 Web sites its clients visited and map URLs to content or category fields. Although it might not get down to the detail of knowing that the specific book was *Gardening for Dummies,* the infomediary could know that this was a look at a gardening book, thereby indicating a possible interest in gardening. In this particular case, a simple rule could suffice: If the URL starts with www.amazon.com and contains the text "ISBN=", then the following string of numbers indicates the ISBN number, which can be uniquely mapped to a book. The infomediary would then need to have access to the ISBN database to match number with title, and ultimately interest category. An additional benefit of having a relationship with Amazon.com, in this case, would be to have the infomediary notified of any structural changes in the page-serving database that would require a database or rules change on the part of the infomediary.

Yet another challenge will be that Web sites don't always use a single page address per topic. For example, a visit to www.audi.com to look at the latest information on the Audi A4 Quattro doesn't give away what model the customer is inquiring about. The page address of www.audi.com/java/models/index. html is the same address for all Audi models, from the A3 to the S8. Consequently, although the infomediary will know that a customer is looking at new cars, it will not know if its customer is exploring a compact or a luxury automobile. Again, an established relationship with a site would help the infomediary gather the information it needed.

Data collected through the reverse cookie can be either sent directly to the infomediary or stored on the client's computer and uploaded regularly. Given the significant amount of data, the preferred solution is to send data to the infomediary on a real-time basis. Customers should be given an opportunity to review and delete any profile data at any point and to set up blocks so that data from certain sites will not be put in the profile. For those that are particularly concerned about privacy, the data can be stored on their PC and edited before transmission to the infomediary. These behavioral data will add depth to an individual's profile that could not be achieved through questionnaires and registration forms alone.

Once received at the infomediary, on-line data will be added to the individual customer's profile. The translation of the data into useful information will be completed by mapping individual site and page visits into both categorical indicators of interest and cumulative measures of recurring or persistent interest in a particular site or category of sites. Profiles can be kept in a standard database, such as Oracle, IBM DB2, or MS SQL Server, and should be accessible across the enterprise, including sales, marketing, and customer support.

Once a profile is developed, the infomediary can use the

data in the profile to create a better experience for the consumer. The infomediary can deliver more relevant content, advertising, and promotions based on both actual and inferred behavioral data. Using the customer who looked up *Gardening for Dummies* as an example, the infomediary could infer that the customer is a novice gardener who might be in need of basic garden tools and consequently deliver a promotional ad to the customer for a special deal on quality garden tools offered by one of the vendors in the network.

When the infomediary has built a critical mass of rich profiles, it can use cross-profile technologies, such as the one developed by Net Perceptions (www.netperceptions.com), to make targeted product recommendations and customized offerings. The Net Perceptions product uses collaborative filtering, which enables a set of profiles to make recommendations to themselves. Consider a simplified example in which AnaRosa bought items A, B, and C and visited sites D and E, and Ned bought items B and C and visited sites D and E. Net Perceptions would recommend item A to Ned, under the assumption that his purchasing and viewing patterns are similar enough to AnaRosa's that he would be interested in the product.

Eventually, emerging technologies, including the set-top box that will make television an access device for network-based content, will provide a platform where behavioral data indicating preferences and interests can be captured as well. The set-top box could capture a customer's behavior over the Internet, and could track television-viewing habits that would greatly enhance the customer's profile. The television networks have extensive data on the demographics and psychographics of program viewers. Whether a customer watches "Days of Our Lives" every day or doesn't watch television at all would be a indicator of lifestyle and preferences.

As technology is refined and as electronic networks become more pervasive (whether they're the Internet, broadband networks, cable networks, wireless systems, or proprietary environments), information-capture opportunities will arise for content providers, network operators, and consumers. Like data captured over the Internet, data captured through set-top boxes and other network devices will be sent to the infomediary, where they, too, will be used to update the customer's profile.

Profile Technologies

Several companies are building the technology behind online profile creation and enhancement. Although each takes a different approach, these companies are on the leading edge of developing and leveraging profiles in order to provide a better experience for customers. One way to categorize these technologies is to look at whether data are gathered across Web sites or within a Web site, and whether profiles are compared with each other or treated individually.

Profile building across Web sites, across customers: Firefly Networks was the first and most well known of the personalization technology companies. Profiles developed through the Firefly Passport product can reside either on the individual's computer or at a more centralized point, such as an infomediary. Individuals can decide what personal information they want released to Web sites, and thus set their own "privacy" rules. The Firefly Passport allows sites to provide customized information to individuals when they log onto participating sites, and if the individual allows his or her profile to be kept centrally, product and content customization are refined based on cross-profile preferences. Microsoft acquired Firefly in early 1998 with the intent of integrating this privacy and personalization technology into Microsoft Web servers and MS Internet Explorer.   (www.firefly.net)

Within a Web site, across customers: Net Perceptions has developed GroupLens, a tool that uses collaborative filtering to make product recommendations to consumers based on their past behavior and the behavior of others with similar interests. For example, a customer who purchases books or CDs on Amazon.com or CDnow will get recommendations from these two companies based on the buying behavior of people who have enjoyed the same books or CDs.   (www.netperceptions.com)

Across Web sites, individual customers: Engage Technologies markets a product that specializes in creating and leveraging user profiles across multiple Web sites. It maintains a database of more than 16 million user profiles with both behavior- and interest-based data, which can be accessed by any Web site participating in the Engage network. Profiles containing customer-identifiable information are kept locally at each Web site, and anonymous profiles (containing a unique user ID but no personal identification) are shared across sites.   (www.engagetech.com)

Across an Enterprise: Home Account Network has developed a complete set of tools for data capture over enterprise networks. Home Account Network has focused primarily on gaining access to databases across an enterprise in order to be able to offer integrated product and service solutions to individual customers. It is primarily focused on the financial services industry. Customers can specify needs, desires, and risk tolerances, and the Home Account Network products work across an enterprise to make recommendations and provide consolidated offerings. (www.homeaccount.com)

. . . and in the physical world

At least two existing physical-world customer data sources could be tapped and integrated with on-line profiles to quickly make the overall customer profile more valuable. An infomediary could draw on existing geodemographic databases from personal data collectors like Axciom, Donnelly Marketing, Metromail, and R. L. Polk to enhance customer database profiles. Doing so would involve sending periodic updates to the infomediary data center, where individual records would be enhanced or modified. Data from these sources are extensive and include information on home ownership, mortgage payments, cars owned, and so on.

Credit card purchases in the physical world are another rich source of profile data, because substantially all credit card transactions are captured and processed in electronic form. The challenge with credit card data is that they indicate which vendors were used, but give no indication of what product was purchased. For example, a $400 purchase at Sears could be a new dishwasher or many, many pairs of socks. Credit card purchase data are not available on the open market; in order to have access to this data source, the infomediary would have to issue its own credit card.

Infomediaries are likely to issue credit cards for several other reasons:

1. They would enable the infomediary to easily capture purchase data both on-line and in the physical world.

2. The infomediary's business model is one of collecting fees for matching buyers and sellers, and doing so through credit card commissions is a natural fit.

3. The infomediary could set up a mechanism to disguise the identity of the credit card user to the vendor, thereby enhancing the promise of privacy.

4. Customers would be inclined to select the infomediary credit card because using it would increase the ability of the infomediary to deliver targeted offerings and would guarantee the retention of privacy.

Smart cards, cards that have an embedded chip and an operating system that manages information in file structures much like those used in a personal computer, will play a significant role in the payments world, effectively enhancing the detail of data captured in physical-world environments and presenting an alternative to cash as a completely anonymous means of payment. Although the technology has been around for many years and is quite popular in Europe, Americans have been hesitant to adopt smart cards, instead using credit and debit cards for their purchasing needs. The smart card, if adopted, can keep track of noncash purchases on the card itself, rather than giving the vendor access to account and customer information.

Growing in popularity are the "club cards" that many grocery stores have begun to issue. These cards allow users to earn points for purchases which can be redeemed for gifts or discounts. What most customers don't realize, though, is that grocery stores are thereby amassing large databases of customer purchasing habits. For example, using data from the Safeway club card, Safeway knows that Sara D. purchases a frozen dinner every Friday and that Chris P. buys beer every time he shops at the store for diapers.

Smart cards have the capability of moving physical-world data, such as that captured by the grocery store club cards, to the infomediary. Using a smart card for purchases, a client could self-monitor purchases and convey these off-line to the infomediary for a more complete profile. The infomediary would need to offer similar benefits to the consumer and would ideally do so in conjunction with the grocery store itself. This would allow consumers to receive a direct benefit from sharing purchasing information, but it would have them sharing the information with their trusted infomediary rather than with a large, impersonal grocery store chain.

Smart cards are also being developed to enable television set-top box decoding, as well as providing secure portable phone access. Behavioral data captured by these devices could contribute to the richness of an individual profile at the infomediary.

Consumer privacy protection technologies

Privacy is an important part of the infomediary's value proposition to its clients. Consequently, the infomediary will need to provide a set of privacy protection tools to its members. These technologies would initially include some combination of anonymization software, cookie suppressors, e-mail filters, and anonymous payment mechanisms. Taken together, the use of some or all of these technologies could prevent the capture of substantially all personal profile and behavioral information without the explicit consent of the customer and could enhance the value of a unique infomediated profile maintained for the benefit of the customer.

Anonymization software. Anonymization software allows consumers to interact anonymously when visiting Web sites, by first passing through an anonymizing Web site that disguises their identity. Such anonymization is likely to be an important component of the privacy protection offered by the infomediary, because it will protect the member's identity from other Web sites and allow the infomediary to mediate interactions between its members and other vendors and content providers.

While members are visiting sites on the World Wide Web, anonymization will allow Web sites to see the infomediary, rather than the individual members, visiting their site. When needed, the infomediary will provide just enough information to realize site customization, make transactions, or get the best service for its members.

The leading provider of anonymization services today is Anonymizer (www.anonymizer.com). Anonymizer offers two main services—anonymous surfing and anonymous e-mail—and one product—the Anonymizing Server. The Anonymizing Server enables anyone to create his or her own anonymizing site.

By stopping at an anonymizing web site before going anywhere else on the Internet, the customer can allow personal information—such as the customer's IP address (IP addresses indicate either employer or Internet service provider)—to be withheld from the receiving site. Anonimizer sites also block system data (such as what operating system and browser are being used) from being sent to web sites, block cookies from being deposited in browsers (see below), and block Java and JavaScript (which can access personal data in browsers). An infomediary would likely turn its own Web site into an anonymization site, so that customers could explore the Internet safely as long as they passed through the infomediary's site before venturing out into the World Wide Web.

A challenge for the infomediary will be to provide this anonymization without disrupting the Internet experience for the customer. As more and more Web sites use personalization to differentiate their sites and make them more valuable to customers, being able to identify oneself becomes important. Custom Web pages, such as MyYahoo!, rely on cookies to identify users each time they return, so users don't have to log into the Web site each time they check their news. The infomediary will have to find a way to identify a user without giving away his or her real identity and, ideally, allow users to view and edit their "anonymous cookies" to determine which they want to keep and which they want to discard.

Cookie suppression. A cookie resides on a customer's hard drive and contains information about the individual that can be read back by the Web site that deposited it or by anyone else with an understanding of that Web site's data format. A cookie can contain any information the Web site wants to include in it: pages viewed, ads clicked, customer identification number, and so on. Cookies are kept in a file called "cookies.txt" for Netscape browsers and in a folder called "cookies" for Microsoft Internet Explorer.

Cookies were initially designed to benefit users, storing information so that repeat visitors to a site wouldn't have to log into or respecify preferences on each visit. Because cookies can also be used to match browsing habits and preferences, they're increasingly being used to target advertisements to specific users. Indeed, DoubleClick, Globaltrash, and ADSmart are examples of companies that use cookies to target advertisements to consumers at their enabled sites.

For example, if a customer visiting the U.S. News & World Report site, clicks on an advertisement for a CD vendor placed by DoubleClick, DoubleClick could drop a cookie in the customer's browser indicating the action. In future visits to the same site or one of over 170 other sites in the DoubleClick network, the Web site could "read" the DoubleClick cookie and deliver other CD advertisements, because the customer would have been "tagged" as someone interested in CDs. Cookies have thereby evolved so that they benefit vendors more than users.

As part of the enrollment process for the infomediary, infomediaries will provide an automated way for members to delete their cookie file as well as change their browser settings so that they will not accept cookies.

E-mail filters and anonymous e-mail. E-mail filtering screens a member's incoming e-mail and lets through only the e-mails that the member has indicated he or she would like to receive. Largely used to screen out junk e-mail, several companies today provide tools that consumers can install on their computer to screen out unwanted e-mail. These include Contact Plus Corporation's product Spam Buster and TSW's product efilter. In addition, several e-mail packages, including Eudora, allow users to filter messages as they are received at the desktop.

The most effective filters are those that allow in only certain e-mails—for example, only e-mail with domain name mycompany.com or from the following e-mail addresses: jennifer@isp.net, barr@company.com, IanD@nonprofit.org. Although this algorithm works for those who have an unchanging network of e-mail correspondents, it would be cumbersome for the bulk of the population because each new e-mail partner would have to be approved.

The more common filtering technology allows all e-mail in except for e-mail from certain domain names (mailalot.com) or e-mail addresses (ObnoxiousOne@spam.com), or with keywords in the subject line (Get Rich Quick!). However, persistent senders frequently change domain name or e-mail address in order to get around these filters, especially because Web-based e-mail accounts, such as those offered by HotMail and Yahoo!, are free and easy to join and leave at any time. Finally, it's difficult to effectively filter using keywords because the likelihood of error is quite high.

Nevertheless, an infomediary has the opportunity to move filtering from the client's desktop to its servers, which would serve the dual purpose of allowing the infomediary to protect members from unwanted solicitations as well as to set up anonymous e-mail services for members.

By centralizing filtering, an infomediary could monitor for likely junk e-mail senders by tracking the number of messages sent to its members from a particular domain name or source and could centrally track when troublesome senders change their source. This would provide better filtering across all members. Many ISPs, including Pacific Bell Internet, have developed their own antispam sensors and can effectively track and block much of the high-volume, unsolicited e-mail that clutters their members' e-mail boxes. Several other companies are also working on antispam products, which an infomediary could implement centrally to reduce unwanted e-mail.

Anonymous e-mail allows members to offer their e-mail address on-line without having to give away their identity. This service is currently available free of charge on the Internet through a collection of companies providing "remailer" services. With these services, the remailer strips off a user's identity before e-mail is sent out and puts on the remailer's identity for delivered e-mail. Replies to the anonymous e-mail go to the remailer, who then matches the anonymous address with the actual e-mail address and delivers the e-mail response securely to the customer.

Customers should have the choice, each time they log on, of a single anonymous e-mail address or a different address that was issued by the infomediary. The former would allow Web sites to build a history of interaction with their Web site, thereby offering personal service, and the latter would completely protect the identity of the consumer.

Anonymous payments. As in the physical world, on-line payments for purchases are the most powerful indicators of preference, yet they also offer a significant opportunity for privacy and security violations. As a result, an important part of an infomediary's value proposition could be offering an anonymous on-line payment option. Three options are possible: an anonymous credit or debit card, a smart card, or on-line cash.

An anonymous credit or debit card would block customer information from the vendor entirely. From the vendor's perspective, the buyer would appear to be the infomediary for either a credit or a debit card transaction. The vendor would charge the infomediary, and the infomediary would charge the customer. The same would work for a smart card.

Several stored-value digital cash options are also available, primarily Digicash and Cybercash. Cash would be held for the infomediary's customers in an account that was anonymous to the vendor, and payment would be made and goods exchanged without revealing anyone's identity. Digital cash, and any number of other emergent technologies, would be a value-added, but not critical, portion of the overall consumer offer.

In order to keep the buyer's identity private, electronic content and goods would be sent to the buyer through the infomediary, and physical goods could be either shipped to the infomediary, who then would forward them, or delivered directly to the buyer through an anonymous third-party delivery service.

Using technology standards

In using profiling and privacy technologies to deliver their value proposition to clients, infomediaries will be heavily dependent on certain technology standards that are under development today. Whether it's an industry standard such as the Open Profiling Standard or a new, more powerful programming language such as XML, the tools and technologies on which the infomediary will be built aren't that far away.

Extensible Markup Language

eXtensible Markup Language (XML) has been called the "killer app" for electronic commerce on the Internet. It forms the foundation for nearly all the Internet commerce standards being developed today and is an evolution of programming languages that provide context to data through a tagging system for on-line content. Whereas Hypertext Markup Language

(HTML), today's programming language of the World Wide Web, is a powerful programming language that describes data (pictures, text, video clips), XML extends this capability by also indicating the function of data (cover photo, city name, price).

XML allows a Web site to classify the content of its Web pages, thereby making it easier for users to find what they want. Web sites then become virtual databases of information that can be searched, categorized, ranked, and accessed without need for replication or indexing.

A strong infomediary will be in the position to establish a set of standard tags that vendors can use to mark and describe their data. As the infomediary increases the number of vendors participating in its web, having a set of common tags will free the infomediary of having to develop terabytes of replicated databases of vendor information. If each vendor tags its prices as "prices," and its laptop computers as "notebook computers," then the infomediary can search the vendor databases as efficiently as it would search its own. While eliminating the need for the infomediary to store additional data, virtual databases also provide access to the primary data sources, thereby reducing the challenges of managing and updating replicated databases.

Several industry groups are in the process of defining their own set of tags, and the infomediary will want to take advantage of that. The computer industry, for example, has a standards-setting organization called RosettaNet (www.rosettanet.org), which is creating standard tags for every aspect of a computer, from make and model to color and weight, to be used throughout the supply chain.

However, until XML becomes pervasive on the Internet, a couple of companies have developed a way to simulate XML functionality using HTML data. One of these companies is Junglee (www.junglee.com). Junglee has developed a technology to "wrap" a Web site's HTML data so that it is accessible in a way that provides context. For example, if Junglee were to "wrap" the CDnow.com Web site, Junglee would look at the Web page structure and identify how pricing data are displayed ($X.XX, $X, or $ X.XX), how products are identified (CD title comes directly before artist's name), and so on until a map of the site was created. Junglee would then cross-reference these elements to Junglee's shared terminology database (Price = $X.XX = Price w/out delivery = Offer Price) for each page. Because Junglee provides Webwide search agents for several Web sites, it's able to leverage its work of wrapping individual sites across a network of customers.

An infomediary could use Junglee to provide the initial platform for agent searches until XML becomes widely available and vendors implement it with the infomediary's tagging system. This would allow customers to find the products they needed quickly and effectively, with or without XML. Using Junglee, a customer could indicate that she needed a refrigerator, and the agent could search vendors/partners for refrigerators that match the customer's profile needs, as well as look through nonmember vendor sites for refrigerators in general.

As XML becomes more integrated into Web sites, Junglee is building XML into its Virtual Database Management System. This will allow faster, more accurate searching across sites. The Junglee technology will be needed until 100 percent of commerce sites have converted to 100 percent XML, which will likely take several years.

Information and content exchange

Focusing on the electronic commerce space, Information and Content Exchange (ICE) is an XML tag set being developed by a consortium of enabling technology companies to standardize the way businesses can set up business-to-business on-line relationships to exchange information in a controlled, measured, targeted fashion. Businesses can use the ICE standards to quickly establish the on-line interserver communications needed for syndicated publishing networks, Web superstores, and on-line reseller channels.

ICE enables on-line publishers, content aggregators, and retailers to acquire articles, product specifications, and other "media assets" in a more time- and cost-effective manner than they do now. This can turn the process of adding a new trading partner from a million dollar project to a fairly simple task.

ICE is important to infomediaries in that it could be the standard XML tag set to run their business. This would allow the infomediary to offer customized content and on-line services to its members in a relatively simple way. When the infomediary adds a new media trading partner, such as CNN, to its portfolio of vendors, employing the ICE standards would enable CNN to deliver targeted content to the infomediary's customers quickly and easily.

As the infomediary adds vendors that offer customized content or nonphysical products, such as Preview Travel, to its network of partners, both infomediary and partner will have to agree on a data-sharing protocol, which is a relatively simple task if both follow the ICE standards. The ICE standards would also enable easy communication between a vendor's product information and the infomediary's client base.

The ICE consortium includes technology firms such as Adobe, JavaSoft, Microsoft, National Semiconductor, and Vignette, as well as asset-exchanging companies such as CNET, Hollinger International, News Internet Services, Preview Travel, Tribune Media Services, and ZD Net.

Open profiling standard

The simplest profiling standard, which is moving forward quickly, is Open Profiling Standard (OPS). Being developed by

Platform for Privacy Preferences (P3P), OPS will allow consumers to preprogram personal data, such as age, gender, and address, into their Web browsers. These data will then be easily accessible by any Web site that employs OPS on its server and will eliminate the need for customers to repeatedly enter this information into the Web sites they visit.

Member companies of P3P are Netscape, Microsoft, Firefly, and IBM. The expectation is that OPS technology will become a standard component of all Web browsers and servers.

As personal data become more pervasive on the Internet, protecting one's identity will become a more central concern of Internet users. This concern helps to validate the infomediary's role of protecting member data, through OPS files or otherwise, from being released directly to other Web sites. Rather then releasing the customer's personal OPS data, the infomediary would release disguised data that would provide the benefit of being able to register for information on a Web site, but not give away true identity.

Open financial exchange

Launched in early 1997, Open Financial Exchange (OFX) was developed by Microsoft, Intuit, and Checkfree as a standard for on-line financial transactions. It has won broad industry acceptance, including support from Citibank, Wells Fargo, Chase, Fidelity, and Schwab.

OFX will initially include standards for basic banking transactions on-line, including bill payment and investment positions, and will evolve into on-line trading.

So how does this affect the infomediary? OFX will allow the infomediary to gather data from all of a customer's financial institutions and create a unified financial statement. It will strengthen the infomediary as the destination of choice on the Internet, because multiple bank balances can be checked, stocks traded, and bills paid all in one place. It would also give the infomediary access to financial account balances, mortgage rates, and other customer financial information, allowing the infomediary to become a virtual financial adviser as well as a shopping agent. In addition, it would allow payments to be made directly from a member's savings account, rather than relying on digital cash or credit cards.

Where we're headed

As standards evolve and technologies develop, capturing profile information over a network, whether it be the Internet, cable television, wireless private networks, or broadband, will become easier and easier as the barriers to cross-entity communication come down. With this ease of data capture, protecting privacy will become of greater concern, and technologies will continue to develop to fill this need.

Nonetheless, many technologies available today can be brought together to create an initial, integrated suite of tools for both data capture and privacy protection. As the market evolves, infomediaries will need to take advantage of the new technologies and standards in order to survive—both competitively and by minimizing operating costs. The market will be a competitive and dynamic one, and the less time an infomediary has to spend on defining data structures and technology platforms, the more time it will have to leverage the data it does have to stay in the lead.

further reading

Core Readings

Agre, Philip E., and Marc Rotenberg, eds. *Technology and Privacy: The New Landscape*. Cambridge, Mass.: MIT Press, 1997.

Alderman, Ellen, and Caroline Kennedy. *The Right to Privacy*. New York: Knopf, 1995.

Arthur, W. Brian. "Increasing Returns and the New World of Business." *Harvard Business Review* 74, no. 4 (July–August 1996).

———. *Increasing Returns and Path Dependence in the Economy*. Ann Arbor: University of Michigan Press, 1994.

Axelrod, Robert M. *The Complexity of Cooperation: Agent-Based Models of Competition and Collaboration*. Princeton, N.J.: Princeton University Press, 1997.

Bacard, Andre. *The Computer Privacy Handbook: A Practical Guide to E-Mail Encryption, Data Protection and PGP Privacy Software*. Berkeley, Calif.: Peachpit Press, 1995.

Barney, Jay B., and William G. Ouchi, eds. *Organizational Economics: Toward a New Paradigm for Understanding and Studying Organizations*. San Francisco: Jossey-Bass, 1988.

Beinhocker, Eric D. "Strategy at the Edge of Chaos." *McKinsey Quarterly*, no. 1 (1997).

Bennett, Colin J. *Regulating Privacy: Data Protection and Public Policy in Europe and the United States*. Ithaca, N.Y.: Cornell University Press, 1992.

Blackwell, Roger D. *From Mind to Market: Reinventing the Retail Supply Chain*. New York: HarperBusiness, 1997.

Blattberg, Robert C., Rashi Glazer, and John D. C. Little, eds. *The Marketing Information Revolution*. Boston: Harvard Business School Press, 1994.

Boisot, Max H, ed. *Information Space: A Framework for Learning in Organizations, Institutions and Culture*. London: Routledge, 1995.

Boyle, James. *Shamans, Software, and Spleens: Law and the Construction of the Information Society*. Cambridge, Mass.: Harvard University Press, 1996.

Bradley, Stephen P., and Richard L. Nolan, eds. *Sense and Respond: Capturing Value in the Network Era*. Boston: Harvard Business School Press, 1998.

Brandenburger, Adam M., and Barry J. Nalebuff. *Co-opetition: A Revolutionary Mindset That Combines Competition and Cooperation*. New York: Currency Doubleday, 1996.

Branscomb, Anne W. *Who Owns Information? From Privacy to Public Access*. New York: Basic Books, 1994.

Buchanan James M., and Yong J. Yoon, eds. *The Return to Increasing Returns*. Ann Arbor: University of Michigan Press, 1994.

Burnham, David. *The Rise of the Computer State: The Threat to Our Freedoms, Our Ethics, and Our Democratic Process*. New York: Random House, 1983.

Butler, Pat, Ted W. Hall, Alistair M. Hanna, Lenny Mendonca, Byron Auguste, James Manyika, and Anupam Sahay. "A Revolution in Interaction." *McKinsey Quarterly*, no. 1 (1997).

Cate, Fred H. *Privacy in the Information Age*. Washington, D.C.: Brookings Institution Press, 1997.

Cavoukian, Ann, and Don Tapscott. *Who Knows: Safeguarding Your Privacy in a Networked World*. New York: McGraw-Hill, 1997.

Cheong, Fah-Chun. *Internet Agents: Spiders, Wanderers, Brokers, and 'Bots*. Indianapolis: New Riders, 1996.

Coase, R. H. *The Firm, the Market, and the Law.* Chicago: University of Chicago Press, 1988.

Coyne, Kevin P., and Somu Subramaniam. "Bringing Discipline to Strategy." *McKinsey Quarterly*, no. 4 (1996).

Davies, Simon. *Monitor: Extinguishing Privacy on the Information Superhighway.* London: Pan Books, 1996.

Davis, Stan, and Christopher Meyer. *Blur: The Speed of Change in the Connected Economy.* Reading, Mass.: Addison-Wesley, 1998.

Day, Jonathan D., and James C. Wendler. "The New Economics of Organization." *McKinsey Quarterly*, no. 1 (1998).

Diffie, Whitfield, and Susan Landau. *Privacy on the Line: The Politics of Wiretapping and Encryption.* Cambridge, Mass.: MIT Press, 1998.

Downes, Larry, and Chunka Mui. *Unleashing the Killer App: Digital Strategies for Market Dominance.* Boston: Harvard Business School Press, 1998.

Dyson, Esther. "Privacy Protection: Time to Think and Act Locally and Globally." *Release 1.0,* 23 April 1998.

———. *Release 2.0: A Design for Living in the Digital Age.* New York: Broadway Books, 1997.

Ernst, Morris L., and Alan U. Schwartz. *Privacy: The Right to Be Let Alone.* New York: Macmillan, 1962.

Flaherty, David H. *Protecting Privacy in Surveillance Societies: The Federal Republic of Germany, France, Canada, and the United States.* Chapel Hill: University of North Carolina Press, 1989.

Forrest, Edward, and Richard Mizerski, eds. *Interactive Marketing: The Future Present.* Lincolnwood, Ill.: NTC Business Books, 1995.

Fukuyama, Francis. *Trust: The Social Virtues and the Creation of Prosperity.* New York: Free Press, 1995.

Gandy, Oscar H. *The Panoptic Sort: A Political Economy of Personal Information.* Boulder: Westview Press, 1993.

Goldhaber, Michael H. "The Attention Economy: The Natural Economy of the Net." Article available in the on-line journal First Monday at http://www.firstmonday.dk/univers2/issues/issue2_4/goldhaber/

Hagel, John. "Spider vs. Spider." *McKinsey Quarterly*, no. 1 (1996).

Hagel, John, and Arthur G. Armstrong. *Net Gain: Expanding Markets through Virtual Communities.* Boston: Harvard Business School Press, 1997.

Hagel, John, Todd Hewlin, and Todd Hutchings. "Retail Banking: Caught in a Web?" *McKinsey Quarterly*, no. 2 (1997).

Hagel, John, and Jeffrey Rayport. "The Coming Battle for Customer Information." *Harvard Business Review* 75, no. 1 (January–February 1997).

———. "The New Infomediaries." *McKinsey Quarterly*, no. 4 (1997).

Hagel, John, and Toni Sacconaghi. "Who Will Benefit from Virtual Information?" *McKinsey Quarterly*, no. 3 (1996).

Hixson, Richard F. *Privacy in a Public Society: Human Rights in Conflict*. New York: Oxford University Press, 1987.

Holland, John H. *Emergence: From Chaos to Order*. Reading, Mass.: Addison-Wesley, 1998.

———. *Hidden Order: How Adaptation Builds Complexity*. Reading, Mass.: Addison-Wesley, 1995.

Huber, Peter. *Law and Disorder in Cyberspace: Abolish the FCC and Let Common Law Rule the Telecosm*. Oxford: Oxford University Press, 1997.

Jennings, Nicholas R., and Michael J. Wooldridge, eds. *Agent Technology: Foundations, Applications and Markets*. Berlin: Springer-Verlag, 1998.

Kauffman, Stuart. *At Home in the Universe: The Search for Laws of Self-Organization and Complexity*. New York: Oxford University Press, 1995.

———. "The Evolution of Economic Webs." In *The Economy as an Evolving Complex System*, edited by Philip W. Anderson, Kenneth J. Arrow, and David Pines. Redwood City, Calif.: Addison-Wesley, 1988.

Kelly, Kevin. *Out of Control: The Rise of Neo-Biological Civilization*. Reading, Mass.: Addison-Wesley, 1994.

Klein, Daniel B., ed. *Reputation: Studies in the Voluntary Elicitation of Good Conduct*. Ann Arbor: University of Michigan Press, 1997.

Larson, Erik. *The Naked Consumer: How Our Private Lives Become Public Commodities*. New York: Holt, 1992.

Leonard, Andrew. *Bots: The Origins of New Species*. San Francisco: Hard-Wired, 1997.

Linowes, David F. *Privacy in America: Is Your Private Life in the Public Eye?* Urbana: University of Illinois Press, 1989.

Ludlow, Peter. *High Noon on the Electronic Frontier: Conceptual Issues in Cyberspace*. Cambridge, Mass.: MIT Press, 1996.

Lyon, David. *The Electronic Eye: The Rise of the Surveillance Society.* Minneapolis: University of Minnesota Press, 1994.

Lyon, David, and Elia Zureik, eds. *Computers, Surveillance, and Privacy.* Minneapolis: University of Minnesota Press, 1996.

Malone, Thomas W., J. Yates, and R. I. Benjamin. "Electronic Markets and Electronic Hierarchies." *Communications of the ACM* 30, no. 6 (1987).

McKenna, Regis. *Real Time: Preparing for the Age of the Never Satisfied Customer.* Boston: Harvard Business School Press, 1997.

————. *Relationship Marketing: Successful Strategies for the Age of the Customer.* Reading, Mass.: Addison-Wesley, 1991.

Nocera, Joseph. *A Piece of the Action: How the Middle Class Joined the Money Class.* New York: Simon & Schuster, 1994.

Packard, Vance. *The Naked Society.* New York: Pocket Books, 1964.

Peppers, Don, and Martha Rogers. *Enterprise One to One: Tools for Competing in the Interactive Age.* New York: Currency Doubleday, 1997.

————. *The One to One Future: Building Relationships One Customer at a Time.* New York: Currency Doubleday, 1993.

Pfaffenberger, Bryan. *Protect Your Privacy on the Internet.* New York: Wiley, 1997.

Phlips, Louis. *The Economics of Imperfect Information.* Cambridge: Cambridge University Press, 1988.

Pine, B. Joseph III. *Mass Customization: The New Frontier in Business Competition.* Boston: Harvard Business School Press, 1993.

Rayport, Jeffrey F., and John J. Sviokla. "Exploiting the Virtual Value Chain." *Harvard Business Review* 73, no. 6 (November–December 1995).

————. "Managing in the Marketspace." *Harvard Business Review* 72, no. 6 (November–December 1994).

Regan, Priscilla M. *Legislating Privacy: Technology, Social Values, and Public Policy.* Chapel Hill: University of North Carolina Press, 1995.

Reichheld, Frederick F., with Thomas Teal. *The Loyalty Effect: The Hidden Force Behind Growth, Profits, and Lasting Value.* Boston: Harvard Business School Press, 1996.

Rothfeder, Jeffrey. *Privacy for Sale: How Computerization Has Made Everyone's Private Life an Open Secret.* New York: Simon & Schuster, 1992.

Schneier, Bruce, and David Banisar, eds. *The Electronic Privacy Papers: Documents on the Battle for Privacy in the Age of Surveillance.* New York: Wiley, 1997.

Schwartz, Evan I. *Webonomics: Nine Essential Principles for Growing Your Business on the World Wide Web.* New York: Broadway Books, 1997.

Senge, Peter M. *The Fifth Discipline: The Art and Practice of the Learning Organization.* New York: Doubleday/Currency, 1990.

Shapiro, Carl, and Hal Varian. *Information Rules: A Strategic Guide to the Network Economy.* Boston: Harvard Business School Press, 1999.

Singleton, Solveig. "Privacy as Censorship: A Skeptical View of Proposals to Regulate Privacy in the Private Sector." *Cato Institute Policy Analysis,* no. 295, 22 January 1998.

Smith, H. Jeff. *Managing Privacy: Information Technology and Corporate America.* Chapel Hill: University of North Carolina Press, 1994.

St. Laurent, Simon. *Cookies.* New York: McGraw-Hill, 1998.

Taylor, Jim, and Watts Wacker, with Howard Means. *The 500-Year Delta: What Happens After What Comes Next.* New York: HarperBusiness, 1997.

Vinge, Vernor. *"True Names" in True Names . . . and Other Dangers.* New York: Baen Books, 1987.

Wayland, Robert E., and Paul M. Cole. *Customer Connections: New Strategies for Growth.* Boston: Harvard Business School Press, 1997.

Weiss, Michael J. *The Clustering of America.* New York: Harper & Row, 1988.

Westin, Alan F. *Privacy and Freedom.* New York: Atheneum, 1967.

Westin, Alan F., and Michael A. Baker. *Databanks in a Free Society: Computers, Record-Keeping, and Privacy.* New York: Quadrangle Books, 1972.

Whiteley, Richard, and Diane Hessan. *Customer Centered Growth: Five Proven Strategies for Building Competitive Advantage.* Reading, Mass.: Addison-Wesley, 1996.

Wiersema, Fred. *Customer Intimacy: Pick Your Partners, Shape Your Culture, Win Together.* Santa Monica: Knowledge Exchange, 1996.

Williamson, Oliver E. *The Mechanisms of Governance.* New York: Oxford University Press, 1996.

————. *The Economic Institutions of Capitalism: Firms, Markets, Relational Contracting.* New York: Free Press, 1985.

————. *Markets and Hierarchies: Analysis and Antitrust Implications.* New York: Free Press, 1975.

Newsletters and Magazines

With few exceptions, most of the citations above are books. The interested reader should also consult a broad range of industry publications for more detailed and current coverage of the topics discussed in this book.

In the marketing arena, the following publications are helpful: *Credit, Direct Marketing, The Friday Report, Journal of Advertising Research, Journal of Consumer Marketing, Journal of Consumer Research, Journal of Marketing, Privacy and American Business, Privacy Journal,* and *Privacy Times.*

For coverage on the Internet and information capture on electronic networks, the following publications are useful: *ComputerLetter, Forbes ASAP, Industry Standard, Interactive Week, Internet World,* and *Release 1.0.*

index

access
conditional, 230
costs, 147, 178, 244
providers, 220
See also customer profiles: access to; information: access
acquisitions. *See* customer acquisition; merger and acquisition strategies
advertising, 15, 36, 91, 125
in conventional media, 243–244
expenditures, 238–244
generated by infomediaries, 243
mass market, 232, 238, 245
revenues, 241, 243, 244, 249
targeted, 268, 275
See also direct marketing; marketing messages; targeted marketing services; telemarketing
advocacy, 4, 24–28, 252
affiliate programs, 199, 200, 220, 252

agent services, 33–35, 43, 121, 168, 231
provided by infomediaries, 24–26, 52, 74, 123, 124–127, 150–151, 157–158, 159, 172, 188, 191–192, 195, 196, 245, 257
aggregated purchases. *See* purchases/purchasing patterns: aggregated; transaction aggregators
alliances, 58, 83, 118, 138, 167.
See also joint ventures
America Online, 6, 23, 86, 190
analytic services, 67, 68, 118, 138, 168. *See also* customer profiles: analysis of; information: analysis; product(s): evaluation of
anonymity/anonymization software, 17–18, 68, 130, 161, 256, 262, 273–274
user IDs, 270, 274, 275, 277

anonymous payment mechanisms, 17, 29, 31, 34, 35, 37–39, 72, 161, 163, 167, 271, 273, 277–278
antispam technology, 277
antitrust concerns, 253–254
auctions, 26, 232
audience focus, 98–99
automobiles. *See* transportation market

banking industry, 68, 80, 95, 96, 207, 208, 216, 224–225, 227, 229
   conventional, 223–224
   credit cards issued by, 217
   on-line transactions, 282–283
   personal shopper services offered by, 236
   See also financial services
barriers to competition, 254
barriers to cross-entity communication, 283
barriers to entry, 11, 15, 119, 177
   increasing returns to scale and, 122, 184
   predatory pricing as, 184
   size of company and, 245
   speed to market and, 175, 176
billing services, 100, 118, 138, 146, 195, 262. *See also* anonymous payment mechanisms; transaction-processing services
brand names, 58, 79–80, 98, 100, 101, 102, 106, 141, 190, 217, 230
   conventional advertising, 243
   customer-centric, 235–237, 238, 240–241
   product-centric, 235
   reengineering of, 233–238
   vendor-centric, 237–238

   See also advertising; marketing; targeted marketing services
broadband networks, 262, 268, 283
browsing, 12, 30, 31, 37, 38, 45, 70, 133, 239, 242
   anonymous, 68, 274, 275
   duration rates, 265
   profiles, 59, 168
   "push" environments for, 168
   software, 262, 264, 265
   See also search(es)
bundling of products and services, 52, 198, 210, 212–213, 215–219
   effect on pricing, 52
   by infomediaries, 235, 236
   unbundling of traditional businesses, 214–224, 225, 226–227
   unbundling of traditional organizational structures, 198, 206, 207–214
business ecology, 23, 85, 135
business models, 241–243, 259
   mixed, 219–224
   See also content: aggregators; economic model of infomediation; portals/portal companies; transaction aggregators; virtual communities
business-to-business relationships, 106, 135, 171, 280–281
buying power. *See* transaction aggregators

cars. See transportation market
cash flow, 187, 196–198
catalog companies, 97. *See also* direct mail
churn rates, 43, 84, 87, 88, 112, 194, 200
click-stream data, 129–130, 154, 265, 266

click-through rates, 174

"club cards," 272

clusters, 126, 227

  of customers/clients, 117, 164, 173–174, 180

  See also critical mass

Coase, Ronald, 210

collective will concept. *See* consumer influence

commercialization businesses, 206, 208, 209, 211, 213, 215–216, 217–218, 222, 224, 225, 243, 245

commercial transactions

  laws restricting, 259

  non-infomediary, 127, 129, 154

  on-line environments for, 54

  See also credit card(s); information, types of: transaction history; private information sources: commercial transactions; purchases/purchasing patterns

commissions

  to agents, 24, 25

  to infomediaries, 22, 40, 41, 271

  to transaction aggregators, 89, 90, 171

  See also fees

comparison shopping, 26–27, 34, 40, 41, 42, 51, 139, 232

computer industry, 134, 136, 139, 178, 205–206, 216, 219, 227

  market, 8, 53, 69–70, 126

  personal computers, 8, 185, 262, 267, 272

concentration

  of industries, 119, 139, 175, 181–182, 186, 225, 253

  of markets, 176, 177

  See also bundling of products and services

connection services, 201, 220. *See also* portals/portal companies

consulting services, 138, 185. *See also* evaluation services

consumer advocacy, 4, 24–28, 252

consumer influence, 19–20

  over commercial practices, 248, 250–253, 259

  over government and public policy, 248, 253–259

  over information transparency, 248–250

content, 19, 52, 133

  aggregators, 241, 242, 281

  customization, 269

  definition "tags," 133, 134, 150, 151, 278–279

  display/presentation, 129–130, 131, 133, 134, 151

  exchange, 280–281

  providers, 269, 273

  published, 88

  sites, 91, 266

contracts, 83, 136, 138, 183

cookie cutters/cookie files, 29–30, 264–265, 274

cookie suppressors, 17, 262, 273, 274, 275

core processes. *See* operations/ operating systems: core

corporations, traditional-market, 85, 103–106, 224–228

  database marketing, 89

  infomediary potential for, 94–103

  web-based strategies, 84

creative talent, 211, 215, 225

credibility issues, 84, 85

credit bureaus, 22, 102, 103, 142, 244

credit card(s), 262, 277–278, 283

  companies, 68, 199, 216, 217, 244

  issued by infomediaries, 271–272

  purchases, 29, 30, 31, 223, 264, 271

credit card(s) *(continued)*
  See also anonymous payment
    mechanisms; debit cards;
    private information sources:
    commercial transactions;
    private information sources:
    credit histories; smart cards
credit information providers, 94, 101
critical mass
  of application software, 114
  of clients and vendors, 79, 89, 90,
    113, 115, 116, 146, 169–173,
    197, 200–201
  of customers/clients, 58, 119,
    120, 121–122, 175, 180,
    190–191, 247, 264–268, 272,
    281
  of data, 166
  of users, 113–114, 115, 116, 117,
    135, 136–137
  See also clusters
cross-profile preferences, 269
cross-selling, 43, 46, 112, 166
cumulative production, 113–114
customer acquisition, 220, 221
  cost of, 42–43, 51, 52, 79, 110,
    112, 116, 122, 174–177, 193,
    197, 199
  as entry strategy, 120–122
  by infomediaries, 171, 174–175,
    190
  preemptive strategies for, 194
  services, 43–44
customer base. *See* critical mass: of
    customers/clients
customer needs and preferences
  agent services and, 52
  assessment of, 110
  in customer profiles, 31, 34,
    35–36, 37, 125, 126, 127, 192
  filter services and, 52
  product development based on,
    145, 244–245
  research on, by vendors, 47, 231

selection and comparison, 7–12
  targeted information to, 61–62,
    70, 174
  unmet, 48, 67
  See also information, types of:
    direct preference measures
customer profiles, 31, 142
  access to, 41, 42–48, 106, 169,
    181, 184, 194, 230, 244, 255,
    272
  accurate inferences from, 149,
    164, 268
  aggregated, 176, 239, 258
  analysis of, 180–181, 185, 192
  anonymous, 270
  assembled and controlled by cus-
    tomer, 18, 20, 47, 68, 165,
    229, 230–231, 241, 267, 269
  assembled by infomediaries, 22,
    30–33, 36–37, 42, 45, 47, 64,
    67, 72, 78–79, 106, 110, 124,
    125–126, 142, 147, 157, 191,
    192, 241, 264, 269
  assembled by portal companies,
    87
  assembled by vendors, 31, 42
  broad-based, 130
  competition for, 145, 146
  contents/types of information in,
    31, 127–129, 159–161, 180,
    264
  criteria for, 149, 150
  deleting information from, 256,
    267
  enhancement of, 45, 184, 262,
    267, 269, 271
  evaluation of, 51, 84, 139
  as indicator of revenues, 68
  integrated, 43, 96, 130, 131, 134,
    137, 152, 172, 174, 224, 230,
    254
  international access to, 255, 257
  learning process for, 192,
    194–195

limitations of, 81–82, 129–131, 176

maintenance and management of, 116, 147, 159, 195, 214–215, 222, 261

offered to vendors, 121

range of infomediary services and, 155, 157–158

selective use of, 161, 229–230

services based on, 33–40

as shaping platform, 135–138, 178, 180

in standard data formats, 136, 147, 152–155, 159–161, 178

transaction-based, 29–33, 39–40, 90–91, 126

use of, 28–29, 169, 182, 184, 201, 229–230, 244, 254–256, 262, 267–268

value of and from, 13–14, 29, 33–40, 47, 109, 146, 152, 259

See also critical mass: of customers/clients; information; information, types of

customer relations, 20, 83, 118, 122, 198, 212

with infomediaries, 19–20, 82, 121

with vendors, 79, 82, 178

customer relationship businesses, 95–101, 206, 207, 209, 210–211, 213–214, 219, 221, 223, 264

economies of scope and, 225, 227

infomediaries as, 214–215, 237

management, 220, 224

specialized, 222

customer(s), 247

aggregation of, 117, 248–250

attention, 235, 247

core, 224

direct connection to vendors, 24, 217

loyalty, 53, 71–72, 164–165, 232

potential, 44–45, 52, 81, 112

profitability, 52–53, 67, 139, 210

subsidization of other customers by, 53

vendor-focused view of, 87, 92

See also consumer influence

customer trust, 32, 84, 119, 273

attached to product attributes, 97

building, 78, 79–80, 113, 237

customer database companies and, 102

as factor in information capture, 98, 99

relations with infomediaries based on, 78–80, 83, 85, 87–89, 90, 92, 121–122, 124, 142, 147, 184, 188, 192, 193, 194, 195, 197

transfer, 121

value and, 113, 121–122

data

aggregation, 47, 165

census tract, 110

compatibility of, 133–134

function of, 279

management and analysis of, 33, 39–40

mining, 102, 185

survey, 110

"wrapping," 27, 279–280

See also content; customer profiles; standard data formats; *information listings*

database(s), 4, 21, 94, 101–103

international, 255, 256

limitations of, 81–82

management, 94, 102, 222, 279

matching of potential customers to vendors, 44–45, 52

proprietary, 133, 136

relational, 264

virtual, 279, 280

database(s) *(continued)*
  See also critical mass; customer
    profiles
debit cards, 272, 277–278
delivery services. *See* distribution of
    products and services: delivery
desktop operating systems, 86, 99,
    146, 175, 276
digital cash, 17, 262, 277, 278, 283
digital information, 19
digital networks, 54, 216
direct mail, 15, 42, 110
direct marketing, 4, 21, 22, 94,
    97–98, 125, 238, 239
  response rates, 44
  skills, 101, 180
  See also advertising; marketing
    messages; targeted marketing
    services
discounts, 22, 63, 171
  for information, applied to
    purchases, 38, 42
  loyalty, 164
distribution of products and services,
    138, 165, 166, 167, 218–219,
    220
  capacities, 245
  channels, 49–50, 211, 245
  costs, 51–52, 73, 114
  delivery, 66, 167, 176, 181, 218,
    234, 278
  See also inventory
divestiture, 226–227

early adoption drivers, 146, 178
economic incentives
  to adopt standard data formats,
    138, 139, 140, 141, 145
  for complementary products, 205
  created by infomediaries, 83
  for infomediary growth and
    profitability, 174–175
  to join economic webs, 140–141

  to join shaping platforms, 179
  to share information, 215
  to vendors, 172
  See also economic webs
economic model of infomediation,
    23, 60, 109, 176, 187
  cash flows, 187, 196–198
  context for, 188–189
  economic profile of the infome-
    diary, 189–198
  operating costs, 187, 193–197,
    198
  performance drivers, 187,
    199–201
  revenues, 187, 189–192,
    196–197
  See also business models
economic webs, 135, 178, 199, 234
  access to, 147
  architecture, 136
  benefits of, 137–140
  competition among, 184, 186
  development and deployment
    strategies for, 141, 147–152
  incentives for, 135, 136, 137, 186
  roles and participation in,
    136–137, 140–145
  shaping platforms and, 178
economies of scale, 184, 211,
    212–213, 218
economies of scope, 113, 116–117,
    157, 197
  bundling and, 212–213
  economic drivers for, 173–175
  for infomediaries, 130
  as shaper of culture, 210–211
electronic commerce, 23, 139, 216.
    See also network(s): electronic
e-mail, 17, 29, 30, 38, 88, 262, 273,
    275–277
employment laws and services, 243,
    247, 259
encryption of data, 130, 256, 265
enterprise resource planning, 264

entertainment market. *See* travel and
entertainment markets
entrepreneurs/entrepreneurial
companies, 20, 103–106
infomediary potential for, 84,
85–86
as spinouts, 198
"trust transfer" and, 121
uncertain market environments
and, 139
See also web-based companies
entry strategies, 83, 106, 116
accelerated, 79, 117–119, 142,
189
customer acquisition for,
120–121
economic incentive for, 117–118
network-based, 118
sequenced, 106, 112–113
See also preemptive positioning;
speed: to market
evaluation services, 72, 100–101,
185, 234
for performance, 248–250
provided by infomediaries, 19,
101, 125, 248–250
provided by third parties, 185
See also product(s): evaluation of
eXtensible Markup Language
(XML), 134, 278–280, 281

fees
collected by infomediaries, from
clients, 40–41, 237, 271
collected by infomediaries, from
vendors, 36, 41, 42, 43, 147,
150, 167, 171, 174, 192–193,
230, 244, 271
explicit, 52
subscription, 242
usage, 242
See also commissions; interaction
costs

fiduciaries. *See* financial services;
health care industry
filtering services, 17, 29, 33–34, 54,
69, 121, 126, 262
blanket, 127
information-based, 53–54
provided by infomediaries, 40,
52, 124, 125, 126–127, 188,
273, 275–277
selective, 127
filtering technology, 29–30, 273,
275–277
collaborative, 116–117, 130,
163–164, 173, 268
financial services, 122, 139, 207,
208, 222–223, 230, 270,
282–283
agents, 25
companies, 59, 68, 75, 94, 95–98
market, 50, 51, 66–68
vendors, 142

gateways. *See* portals/portal
companies

hardware. *See* operations/operating
systems
health care industry, 75, 80, 94, 95,
122, 230, 237–238
consolidation of, 96
cost reduction strategies, 65
HMOs, 10–11, 96, 250, 252
legacy information systems, 96
markets, 50, 64–66
trust-based customer relations, 95
HMOs. *See* health care industry
Hypertext Markup Language
(HTML), 133, 278–279

impulse buying, 130, 161, 163, 168,
239, 242. *See also* purchases/
purchasing patterns

increasing returns dynamics, 113,
169, 181–182, 197
  accelerated entry strategies,
    117–119
  amortization effects, 113, 114,
    115–116
  barriers to entry and, 175–177,
    184
  benefit to infomediaries,
    115–116, 169–171
  brand names and, 235
  economic webs and, 136–137,
    146
  economies of scope and, 173–175
  inflection points, 114, 117–127
  to infomediaries, 157, 159
  of infomediary businesses, 188
  learning effects, 113, 114–115,
    116
  to lock in clients and vendors,
    199–200
  network effects, 113, 115, 121,
    122, 123, 169, 199
  preemptive positioning and,
    117–118, 119
inflection points, 114, 119–127
influence/influence vendors, 83, 258.
    See also consumer influence
infomediaries, 19–20, 53–54, 83,
    103–106, 116, 117, 283
  ability to "look across" customer
    profiles, 46, 154–155, 166,
    173
  ability to "look across" product
    and service categories, 66,
    72–73, 112, 117, 151, 158,
    230, 234
  analytic tools, 68
  beachhead strategies, 137, 138,
    147
  benefits to clients, 24–26, 40–42,
    112, 123–124, 126, 130, 138,
    169–173, 174, 199–200, 233,
    258, 259, 273

benefits to vendors, 42–48, 112,
    125, 130, 145, 169–173, 200
  billing systems, 116
  as catalyst for unbundling,
    214–224
  collaboration marketing and,
    240–241, 242
  competition among, 83, 84–103,
    189
  as distribution channel, 201
  as driver of change, 207
  economic profiles of, 189–198
  effect on conventional markets,
    231
  financial, 66–68
  geography-focused, 116, 117, 128
  information generated by, 234
  international operations, 188,
    255–259
  liability concerns, 253–256
  limitations of, 166
  management of inflection points
    by, 119–127
  market value of, 77
  mind-set, 83, 185–186
  as portal, 183
  range of services provided by, 19,
    32, 33–40, 47, 50–51, 80, 113,
    116, 117, 121, 146, 147, 155,
    157–158, 168–169, 180, 181,
    184, 196, 201, 224, 231, 261,
    281
  requirements for, 77–78, 101
  role in protecting privacy of
    clients, 19–20, 28–30, 32, 40,
    45, 66, 67, 80, 121, 124, 125,
    149, 161, 183, 253, 257, 259,
    271–272, 282
  role of, 20, 22–23, 138, 223
  specialized, 236–237
  "vendor-facing," 32
  web-based strategies, 157–158
  See also customer profiles:
    assembled by infomediaries;

economic model of infomediation; information: compensation to customer for; *specific services*

infomediary businesses

consumer marketing expenditures, 232

customer relationships as base of, 78–79

economic thresholds for, 119–120

economies of scope and, 116–117

entry strategies for, 147–152

expansion of, 99

increasing returns dynamics in, 115–116, 188

initial and cumulative investments, 79, 114, 116, 119, 176, 187, 196, 197

infomediary revenues, 77, 152, 169, 187, 189–192, 200

from agent services, 174

economic drivers for, 174

economies of scope and, 173–175

from marketing, 174, 242

from new clients, 177

per customer, 67, 130, 175, 190, 191, 197, 210

potential amounts, 176

size of company as determinant of, 169–177

See also fees

infomediary webs, 242, 254, 259.

See also economic webs; shaping platforms

information

abuse of, 21, 28, 32, 80, 109

access, 81–82, 230, 233, 271, 272

accuracy of, 5, 31, 110, 160, 166

analysis, 33, 39–40, 91, 102, 183, 238

compensation to customer for, 15, 17, 18, 19, 30, 38, 40, 41, 42, 47, 109, 237

concentrated flow of, 183

content, 53–54, 267

definition "tags" for, 133, 134, 150, 151, 278–279

flows, in economic webs, 179–180, 182

levels of, 266

packaging, 83, 91, 101, 102

perfect, 110

presentation of, 151, 152, 163, 167, 182, 184

proprietary, 133, 136, 230

requested by customer, 237

storage, 116, 195, 267

supply chain, 20, 172

transparency, 248–250

unauthorized release of, 254–255

uses of, 16, 21, 22–23, 24, 38–39, 47

for value creation, 244–245

See also customer profiles; selective disclosure

information, types of

asymmetrical, 8, 10, 28, 115, 137, 231

behavioral, 31, 43, 45, 81, 91, 130, 134, 264–269, 270, 273

demographic, 46, 47, 65

descriptive data, 31, 43, 110, 112, 123, 127, 150, 151, 159, 160, 270, 279

direct preference measures, 112, 124, 127, 150, 151, 152, 154, 159–160, 163, 164, 165, 166, 169, 230, 237, 268

financial arrangements, 271

frequent use profiles, 38, 46, 71–72, 81–82, 200, 229–230, 264–265

"intelligent," 27

media usage profiles, 159

physical-world, 264

potential customer, 13–15, 42

sell-through, 43, 46, 112, 166

information, types of *(continued)*
transaction history, 112, 123,
150, 151–152, 159, 163, 185,
223, 239, 271
trigger events, 112, 124, 126,
150, 152, 154, 159, 164–165,
223, 231
See also commercial transactions;
customer profiles; private
information sources
information and content exchange
(ISE), 280–281
information capture, 14, 15–16, 83,
139, 238, 241, 283
by advertising networks, 91–92
customer control over, 16–18
by customers, 230–231, 272–273
implicit and explicit, 264
by infomediaries, 23–24, 39, 91,
115, 123–124, 138, 139, 149,
181, 267
by intermediaries, 23–24, 39
laws/government regulation of, 5,
16, 42, 253, 259
across multi-media properties,
98, 101–103
from physical-world sources,
271–273
by portal companies, 87
prevention of, 28–30, 32, 267
by retailers and direct marketers,
98
in selected formats, 183
by software agents, 27–28
through loyalty programs, 98
across and within web sites, 269,
270
information management, 116, 272
by infomediaries, 19–20, 22,
39–40
See also selective disclosure
information technology, 11, 17–18,
20, 49–50, 91, 206, 262–269.

See also technology; technology tools
infrastructure management businesses, 91, 207, 208, 209, 211,
213, 214, 215, 219, 220, 221,
224, 226–227, 262
economies of scale and, 225, 227
innovation. *See* product(s): innovation; speed: of innovation
insurance/insurance companies, 22,
64, 96, 126
Intel, 84, 135, 136, 141, 157, 178
interaction costs, 19, 49–50, 112,
207, 231–232, 242
for automobile purchases, 63–64
of comparison shopping, 34, 40
as competitive advantage, 229
computer market, 70
customer loyalty and, 232
defined, 205
effect on restructuring, 227
in health care market, 65
by infomediaries, 195
market inefficiencies and, 50
reduced by information technology, 206
reduced by use of infomediaries,
28, 37, 40, 41
interest revenue, 52
Internet, 19, 20, 207, 262, 264, 268,
283
access, 8, 23, 86–88, 243
competitive dynamics, 15–16
service providers, 199
web-based companies, 85–93
Intuit, 67, 68, 99–100, 222, 223
inventory, 22, 138, 214, 218–219
management, 47, 138
risk, 97, 138
See also distribution of products
and services
investment/investment strategies,
25, 79, 87, 147, 240, 242, 251.

See also infomediary businesses: initial and cumulative investments

joint ventures, 83, 118, 136, 138, 167. *See also* alliances
junk mail (spam), 3–4, 7, 15, 102, 124, 276
    filtering of, 17, 29, 34, 36
    generated from third-party list companies, 21

leveraging
    of assets, 47, 94–95
    of customer profiles, 106, 147, 165, 172, 269
    of data, 94–95, 283
    for efficiency, 116
    of expertise, 218
    of information, 161, 241
    of market position, 90
    of resources, 240, 242
    of resources of other companies, 103, 106, 118, 136, 140, 220
    skills, 86–87
    of technology, 206, 262
    of unbundling process, 225, 227
liability concerns, 253–256
lock-in of clients and vendors, 122, 177–178, 182, 184, 199, 230
logistics, 208, 209, 213, 218, 227, 244
loyalty/loyalty programs, 12, 13, 88, 98, 166, 229

mailing lists. *See* direct mail; third-party list companies
management, 195
    in entrepreneurial ventures, 106
    increasing returns to scale and, 114

innovative, 84–85
    services, 220, 221, 222
    teams, 84, 90, 106
    in traditional corporations, 105
manufacturing operations, 208, 227, 244
marketing, 212
    collaboration, 239–240, 242
    data-based, 13, 87
    deep, 102
    expenditures, 43, 193–194, 195, 198, 238–244
    gulf between consumers and marketers, 12–13, 15, 16, 20, 27–28
    loyalty programs, 12, 13
    mass, 180
    new products and services, 208
    permission, 13, 14–16
    relationship, 4, 13–14
    response rates, 110
    skills, 82–83, 84, 86, 88, 89, 181, 245
    strategies, 5
marketing information providers, 94, 101, 142
marketing messages, 3–4, 7
    conventional media, 34, 38, 43, 243
    customer profile criteria for, 149, 192, 244
    delivered by infomediaries, 22, 217
    environments for, 242
    filtering of, 33–34, 36, 38, 127, 192
    first wave, 165
    with immediate purchase option, 45
    network businesses, 91–92
    predatory, 27–28
    relationships, 99
    relevant context for, 165–168

marketing messages *(continued)*
  response rates, 7, 15, 42, 44, 45,
    174, 192
  second wave, 159, 161–168
  solicited by customer, 154–155,
    192
  targeted to customer needs and
    preferences, 37, 40, 44, 61–62,
    72, 91, 154, 168, 244–245
  as unwanted intrusions, 3–4, 14,
    15, 26, 28, 232, 276–277
  unwanted/irrelevant, 14, 30,
    33–34, 36, 37, 42, 102, 125,
    192, 194–195
  See also advertising; targeted
    marketing services
marketing services, 18
  provided by infomediaries,
    157–158, 159, 160, 161–168,
    261
market research services, 19, 43,
    46–47, 167, 208
  fees charged to vendors for,
    192–193
  provided by infomediaries, 172,
    180, 183, 195
market(s)
  business-to-business, 171
  capitalization thresholds, 198
  characteristics, 54–58
  competitive, 86, 88, 89
  conventional/traditional, 22, 25,
    26, 30, 85, 90, 188, 230–232,
    233–238
  global, 11
  inefficiencies, 50, 51
  infomediated, 48, 49–75, 50,
    54–58, 182, 230
  for infomediation, 48, 50, 54–58,
    182
  invisible hand concept of, 137
  local, 11
  opportunities, 165–166
  product-focused, 96

restructuring, 205
revenues/market share, 185
segments, 235–236
value, 206
vendor-centric, 230, 231
See also preemptive positioning;
  reverse markets; *specific prod-*
  ucts and services
media, 94, 98–99, 216–217, 227,
  232, 249
  conventional, 43, 243–244
  See also advertising
merger and acquisition strategies,
  103–106, 119, 177, 189, 198,
  226
Microsoft, 8, 84, 99–100, 135, 136,
  141, 157, 175, 222, 223,
  269–270
  market share, 188–189
  technology standards, 178
Microsoft/Intel web, 142, 143, 144,
  180, 181
monitoring services, 49, 60, 168–169
monopolist strategies, 184
moral hazard issues, 8, 10–11, 28,
  65, 137, 231
mortgages, 51, 53, 60–62, 80, 208.
  See also real estate market

network(s)
  effects, 113, 115, 121, 122, 123,
    169, 199
  electronic, 207, 233, 268–269
  infomediaries and, 23–24
  management of, 214
  See also economic webs
niche players, 139, 177, 218

offshore operations, 257
one-to-one marketing, 4, 13–14
on-line environments (general discussion), 23, 29, 31–33, 100,
  240–242

Open Financial Exchange (OFX),
282–283
Open Profiling Standard (OPS),
281–282
operations/operating systems, 114,
145, 189
core, 175, 209–210, 212–213,
214, 216
costs, 114–115, 187, 193–196,
212, 215, 217, 226
licensing of, 185
revenues, 185
standardized, 136, 178
outsourcing, 216, 218, 222,
226–227

paranoia, institutional, 78, 85
performance drivers, 187, 199–201
performance inefficiencies, 209
personal computers. *See* computer
industry
personalization technology companies, 269, 274
personal shoppers, 25, 236
pharmaceutical companies, 65, 114,
218, 219
platforms. *See* shaping platforms
portals/portal companies, 43–48, 61,
86–88, 89, 121, 220, 241.
See also connection services
portfolios, product and service, 224,
227
preemptive positioning, 84, 87, 88,
90, 117–119, 188, 194, 232.
See also entry strategies;
market(s)
pricing, 19, 133, 230
arbitrated, 256
competition, 146
differentials, 63
discriminate, 52
distortions, 50, 52, 53, 248
of financial services, 67

predatory, 184
product, 53
See also antitrust concerns
privacy, 3–7, 12–13, 50, 122, 139,
239
backlash, 16, 42, 140
commercial, 256–258
compromise of, 27–28
consumer influence over, 253
identity protection, 17–18, 26, 41
laws/government regulation, 4,
5–6, 256–258
liability concerns, 253–256
offshore operations and, 257
sale of, to marketers, 16
small businesses and, 74
tool kits, 28–30, 33, 37, 40, 81,
99, 138, 139, 144, 184, 185,
261, 262, 273–278, 283
voluntary privacy standards, 5–6
See also anonymity/anonymiza-
tion software; infomediaries:
role in protecting privacy of
clients; private information
sources; selective disclosure
private information sources
commercial transactions, 4, 6, 18,
28, 29, 31, 38, 39, 90, 98,
125–126, 130, 168, 238, 255,
256, 264, 265
credit histories, 4, 101, 102, 103
customers themselves, 16, 29, 39,
47, 92, 102, 126, 264
filter services, 126–127
financial arrangements, 4, 16–17,
66–68, 80, 95, 229, 282–283
medical records, 4, 6–7, 16,
65–66, 80, 95, 96, 122
software agents, 26–28
surveys and questionnaires, 4, 5,
15, 27, 31, 81, 111, 123, 264,
267
telephone and utility bills, 4, 100
virtual communities, 88

private information sources
(continued)
web site visits, 4, 29–32, 129,
264–265, 267, 273–274, 277
See also information, types of
product(s), 11–12, 50, 65, 161
attributes, 51, 97, 146, 151, 245
browser, 86
categories, 54–58, 59–62, 69–70,
83, 116, 117, 122, 126, 130,
146, 149, 151, 152, 161, 168,
218, 236, 252
complementary, 142, 145, 147,
166–167, 175, 179–180, 205
complex, 7–11, 19, 34, 123–124,
126
consumption and lifestyle, 58,
68–73
customized, 43, 47, 141,
166–167, 269
definition "tags," 133, 134, 150,
151, 278–279
development, 43, 138, 145,
179–180, 208, 244–245
essentials, 58–68
evaluation of, 12, 51, 54, 70, 101,
234, 245, 248–250
focused, 225
information, 19, 26, 45, 51,
53–54, 131, 166–167, 183,
237, 280, 281
innovation, 85, 141, 142,
166–167, 206–209, 211,
213–220, 222, 224, 225,
244–245
inventories, 22, 138, 167
new, 173, 181, 183
new applications for, 141,
166–167
ownership of, 89
potential interest in, 30, 35–37
presentation, 44, 182, 183, 184
production cost of, 114, 115

remote purchase of, 54
replenishment, 73, 130, 150, 154,
161, 230–232
returns, 39, 46, 234
"shopping," 73, 168
special-interest, 94
targeted marketing services for,
163–164
testing/test marketing of, 85,
167, 173, 183
See also brand names; bundling of
products and services; distribution of products and services;
increasing returns dynamics;
market(s); purchases/purchas-
ing patterns
profiling
services, 231
standards, 281–282
tool kits, 68, 81, 129, 138, 144,
184, 185, 261, 269–278
profitability. *See* customer(s): profitability; economic incentives;
increasing returns dynamics;
inflection points; revenues
programming languages, 133,
278–280
propensity scores, 125, 127
proprietary technology and
environments, 86, 229, 262,
268–269
purchaser identification services, 33,
37–39, 40, 41, 67, 68, 69, 124,
168
commercial transactions and,
151–152
limited, in offshore operations,
257
presentation standards and, 184
provided by infomediaries,
167–168, 171, 195
standard data formats for,
151–152

purchases/purchasing patterns, 18, 32–33, 46, 75, 81, 90–91, 151, 154, 165, 166, 180, 272–273
aggregated, 73, 232, 252
analysis of, by infomediaries, 39, 40, 72–73
brand names and, 233–234
categories, 81, 82, 90
estimates of, 126
leading indicators of, 33
off-line, 272–273
point-of-purchase, 69
"propensity scores," 125, 127
search-related, 73, 126
See also commercial transactions; impulse buying; information, types of: transaction history; private information sources; product(s)

qualified leads, 35–36, 43, 44, 220

rating service companies, 100–101, 241. *See also* evaluation services
real estate market, 51, 59–62, 62, 75, 125, 126
regulation, 139
of financial services companies, 97
of information, 4, 5–6, 16, 42, 253, 256–259
public policies, 248, 253–259
of utilities companies, 100
relationship management
marketing, 4, 13–14
skills, 82, 83, 84, 89, 92, 94
research. *See* market research services
restructuring, 222, 227–228. *See also* bundling of products and services

retail businesses, 53, 94, 97–98, 150, 165, 166, 172, 208, 213–214, 215, 243–244, 245
revenues, 194
advertising, 92
per customer, 67, 130, 175, 190, 191, 197, 210
reinvestment of, 200
reverse cookies/reverse engineering, 17, 18, 136, 262, 264–265, 266, 267
reverse markets, 25, 26, 72, 232
customer switching and, 231
effect on marketing expenditures, 238–244
need for shelf space and, 233–234, 245
shifting sources of advantage, 244–245
risk
assessment, 259
to consumers, 8–11
credit, 22
investment, 140
management, 137, 139
minimized by new technologies, 143–144
multiple shaping platforms and, 142–143
sharing, 140
size of company and, 144
of web-based strategies, 141–142
risk-taking behaviors, 78, 84, 87, 90, 92
by infomediaries, 83
in virtual communities, 88

search engines, 86, 143
search(es)
assets, 86
client history of, 154
customer-initiated, 36

search(es) *(continued)*
    text-based, 133–134
    words, 45
search services, 26, 27, 174, 280
    cost of, 28, 47, 51–52, 112, 231
    gulf between consumers and
        marketers, 27–28
    privacy compromised by, 35
    provided by infomediaries, 37,
        40, 41, 43, 50–51, 54, 66, 68,
        109, 125, 127, 128, 133–134,
        171, 174
    for travel needs, 71
secure mode/areas, 130, 265–266
selective disclosure, 26, 41, 161, 168,
    183, 192, 229–230, 269
services/service companies, 61, 139
    categories of, 54–58, 117, 122,
        126, 130, 252
    cost of, 114
    customized, 43, 47
    information-based, 19
    innovative, 85
    test marketing of, 167, 173
    value-added, 90
shaping platforms, 32, 157, 283
    advantages of, 181–183, 186
    customer profiles as, 135–138
    economic incentives of, 181, 182,
        186
    enhancement of, 179, 181
    functionality of, 178–179, 182
    late-stage, 177–186
    multiple, 142–143
    owner/participant interaction,
        179
    revenues from, 179
    sources of advantages, 183–185
    in standard data formats (early-
        stage), 140–142, 145–147
    switching barriers for, 179
    used to influence behavior, 179,
        180, 182–183
    value creation from, 183–184

shareholders/shareholder value, 187,
    197–198, 206, 251–252, 254
shopping clubs, 25–26
smart cards, 17, 18, 29, 30, 31, 39,
    244, 262, 272–273, 278
software, 137
    agents, 26–28
    application, 114
    compatibility, 114
    customer relationship manage-
        ment, 264
    market, 69–70
    profiling, 31–33
    protocols, 182
    revenues, 185
    search agent, 43, 109
    "wrapping the data," 27,
        279–280
    See also computer industry; pri-
        vacy: tool kits; profiling: tool
        kits; purchaser identification
        services; technology tools
speed, 215
    bundling and, 212–213
    of implementation, 181
    of influencers in economic webs,
        141–142
    of innovation, 83
    to market, 138, 175, 176, 211,
        225
spending patterns. *See* purchases/
    purchasing patterns
standard data formats, 44, 85, 131,
    133–136, 184, 261–262, 278
    adoption of, 148, 149–150, 152,
        182
    in customer profiles, 136,
        152–155
    deploying web-based strategies,
        137–140, 146, 147–152
    economic incentives for, 167
    economic webs and, 136–144
    for information presentation,
        151, 163

for purchaser identification, 151–152, 167

See also shaping platforms

support services, 118, 166, 167, 208, 214, 221–222, 224, 267

for customer accounts, 193, 195, 196, 198

surfing. *See* browsing

surveys and questionnaires.

See private information sources: surveys and questionnaires

switching, 179, 194–195, 232

barriers to, 179

costs, 177, 230

See also churn rate

targeted marketing services, 19, 33, 35–37, 40, 41–42, 43, 44–45, 67, 68, 69, 89, 97, 101, 110, 125, 217, 242

cost of, 183

customer acquisition costs and, 52

fees charged to vendors for, 192–193

first wave, 154, 180

limited, in offshore operations, 257

profile-based, 64

provided by infomediaries, 72–73, 125, 147, 149–151, 160, 161–169, 171, 172, 174, 180–181, 188, 191, 195, 196, 238–239, 243, 244

response rates, 154, 180

standard data format adoption and, 149–151

See also advertising; marketing messages: targeted to customer needs and preferences

taxes, 68, 197, 198, 256, 258–259

technology, 17–18, 63, 64

architectures, 85, 139, 144, 145–146, 182, 184, 205

competencies, 225

cryptographic, 130

for information control, 17–18, 268–269

innovations, 176

integrated, 283

investments, 96

proliferation of products and, 11

proprietary, 262

standards, 135, 178, 283

vendors/companies, 118, 143–144, 146, 185

webs, 136, 178, 205–206

See also filtering technology; information technology; software

technology tools, 30–33, 34, 40, 99, 139, 261–262, 269–278

cross-profile, 268

information capture, 262–269

standards for, 278–283

telemarketing, 4, 5, 15, 102, 110, 123

telephone companies, 53, 100, 213–214

television

networks, 99, 243, 268, 283

set-top boxes/viewing meters, 17, 18, 262, 268, 269, 273

See also advertising; media

third-party list companies, 16, 18, 21, 81, 101–103, 110

contracts preventing sales to, 38–39

traditional businesses. *See* corporations, traditional-market; market(s): conventional/traditional

traffic. *See* transaction aggregators

transaction aggregators, 23, 86–87, 88, 89–91, 150, 171, 231–232, 241, 242

transaction aggregators *(continued)*
infomediaries as, 22–23, 150,
171, 231–232
transaction costs. *See* interaction
costs
transaction processing services, 23,
101, 217, 220, 224
transportation market, 51, 62–64,
74, 113–114, 126, 220–222
travel agents, 25–26, 82
travel and entertainment markets,
70–73, 74, 75, 81–82
trust. *See* customer trust

uncertain market environments, 65,
84, 92, 183
concentration of information
flow and, 180, 182
for economic webs, 143
risk management and, 139
technology changes as cause of,
63, 70
unions, 248
URLs. *See* click-stream data
utilities companies, 250

value
destruction, 241
exchange, 122–123, 149, 237
propositions, 252–253
value creation, 39, 259
analysis of, 185–186
customer profiles as basis for,
146, 149
in economic webs, 141, 146, 181,
182
by entrepreneurial ventures,
105–106
by infomediaries, for clients,
13–14, 17, 47–48, 231

maximization of, 185–186
by shaping platforms, 178–179
shifts, 206, 231, 254, 259
by vendors, 47–48
vendor profiles, 39, 185, 231
vendor relationships, 99, 102
cost of, 176–177
with infomediaries, 149–151,
169–173, 266
skills, 97
vendors, 10, 12, 15, 18, 27, 28, 79,
200, 247
access to customer profiles, 272
advertising by, 91–92
analysis of customer profiles, 185
analytic skills of, 180–181
benefits to customers, 47–48, 88
bids by, 34, 45, 53, 150,
231–232
collaboration marketing by,
239–240
competition among, 14–15
cost of customer acquisition,
42–43
cost to acquire, 193, 200
customer database companies
and, 101–103
evaluation of, 185, 231, 241
information skills, 244–245
marketing expenditures by,
238–244
privacy policies and, 182
restrictions on, 38–39
shift of power to customer,
16–18, 231 (*See also* reverse
markets)
standard data formats and, 131,
137, 138, 149–150, 152, 157
use of customer profiles, 169,
229–230
use of distribution channels, 245
See also fees: collected by infomediaries, from vendors

vertically integrated companies, 138,
140, 206
virtual communities, 88–89, 241, 242

warehouse clubs, 25–26
web-based companies
    as adapter, 141–143, 144
    initial investment risk, 140
    strategies, 83, 206
    as web shaper, 140–141,
        144–145, 157 (*See also* shaping
        platforms)

See also economic webs
World Wide Web, 5, 26, 133, 206,
    273
    home pages, 29
    related content sites, 32–33

XML. *See* eXtensible Markup
    Language

Yahoo!, 23, 45, 61, 86, 206, 220

about the authors

JOHN HAGEL III is a principal at the Silicon Valley office of McKinsey & Company, Inc., and leader of McKinsey's Electronic Commerce Practice. His work is primarily with clients in the electronics, telecommunications, and media industries, with a focus on strategic management and performance improvement. Prior to joining McKinsey, he served as senior vice president for strategic planning at Atari; as president of Sequoia Group, a systems house selling turnkey computer systems to physicians; and as a consultant with the Boston Consulting Group. Mr. Hagel is the author of legal and business books and articles. His book coauthored with Arthur G. Armstrong, *Net Gain: Expanding Markets through Virtual Communities,* has been on business book bestseller lists and has been translated into nine languages.

MARC SINGER is a principal at the San Francisco office of McKinsey & Company, Inc., and coleader of the firm's Continuous Relationship Marketing practice. He works mainly with clients in the financial services, consumer goods, and health care businesses, with a focus on strategy and marketing. He has published articles in the *McKinsey Quarterly, Harvard Business Review,* and other publications.